The Tyndale Old Testament Commentaries

General Editor:
PROFESSOR D. J. WISEMAN, O.B.E., M.A., D. Lit., F.B.A.,
F.S.A.

OBADIAH, JONAH
and MICAH

OBADIAH

AN INTRODUCTION AND COMMENTARY
by
DAVID W. BAKER, A.B., M.C.S., M.PHIL., PH.D.
*Associate Professor of Old Testament and Hebrew,
Ashland Theological Seminary, Ohio*

JONAH

AN INTRODUCTION AND COMMENTARY
by
T. DESMOND ALEXANDER, B.A., PH.D.
Lecturer in Semitic Studies, The Queen's University of Belfast

MICAH

AN INTRODUCTION AND COMMENTARY
by
BRUCE K. WALTKE, B.A., TH.D., PH.D.
*Professor of Old Testament, Westminster Theological Seminary,
Philadelphia*

INTER-VARSITY PRESS
LEICESTER, ENGLAND
DOWNERS GROVE, ILLINOIS, U.S.A.

Inter-Varsity Press
38 De Montfort Street, Leicester LE1 7GP, England
P.O. Box 1400, Downers Grove, Illinois 60515, U.S.A.

Obadiah © *1988 David W. Baker*
Jonah © *1988 T. Desmond Alexander*
Micah © *1988 Bruce K. Waltke*

Inter-Varsity Press, England, is the publishing division of the Universities and Colleges Christian Fellowship (formerly the Inter-Varsity Fellowship), a student movement linking Christian Unions in universities and colleges throughout the United Kingdom and the Republic of Ireland, and a member movement of the International Fellowship of Evangelical Students. For information about local and national activities in Great Britain write to UCCF, 38 De Montfort Street, Leicester LE1 7GP.

InterVarsity Press, U.S.A., is the book-publishing division of InterVarsity Christian Fellowship, a student movement active on campus at hundreds of universities, colleges and schools of nursing. For information about local and regional activities, write Public Relations Dept., InterVarsity Christian Fellowship, 6400 Schroeder Rd., P.O. Box 7895, Madison, WI 53707-7895.

Distributed in Canada through InterVarsity Press, 860 Denison St., Unit 3, Markham, Ontario L3R 4H1, Canada.

Text set in 10/10pt Baskerville
Phototypeset by Input Typesetting Ltd., London SW19 8DR
Printed in the United States of America ∞

UK ISBN 0-85111-643-4 (hardback)
UK ISBN 0-85111-841-0 (paperback)

USA ISBN 0-8308-1425-6 (hardback)
USA ISBN 0-87784-275-2 (paperback)
USA ISBN 0-87784-880-7 (set of Tyndale Old Testament Commentaries, hardback)
USA ISBN 0-87784-280-9 (set of Tyndale Old Testament Commentaries, paperback)

Library of Congress Cataloging-in-Publication Data
Baker, David W. (David Weston), 1950-
    Obadiah: an introduction and commentary/by David W. Baker.
    Jonah: an introduction and commentary/by T. Desmond Alexander.
    Micah: an introduction and commentary/by Bruce K. Waltke.
        p.   cm.—(Tyndale Old Testament commentaries)
    Includes bibliographies.
    ISBN 0-8308-1425-6.   ISBN 0-87784-275-2 (pbk.)
    1. Bible. O.T. Obadiah—Commentaries.   2. Bible. O.T. Jonah—
Commentaries.   3. Bible.   O.T. Micah—Commentaries.
I. Alexander, T. Desmond.   Jonah.   1988.   II. Waltke, Bruce K.
Micah. 1988.   III. Title.   IV. Series.
BS1560.B24 1988
224'.9—dc 19
                                                                                    88-9041
                                                                                    CIP

British Library Cataloguing in Publication Data

Obadiah/Jonah/Micah.—(The Tyndale Old Testament
commentaries).
    1. Bible. O.T. Obadiah. Critical studies
    2. Bible. O.T. Jonah—Commentaries
    3. Bible. O.T. Micah—Commentaries
    I. Baker, David W. (David Weston), 1950—Obadiah
    II. Alexander, T. Desmond (Thomas Desmond), 1955—
Jonah   III. Waltke, Bruce K. (Bruce Kenneth),
    1930—Micah   IV. Series
    224'.9106

17   16   15   14   13   12   11   10   9   8   7   6   5   4   3   2   1
99   98   97   96   95   94   93   92   91   90   89

GENERAL PREFACE

THE aim of this series of *Tyndale Old Testament Comment-aries* as it was in the companion volumes on the New Testament, is to provide the student of the Bible with a handy, up-to-date commentary on each book, with the primary emphasis on exegesis. Major critical questions are discussed in the introductions and additional notes, while undue technicalities have been avoided.

In this series individual authors are, of course, free to make their own distinct contributions and express their own point of view on all debated issues. Within the necessary limits of space they frequently draw attention to interpretations which they themselves do not hold but which represent the stated conclusions of sincere fellow Christians.

The books of Obadiah, Jonah and Micah cover an important but turbulent epoch in the history of Israel in which prophets warned of coming judgment if Israel refused to turn back to God from her apostasy and to practise effective social justice. This culminated in the fall of Jerusalem in 587 BC and in the exile in Babylon.

In the Old Testament in particular no single English trans-lation is adequate to reflect the original text. The version on which these three commentaries are based is the New International Version, but other translations are frequently referred to as well, and on occasion the authors supply their own. Where necessary, words are transliterated in order to help the reader who is unfamiliar with Hebrew to identify the precise word under discussion.

It is assumed throughout that the reader will have ready access to one, or more, reliable rendering of the Bible in English.

Interest in the meaning and message of the Old Testament continues undiminished and it is hoped that this series will thus further the systematic study of the revelation of God and his will and ways as seen in these records. It is the prayer of the editor and publisher, as of the authors, that these books will help many to understand, and to respond to, the Word of God today.

D. J. Wiseman

CONTENTS

OBADIAH

JONAH

CONTENTS

MICAH

CHIEF ABBREVIATIONS

Bible translations and versions

AV	Authorized Version (King James), 1611.
BHS	A. Alt *et al.* (eds.), *Biblica Hebraica Stuttgartensia* (Deutsche Bibelstiftung Stuttgart, 1967/77).
EVV	English versions.
GNB	Good News Bible, 1976.
Heb.	Hebrew.
JB	Jerusalem Bible, 1966.
LXX	The Septuagint (Greek version of the Old Testament).
MT	Massoretic Text.
NAB	New American Bible, 1970.
NEB	New English Bible, 1970.
NIV	New International Version, 1973, 1978, 1984.
RSV	Revised Standard Version, 1952.
RV	Revised Version, 1885.
Syr.	Syriac.
Vulg.	Vulgate.

Other reference works

ANET	J. B. Pritchard, *Ancient Near Eastern Texts Relating to the Old Testament* (Princeton University Press, ^{2}1955; ^{3}1969).
CAH	*Cambridge Ancient History* (^{3}1970–).
G-K	Gesenius-Kautzsch, *Hebrew Grammar*, ET, 1910.
HDB	J. Hastings (ed.), *Dictionary of the Bible*, 5 vols. (Edinburgh, 1898–1904).
IBD	J. D. Douglas *et al.* (eds.), *The Illustrated Bible Dictionary*, 3 vols. (IVP, 1980).
IDB	G. A. Buttrick *et al.* (eds.), *The Interpreter's Dictionary of the Bible*, 4 vols. (Abingdon Press, 1962).
IDBS	K. Crim *et al.* (eds.), *The Interpreter's Dictionary of the Bible*, Supplementary volume (Abingdon Press, 1976).

NBA	J. Bimson *et al.* (eds.), *New Bible Atlas* (IVP, 1985).
NBC	D. Guthrie and J. A. Motyer (eds.), *New Bible Commentary* (IVP, ³1970).
NBD	J. D. Douglas *et al.* (eds.), *The New Bible Dictionary* (IVP, ²1982).
POTT	D. J. Wiseman (ed.), *Peoples of Old Testament Times* (Oxford University Press, 1973).
TDNT	G. Kittell and G. Friedrich (eds.), *Theological Dictionary of the New Testament*, 10 vols., trans. G. W. Bromiley (Eerdmans, 1946–76).
TDOT	G. J. Botterweck and H. Ringgren (eds.), *Theological Dictionary of the Old Testament*, vols. 1–2, trans. J. T. Willis (Eerdmans, ²1977); vol. 3, trans. J. T. Willis, G. W. Bromiley, D. E. Green (Eerdmans, 1978); vol. 4, trans. D. E. Green (Eerdmans, 1980); vol. 5, trans. D. E. Green (Eerdmans, 1986).
THAT	E. Jenni and C. Westermann (eds.), *Theologisches Handwörterbuch zum Alten Testament*, 2 vols. (Chr. Kaiser Verlag and Theologischer Verlag, 1971–76).
TWOT	R. L. Harris, G. L. Archer, B. K. Waltke (eds.), *Theological Wordbook of the Old Testament*, 2 vols (Moody Press, 1980).

Journals

BA	*Biblical Archaeologist.*
BAR	*Biblical Archaeology Review.*
BASOR	*Bulletin of the American Schools of Oriental Research.*
Bib	*Biblica.*
BZ	*Biblische Zeitschrift.*
BZAW	*Beihefte zur Zeitschrift für die alttestamentliche Wissenschaft.*
CBQ	*Catholic Biblical Quarterly.*
ET	*Expository Times.*
EvTh	*Evangelische Theologie.*
HAR	*Hebrew Annual Review.*
HUCA	*Hebrew Union College Annual.*
IEJ	*Israel Exploration Journal.*
Int	*Interpretation.*
JBL	*Journal of Biblical Literature.*
JETS	*Journal of the Evangelical Theological Society.*

JJS	*Journal of Jewish Studies.*
JPOS	*Journal of the Palestine Oriental Society.*
JRAS	*Journal of the Royal Asiatic Society.*
JSOT	*Journal for the Study of the Old Testament.*
JSS	*Journal of Semitic Studies.*
JTS	*Journal of Theological Studies.*
OTS	*Oudtestamentlische Studien.*
PEQ	*Palestine Exploration Quarterly.*
PTR	*Princeton Theological Review.*
RB	*Revue Biblique.*
RHPR	*Revue de l'Histoire et de Philosophie Religieuses.*
SJT	*Scottish Journal of Theology.*
TynB	*Tyndale Bulletin.*
TrThS	*Trierer Theologische Studien.*
VT	*Vetus Testamentum.*
VTS	*Supplement to Vetus Testamentum.*
ZAW	*Zeitschrift für die alttestamentliche Wissenschaft.*

SELECT BIBLIOGRAPHIES

Commentaries and works on Obadiah

Allen   L. C. Allen, *The Books of Joel, Obadiah, Jonah and Micah*, New International Commentary on the Old Testament (Hodder & Stoughton/Eerdmans, 1976).

Armerding   C. E. Armerding, *Obadiah* in F. E. Gaebelein (ed.), *The Expositor's Bible Commentary* 7 (Zondervan, 1985).

Bewer   J. A. Bewer, 'Obadiah' in J. M. P. Smith, W. H. Ward and J. A. Bewer, *A Critical and Exegetical Commentary on Micah, Zephaniah, Nahum, Habakkuk, Obadiah and Joel* (T. & T. Clark/Scribners, 1911).

Coggins   R. J. Coggins, ' "Judgment between Brothers" – A Commentary on the Book of Obadiah' in R. J. Coggins and S. P. Re'emi, *Israel Among the Nations* (Eerdmans/Handsel Press, 1985).

Craigie   P. C. Craigie, *Twelve Prophets* 1, Daily Study Bible (Westminster/St Andrew Press, 1984).

Eaton   J. H. Eaton, *Obadiah, Nahum, Habakkuk and Zephaniah*, Torch Bible Commentaries (SCM Press, 1961).

C. F. Keil   C. F. Keil, 'Obadiah' in *The Twelve Minor Prophets* 1, trans. J. Martin (Eerdmans, 1949).

J. Keil   J. Keil, 'The Book of Obadiah', in Y. Rafael *et al.* (eds.), *The Twelve* (Rabbi Kok, 1973).

Rudolph   W. Rudolph, *Joel, Amos, Obadja, Jona*, Kommentar zum Alten Testament (GVGM, 1971).

G. A. Smith G. A. Smith, *The Book of the Twelve Prophets*, The Expositor's Bible (A. C. Armstrong/Hodder & Stoughton, 1898).

R. L. Smith R. L. Smith, *Micah – Malachi*, Word Biblical Commentary (Word Books, 1984).

Watts   J. D. W. Watts, *The Books of Joel, Obadiah, Jonah, Nahum, Habakkuk and Zephaniah*, Cambridge Bible Commentary (Cambridge University Press, 1975).

Watts   J. D. W. Watts, *Obadiah: A Critical Exegetical Commentary* (Eerdmans, 1969).

Wolff   H. W. Wolff, *Dodekapropheton 3: Obadja und Jona*, Biblischer Kommentar: Altes Testament (Neukirchener, 1977).

Commentaries and works on Jonah

Allen   L. C. Allen, *The Books of Joel, Obadiah, Jonah and Micah*, New International Commentary on the Old Testament (Hodder & Stoughton/Eerdmans, 1976).

Almbladh   K. Almbladh, *Studies in the Book of Jonah*, Studia Semitica Upsaliensia (Uppsala University, 1986).

Bewer   J. A. Bewer, 'Jonah' in H. G. Mitchell, J. M. P. Smith and J. A. Bewer, *A Critical and Exegetical Commentary on Haggai, Zechariah, Malachi, and Jonah*, International Critical Commentary (T. & T. Clark, 1912).

Calvin   J. Calvin, *Jonah, Micah, Nahum* in *Commentaries on the Twelve Minor Prophets* 3, trans. J. Owen (1847 edn.) (Eerdmans, 1950).

Cohn   G. H. Cohn, *Das Buch Jona im Lichte der biblischen Erzählkunst*, Studia Semitica Neerlandica 12 (Van Gorcum, 1969).

Craghan   J. Craghan, *Esther, Judith, Tobit, Jonah, Ruth*, Old Testament Message (Michael Glazier, 1982).

Fretheim   T. E. Fretheim, *The Message of Jonah* (Augsburg, 1977).

Haller   E. Haller, *Die Erzahlung von dem Propheten Jona*, Theologische Existenz Heute (C. Kaiser Verlag, 1958).

Heschel   A. Heschel, *The Prophets* (Harper and Row, 1955).

Keil   C. F. Keil, 'Jonah' in *The Twelve Minor Prophets* 1, trans. J. Martin (T. and T. Clark, 1885).

SELECT BIBLIOGRAPHIES

Keller   C.-A. Keller, *Jonas* in Commentaire de l'ancien testament, vol. XIa (Delachaux et Niestlé, 1965).

Knight   G. A. F. Knight, *Ruth and Jonah*, Torch Bible Commentary (SCM Press, ²1966).

Lacocque A. and P. E. Lacocque, *The Jonah Complex* (John Knox Press, 1981).

Magonet J. Magonet, *Form and Meaning, Studies in Literary Techniques in the Book of Jonah*, Beiträge zur biblischen Exegesis und Theologie (Lang, 1976).

Maier   G. Maier, *Der Prophet Jonah*, Wuppertaler Studienbibel (R. Brockhaus Verlag, 1976).

Martin   A. D. Martin, *The Prophet Jonah: The Book and the Sign* (Longmans, 1926).

Price   B. F. Price and E. A. Nida, *A Translator's Handbook on the Book of Jonah*, Helps for Translators (United Bible Societies, 1978).

Rudolph W. Rudolph, *Joel, Amos, Obadja, Jona*, Kommentar zum Alten Testament (GVGM, 1971).

Smart   J. D. Smart, 'The Book of Jonah', in *The Interpreter's Bible* 6 (Abingdon, 1956).

Trible   P. L. Trible, *Studies in the Book of Jonah* (unpublished PhD dissertation, Columbia University, 1963).

Vawter B. Vawter, *Job and Jonah: Questioning the Hidden God* (Paulist Press, 1983).

Walton J. Walton, *Jonah*, Bible Study Commentary (Zondervan, 1982).

Watts   J. D. W. Watts, *The Books of Joel, Obadiah, Jonah, Nahum, Habakkuk and Zephaniah*, Cambridge Bible Commentary (Cambridge University Press, 1975).

Weiser   A. Weiser, *Das Buch der zwölf Kleinen Propheten 1: Die Propheten: Hosea, Joel, Amos, Obadja, Jona, Micha*, Das Alte Testament Deutsch (Vandenhoeck & Ruprecht, 1979).

Wolff (1975) H. W. Wolff, *Studien zum Jonabuch* (Neukirchener, ²1975).

Wolff (1977) H. W. Wolff, *Dodekapropheton 3: Obadja und Jona,* Biblischer Kommentar: Altes Testament (Neukirchener, 1977).

Commentaries and works on Micah

Allen L. C. Allen, *The Books of Joel, Obadiah, Jonah and Micah,* New International Commentary on the Old Testament (Hodder & Stoughton/Eerdmans, 1976).

Hillers D. R. Hillers, *Micah: A Commentary on the Book of the Prophet Micah,* Hermeneia (Fortress Press, 1984).

Mays J. L. Mays, *Micah: A Commentary* (SCM Press, 1976).

Renaud (1977) B. Renaud, *La Formation du livre de Michée: Tradition et Actualisation* (Gabalda, 1977).

Renaud (1987) B. Renaud, *Michée, Sophonie, Nahum* (Gabalda, 1987).

Willis J. T. Willis, *The Structure, Setting, and Interrelationships of the Pericopes in the Book of Micah* (unpublished PhD dissertation, Vanderbilt University, 1966).

Wolff (1981) H. W. Wolff, *Micah the Prophet* (Fortress Press, 1981).

Wolff (1982) H. W. Wolff, *Dodekapropheton 4: Micah,* Biblischer Kommentar: Altes Testament (Neukirchener, 1982).

OBADIAH

AN INTRODUCTION AND COMMENTARY

by

DAVID W. BAKER, A.B., M.C.S., M.PHIL., PH.D.

Associate Professor of Old Testament and Hebrew,
Ashland Theological Seminary, Ohio

AUTHOR'S PREFACE

THE truism that 'good things come in small packages' was driven home in the attempt to 'unpack' God's message to his people as contained in this, the smallest Old Testament book. For the privilege of undertaking this study I thank Professor D. J. Wiseman, as well as for his instruction and counsel in so many ways. For help in overcoming some of the infelicities of style I thank the editors and readers of Inter-Varsity Press. For giving up their valuable play time so I could work, I thank two very special 'small packages' to whom this work is dedicated, Adam and Emily.

DAVID W. BAKER

INTRODUCTION

I. EDOM IN SPACE AND TIME

THE land of Edom, also called Seir (Gn. 32:3; 36:20–21, 30; Nu. 24:18), lay south and east of the Dead Sea from the Wadi Zered to the Gulf of Aqabah. Straddling the Arabah rift valley running south from the Sea of Galilee to the Gulf of Aqabah, on the east it was rocky and mountainous, at times reaching *c.* 1,070 metres in elevation. Through it passed two major traffic routes, the King's Highway and the road along the Arabah. Its control over much of the north-south trade fed its coffers and made it a target for attack.

The Bible portrays the Edomites as descendants of Esau (Gn. 36, esp. vv. 1, 9), although archaeological excavations indicate earlier inhabitants of the land. Among the earliest extra-biblical mentions of the area are one in the Amarna letters from Egypt, dating from the fourteenth century BC (see *IBD* 1, pp. 37–39) and several references during the reign of Ramses II (late thirteenth century BC) to people of Seir.[1] The biblical record itself shows continued, though not always amicable, contact between Edom and the Israelites.

After the Exodus, Israel was denied passage through Edom (Nu. 20:14–21; Jdg. 11:17–18) and shortly thereafter Balaam predicted Edom's conquest (Nu. 24:18). Battle was joined with Edom under Saul (1 Sa. 14:47) and the area was conquered under David (2 Sa. 8:13–14 with RSV, NIV marginal emendations; 1 Ki. 11:15–16) and exploited under Solomon (1 Ki. 9:26–28), though not without Edomite opposition (1 Ki. 11:14–22). In the ninth century, Edomites, in confederation with Moabites and Ammonites, raided Judah during Jehoshaphat's reign (2 Ch. 20:1–2). Edom more successfully rebelled against Jehoram (Joram) and enjoyed relative

---

[1] *POTT*, p. 231.

freedom from Israelite domination for about forty years (2 Ki. 8:20–22; 2 Ch. 21:8–10).

Early in the next century, Judah under Amaziah retook Edom with great slaughter (2 Ki. 14:7; 2 Ch. 25:11–12), advancing as far as Sela. Some time later, when Judah was itself under pressure during Ahaz's reign, Edom raided Judah, taking captives (2 Ch. 28:17), and shook herself loose from Israel, never to be subjugated to her again.

During the Assyrian period, from at least 734 BC, Edom was a vassal of Assyria[1] and subsequently also of Babylon. At times they at least planned rebellion (Je. 27), though there is no evidence of trying to realize these plans. The situation at the time of the fall of Jerusalem (587 BC) is not clear from either biblical or extra-biblical sources. 1 Esdras 4:45 blames the Edomites for burning the Jerusalem Temple, but this is unconfirmed (*cf*. La. 4:21–22).

In the sixth century, Edomite power waned, as indicated by archaeological remains, with an apparent abandonment of some towns and migration of population[2] (*cf*. 1 Macc. 5:65). From the late sixth to the fourth centuries BC, Arab influence in the region was predominant (for indications of their presence in this period, *cf*. Ne. 2:19; 4:7; 6:1). This was brought to bear especially by the Nabataeans. Edomites were displaced. Some Edomites settled in the Negev in southern Judah, which became known by the related name Idumaea (1 Macc. 4:29).[3]

Much of this reconstruction is based on conjecture and secondary sources, since documentation and archaeological evidence from the area itself is sparse and ambiguous.

II. OBADIAH: THE MAN AND HIS TIME

Writing prophets in Israel are regularly identified by a notice of the period in which they prophesied, their hometown (or at least the place where the prophecies took place), and their father, or any combination of these. One is identified simply as a prophet (Habakkuk). Only two prophets are not given any contextual framework and not only are they 'without father and mother', they might even be without proper names

[1] *ANET*, p. 282.   [2] *POTT*, p. 243.
[3] For a detailed study of Edomite history, religion and culture, see *POTT*, pp. 229–258.

of their own. Malachi, 'my messenger', could be a designation of the prophet's role as intermediary, and Obadiah, 'servant/worshipper of Yahweh', could indicate the same role. Prophets were often referred to as 'servant' (*e.g.* 1 Ki. 14:18; 2 Ki. 17:23; Je. 7:25; Zc. 1:6). Obadiah is a common Israelite name in the Old Testament, however, so it is probably the name of the prophet.

Nothing further is known about the prophet; not even his time period is mentioned, so our dating of the book must come from clues within the book itself. Since the prophecy concerns Edom, and especially its treachery during an attack on Jerusalem (vv. 10–14), a synoptic study of the histories of Edom and Judah must be done to determine the periods referred to in the prophecy.

The outline of Edomite-Judaean contacts (pp. 21–22) shows that there were several periods when Obadiah would have been relevant. If the canonical sequence of Obadiah among the pre-exilic prophets is seen as significant, the background against which the book is set could be that of Jehoshaphat or Jehoram or Ahaz. The first does not fit the biblical evidence, since 2 Chronicles 20 pictures a victory for Judah through God's intervention rather than the defeat described in Obadiah 10–14. The rebellion against Jehoram mentions nothing of the attack on Jerusalem which is of importance to Obadiah (2 Ch. 21; *cf.* Ob. 11). Neither is it explicitly mentioned as suffering during Ahaz's reign (2 Ch. 28:16–18), although other towns are listed as being taken.

A suggested date in the fifth century BC, based on Arab raids dispossessing the Edomites during that period (see p. 22), is not necessary, since the Arab presence in the area was known as early as the ninth century BC.[1] The most satisfying setting is shortly after the fall of Jerusalem in 587 BC, when refugees were captured in mid-flight (2 Ki. 25:4–6). Although Edom is not explicitly linked with this catastrophe in the canonical text, its satisfaction at the outcome would have matched that of other nations who had opposed Judah in the past.

[1] *POTT*, p. 290.

III. THE BOOK

Obadiah, the fourth of the Minor Prophets, is the shortest book in the Old Testament, consisting of one chapter of twenty-one verses.

The short book is divided into two main sections. The first is particular and specific, consisting of oracles directed against Edom. The second is more general, being oracles concerning Israel and the nations.

Some have proposed that the oracles derived originally from more than one source and were joined for this book. One argument for this is that there are strong resemblances between Jeremiah 49:14–16 and 49:9 and Obadiah 1b–4 and 5 respectively. Rather than proposing a literary dependence of one upon the other, which would be difficult to verify, an independent source could have been used by both. This would account for the variations, especially as regards the order of the elements within the two books.[1]

Some (*e.g.* Wellhausen, Rudolph, Wolff) have proposed a reversal of the two halves of verse 15, since 15a mentions 'the Day of Yahweh' in relation to 'all nations'. The more universal message of the prophecy is found in verses 16–21. Verse 15b is directed specifically to Edom, however, the subject of verses 2–14. In order to place these two half verses close to the related contexts, the reversal was proposed. There is no apparent reason why such a dislocation might have been deliberately done. A scribal error has been suggested, but it is not necessary to suppose any dislocation if the book is from one hand.

Recent research on transitional techniques between paragraphs, by which they are united, has shown that common methods for linking involved repetitions of key words, grammatical forms, or other linguistic material.[2] The latter portion of Obadiah, dealing with 'all the nations', has that as a key concept in verse 16, and it is also found in 15a. This could thus serve as a deliberate transition between the two paragraphs. The direct address, second person singular form 'you', is characteristic of the 'Edom' portion of Obadiah (see all vv.

---

[1] See Allen, pp. 132–133, for further discussion. Pages 133–136 discuss the unity of the book.

[2] See H. van Dyke Parunak, 'Transitional Techniques in the Bible', *JBL* 102 (1983), pp. 525–548.

except 1, 6, 8). This is not used in verse 15a, which uses the more impersonal, third person form 'they', 'he', *etc.* The 'you' form is used in verses 15b and 16a. These shifts in person also serve as links, binding together the two paragraphs. Therefore, rather than indicating a plurality of sources for the prophecy, with a misplacement in verse 15, the evidence more convincingly argues for a deliberate structure. The existing form of the verse shows the unity of the book and of its parts. This is indicated in this commentary by having the discussion of verse 15 in two parts, closing section II and also opening section III (see pp. 38–39).

There are other lexical and theological indicators of unity within the book. A key word throughout is 'day'. Edom can look forward to a 'day' in which she is judged (v. 8), since she stood by on the 'day' that her neighbour, Judah, was attacked (vv. 11, 12 [three times], 13 [three times], 14). Also, on a wider scale, there will be a 'day' which will involve all nations (v. 15) in either judgment or deliverance. All three sections are thus bound by their respective 'days'. Another uniting feature is Edom and Judah being 'cut down' (vv. 9, 14). Finally, the prophecy begins and ends with Yahweh (vv. 1 [twice], 21) and he appears throughout, as speaker (vv. 1 [twice], 4, 8, 18) or actor (vv. 15, 21). His mountain, Zion (v. 17, 21), will gain the ascendancy over the mountain of the enemy of his people, Edom (vv. 8, 9, 19, 21; *cf.* vv. 3–4).

A theological unifier is the concept of *lex talionis*, or the correspondence and appropriateness of the punishment to the crime. This is spelt out explicitly in verse 15b, but can also be seen in examples where the proud (v. 3) is humbled (v. 2), those who passively watched the pillage of a nation (vv. 11–14) will themselves be pillaged (vv. 5–9), those harassing survivors (v. 14) will themselves have none (v. 18) and those who participated in a dispossession (v. 14) will themselves be dispossessed (v. 7, 19).

IV. THE MESSAGE

Obadiah presents a message of hope to God's people. This is done in two different stages, corresponding to the two major divisions of the prophecy. Firstly, Judah can be assured of God's justice in that Edom, a nation who took part in her own humiliation whether as an observer or as a participant

(vv. 11–14), would herself be humiliated (vv. 2–10, 15b). This judgment is due not only to Edom's gloating, but also to her arrogance. She perceived herself as relatively superior to and unassailable by the surrounding nations (vv. 2–4), but forgot the absolute transcendence of Israel's God. Secondly, this can be seen on a wider scale, where all the nations will be judged and Judah will get back from them all that which was taken (vv. 15a, 16–21). God has not forsaken his people, as might have been feared when they suffered defeat. He will continue to support them because he is their covenant God, Yahweh, who met them at Sinai.

Not only is Yahweh willing to help his people, he is also able to do so, since he is sovereign, Lord (v. 1) and king of nations, and not simply of Israel (v. 21). His sovereignty is also shown by his direct intervention in history. While using human agents to carry out his plans for judgment and for blessing, Yahweh is the one who controls these agents and sets them on their path, even though they might not acknowledge him as God (*cf.* v. 7). As Yahweh has fought beside and on behalf of Israel in the past (*e.g.* in the conquest of Canaan), so he will withstand the warriors of her enemies in Obadiah's day. Whether they are relatively minor, such as the Edomites, or major, such as the Babylonians, all are among the nations under Yahweh's power. Nothing now remains of these two particular peoples, Edom and Babylon, but the descendants of those whose capital, Jerusalem, they destroyed survive still.

All of these points have relevance to the contemporary reader of Obadiah. While neither Edom nor Babylon are with us any longer, enemies of God's people are still too evident and sometimes apparently all powerful. The same God whom the prophets proclaimed as not only willing but able to stand on the side of his people and deliver them, is to be declared today.

ANALYSIS

27

COMMENTARY

I. HEADING (1)

A. Title (1a)

The 'revelation' message is spoken to *Obadiah*, the human intermediary. Here *vision* (*ḥāzôn*) is a general term for divine communication (*i.e.* 'revelatory word'), often used in superscriptions to the prophetic books (*cf.* Is. 1:1; Na. 1:1). Elsewhere it is used in the more specific sense of 'vision' (*cf.* Is. 29:7; Ezk. 12:27; Dn. 1:17; 8:1), which the NIV (less accurately) adopts here. The title is the shortest of any Old Testament prophetic book.

B. Message and circumstances (1b–c)

The source of the message is Yahweh, Israel's covenant God, who is *Lord* and sovereign over all nations and keeper of promises, including that of Israel's possession of the land (vv. 19–21; *cf.* Gn. 12:1; 15:7; 28:13). While this typical report formula (*cf.* Ezk. 2:4 and numerous other occasions) refers to the rest of this book, it more narrowly defines verses 2–15, specifically concerning *Edom* (*cf.* Je. 49:7). Edom, Israel's south-eastern neighbour and archetypal enemy, is the subject of several other prophecies (Is. 34; 63:1–6; Je. 49:7–22; Ezk. 25:12–14; 35; Am. 1:11–12; Mal. 1:2–5). It is better understood as the subject of the present oracles rather than their addressee, since Old Testament prophecy is chiefly directed towards Israel. Even Jonah, containing the only recorded prophecy addressed directly to non-Israelites (Jon. 3:4), is in its totality for Israel's use. Obadiah's judgment pronounced on a foreign people is not Israelite nationalistic chauvinism, but rather the recognition of universal responsibility and guilt before the God of both Israel and the nations (*cf.* Is. 2:1–4; Am. 1:3 – 2:16; 9:7, *etc.*)

Ordinarily the report formula ('thus says') immediately precedes the message spoken. In the present text the report is followed by material about Yahweh rather than reporting what he said. This has led some commentators to propose either that the report formula has been displaced from its original position at the beginning of verse 2, or that it was a secondary addition put in the wrong place. A better interpretation, in that it makes sense of the existing text, takes verse 1c as providing the historical-political circumstances surrounding Yahweh's message, which itself starts in verse 2. At the same time that Obadiah was receiving a message concerning Edom itself (vv. 2–15), he hears that the nations round about have been called to action as well.[1]

A *message* or report (1 Sa. 4:19; Is. 28:9; 53:1) from Yahweh is heard. The LXX of the parallel Jeremiah 49:14 reads 'I heard', speaking of the prophet, rather than the *we . . . heard* here. The latter has been interpreted as referring to a group of prophets,[2] although no such group is evident here. It could also refer to all Israel,[3] possibly including the prophet himself in an editorial 'we'.[4] The latter best fits the context, since the prophet seeks to increase his credibility and identification with the audience by using the classical rhetorical device of the ethical appeal (*cf.* Is. 40:3, 8).[5]

The next clause is ambiguous, indicating either that a messenger is sent in addition to the message (RSV, AV), or that the message is given under the circumstances of a messenger being sent (NEB) and as a result of this sending, or, more likely (NIV), it concerns an *envoy*.[6] This envoy, one from among the nations (*cf.* Is. 18:2; 57:9), is most likely sent by one of Edom's enemies to summon other opponents *against her*,[7] to share in her downfall. There is no indication that Yahweh was himself involved in the messenger's commission. He does, however, tell of the forthcoming judgment, and his chosen instruments

---

[1] Craigie, pp. 200–201.   [2] *E.g.* Armerding, p. 341; Wolff, p. 27.
[3] J. Keil, p. 1.
[4] C. F. Keil, p. 351; F. E. Gaebelein, *Four Minor Prophets: Obadiah, Jonah, Habakkuk, and Haggai* (Moody Press, 1970), p. 19.
[5] See Y. Gitay, *Prophecy and Persuasion: A Study of Isaiah 40–48* (Linguistica Biblica, 1981), pp. 37, 67.
[6] M. B. Dick, 'A Syntactic Study of the Book of Obadiah', *Semitics* 9 (1984), p. 12.
[7] *Cf.* Mal. 1:3–4, where Edom is grammatically feminine, and even alternates between feminine and masculine.

include nations not even recognizing him as God (*cf.* Is. 10:5; 45:1; Hab. 1:6–11). Yahweh is sovereign in the history of the entire world, and freely exercises his will therein. The typical battle cry to *rise* up (Je. 6:4, 5; *cf.* Is. 2:5), which is given to the nations to oppose Edom, encourages Obadiah in his prophecy against them as well.

II. ORACLES CONCERNING EDOM (2–15)

A. First oracle: Pride goes before destruction (2–4)

The oracle from Yahweh in which he himself speaks (vv. 1, 4) now begins.

i. Edom's abasement (2). Yahweh directs his audience's attention to the judgment to be meted out to Edom by calling them to *see*, which also emphasizes the following Hebrew word, *small*. This concerns not only population or territorial size but also their intrinsic worth and significance, as shown by the parallel *despised*. This result of God's judgment introduces the central motif of this and the next two oracles which will elaborate on Edom's degradation. While the verbal form commonly denotes a completed action (see AV), it is also used as a prophetic perfect where the threat of God is seen as so certain of fulfilment that it is expressed as already accomplished (RSV, NIV). Here, again, God's sovereignty is evidenced through pagan human activity.

ii. Edom's pride (3–4). 3. Edom's abasement is caused by *pride* (*cf.* Dt. 18:22; 1 Sa. 17:28) or insolence. It is emphasized here by the opening Hebrew clause and also by its blatant evidence in the arrogant questions which close the verse. The word chosen for 'pride' is significant in that a form of the same Hebrew root, *zid*, is found in the description of Jacob defrauding the progenitor of Edom, Esau, of his birth-right through a boiled dish (*nāzīd*, Gn. 25:29).[1] This was the start of the antagonism between Esau's descendants, Edom (vv. 8, 9, 18, 19, 21), and Jacob's, Israel (vv. 10, 17, 18). Edom was *deceived*, leading to her judgment, just as Eve was deceived (Gn. 3:13) and consequently judged (Gn. 3:16).

[1] Armerding, p. 342.

The root of the arrogance is given by describing the Edomite 'dwelling' (rsv)[1] as the *clefts of the rocks*, accentuating the rocky impenetrability as well as the height of the Edomite plateau. This served as a natural barrier and stronghold. There is a word play on 'rock' (*sela'*), which is also the name of an Edomite town (Jdg. 1:36; 2 Ki. 14:7). This could be the site of the later Nabataean capital Petra, also 'rock' in Greek.

The grammatical person changes in mid-verse from 'you' to 'one' (an impersonal subject). Such a change is not irregular in Hebrew (*cf.* Am. 5:12 for a similar change) and does not necessarily indicate a change of addressee. Since such an alternation is not customary in English, most translations keep one person throughout.

The arrogant Edomites reflect in their *heart*, the locus of their pride, that they are invincible (*cf.* Is. 14:13–15). Secure from human attack through no merit of their own, as they are literally elevated above their enemies so they are raised metaphorically above them by pride. With the rhetorical question here, the stage is being set for the Edomites' mortification from an unseen source in the next verse.

4. The oracle climaxes with two conditional clauses, each advancing upon the lofty situation in which Edom prides itself. The first involves soaring (rsv, niv), achieving greater heights than the crags of their dwelling, *like the eagle*, the largest bird in the region (*cf.* Ezk. 17:7), which is renowned for its flying ability (*cf.* Is. 40:31). Picking up on a bird, the second involves nesting *among the stars* as the highest parts of God's creation (Jb. 22:12; Is. 14:13). Structurally, the passage shows a metaphorical development and expansion from rocky heights (v. 3), through the sky where birds cavort, to the very heavens (v. 4). This progression exemplifies the increasing self-assurance of proud Edom. Even from these great heights, Yahweh says he will *bring . . . down* the proud. The same verbal form is used as in the arrogant question of verse 3, showing through the structure that the punishment fits the crime. In her boast, Edom was looking the wrong way. Being beyond man's reach, she forgot the incomparable greatness of God (*cf.* Gn. 11:1–9, esp. vv. 4 and 7, where the folly of the great tower designed

---

[1] The word could involve the idea of 'enthronement' (*cf.* Ex. 11:5; Is. 40:22) as a powerful ruler (Dick, 'A Syntatic Study', p. 14), highlighting Edom's arrogance, as possibly could the word used for 'live' (*škn*), which is associated with the lofty habitation of God himself (*cf.* Is. 33:5; 57:15).

to *reach* to heaven is expressed by God's *descent* from heaven). Pride preceding abasement is not uncommon in the Bible (Pr. 16:18; Is. 14:12–15). The warning of verse 2 is developed from its cause (pride) through its result (abasement; *cf.* 'despised', v. 2). The message of verses 2–4 is a self-contained unit, closing with the final oracle formula reaffirming its divine source.

B. Second oracle: Plunder and treachery (5–7)

The author elaborates upon the first oracle by accentuating the depths to which Edom will plunge.

5. By starting with a conditional particle 'should' (*if*, AV, RSV, NIV), the oracle is connected with that which precedes it (*cf.* v. 4). Rather than the metaphorical possibilities of verse 4, which are not physically attainable, this time the possibilities stated are realizable. The coming of surreptitious *thieves* or forcible *robbers* Edom would know by experience. One would next expect the result, that they would pillage 'enough' for their needs (AV, RSV) or wants (NIV, JB, NEB). This logical progression is broken by the interjection of a lament bewailing Edom's destruction (*cf.* Is. 6:5; 15:1; Ho. 4:6). This lament, a form generally opened by *how* (*'ēk*), is used in dirges (*cf.* 2 Sa. 1:19; Is. 14:4, 12; Je. 9:19). It fits the context as a spontaneous cry of heart-rending shock elicited by the devastation (*cf.* v. 6). Another mark of a dirge is its metre or rhythm, which is in the pattern 3+2 for Hebrew (*e.g.* Am. 5:2–3a). Our oracle section begins[1] and ends[2] with this pattern. If the present interjection is placed after the clause concerning pillage, the same metrical pattern would result in this line too.[3] This relocation also reduces the awkwardness in the thought flow noted above, but does not necessitate seeing the interjection as a secondary, later addition (*cf.* Je. 49:9, where it is lacking). The present text is readily understandable as it now stands, but the proposed slight alteration, though not compelling, achieves a structurally significant pattern. The

[1] Verse 5a:	If-thieves came to-you,		3	
	if-robbers in-the-night –			2
[2] Verse 6:	But-how Esau will-be-ransacked,		3	
	his-hidden-treasures pillaged!			2
[3] Verse 5b:	Would-they not-steal only-as-much-as-they-wanted?		3	
	Oh-what-a-disaster awaits-you.			2

interjection in its proposed new location then separates the two illustrations of pillage used here. The second picture is also taken from Edom's experience. The grape-gatherers (Je. 6:9) pick the fruit, but are expected to *leave* gleanings, as required by Mosaic law (Dt. 24:21).

6. In contrast to the denudation by thief or worker, the plunder of Edom will be total. *Esau*, the father of the Edomite people (Gn. 36:1, 9), will be *ransacked*, completely stripped and searched (*cf.* Gn. 44:12; Zp. 1:12–13). Nothing will remain *hidden* from the voracious conqueror. Israel's punishment, while great, will be partial in that a remnant will remain (*e.g.* Is. 10:20–22; Am. 3:12; 5:3; Zp. 2:3; 3:12–13). Not so Edom, who faces total eradication. The writer uses the dirge form to drive his message home; his hearers join in mourning those who are already as good as dead. This could also explain the change in person between verses 5 and 6. God spoke *to* Edom in verse 5, but *about* him in verse 6, as of one no longer there.[1]

7. Edom is again addressed directly, even emphatically, since 'you/your' occurs seven times in this verse. Now attention is directed to the perfidy inflicted upon Edom by those she trusted (*cf.* Ps. 55:12–14), her *allies* (RSV, NIV) and *friends* (Heb., 'men of peace'). They expelled Edom to her border, possibly referring to the Arab's incursion in the sixth century (see the Introduction, p. 22). Those who were to protect her best interests deceived her, just as Edom's own proud heart had done (v. 3). The ruse could have involved luring the people out from their impregnable strongholds (v. 3). Part of the shock of these events is conveyed by the juxtaposition of treachery on the one hand with friends on the other, the unexpected making the blow rhetorically powerful.

The fourth Hebrew clause is problematic. It could read [*those who eat*] *your bread* (the bracketed portion is lacking), based on a possible parallel with Psalm 41:9. There a 'man of peace' is juxtaposed with 'he that eats my bread'. Eating and drinking together is part of the covenant-making ceremony in Israel and the Near East (*cf.* Gn. 31:54; Ex. 24:11; 1 Cor. 11:23–26),[2] so this meaning would well fit the Obadiah context where allies and friends proved unfaithful. The same Hebrew root *lḥm*, used here of 'bread', has a homonym found

---

[1] Allen, p. 149.

[2] See D. J. McCarthy, *Treaty and Covenant* (Biblical Institute, ²1981), pp. 253–254 and n. 19.

in other passages for 'doing battle' (Pss. 35:1; 56:1–2). This understanding of the word, involving an emendation to the Massoretic vocalization (see *BHS*, Vulg., Targum and several Greek versions), makes explicit the hidden opposition of the fraudulent friends. There could be a word play here on the two uses of the word, showing the assumed friends as veritable foes. This contrast is structurally marked in the Hebrew by a change in word order, *allies* and *friends* closing the clauses in which they are the subject, while the last group of 'foes/friends' commences its clause.

The treachery here involves a *trap* (RSV; NIV) or 'ambush' (*BHS*; *cf.* Vulg.; Syr.; LXX), although this word is also obscure (*cf.* Je. 30:13; Ho. 5:13, where it refers to a 'wound' – so AV here). This treachery will be amazing and beyond comprehension to those betrayed.

C. Third oracle: Judgment day (8–9)

8. Yahweh again speaks in an oracle, as in the first section of the book (*cf.* v. 4). The use of a rhetorical question ties this oracle to the previous one, where two are used (v. 5). The *wise* of Edom are famed (see Job's counsellor Eliphaz of Teman [v. 9], Jb. 2:11; Je. 49:7; *cf.* 1 Ki. 4:30), with wisdom gleaned and dispersed along the important trade routes which crossed through the land. As her allies dispersed, so will wisdom and *understanding* (*cf.* Ex. 31:3; Is. 44:19). This last word formally links this oracle with a key word of the previous oracle (v. 7),[1] showing the structural unity of the final form of this portion of the book. 'Mount Esau' (RSV) is a name unique to Obadiah (vv. 9, 19, 21). It parallels *Edom*, so it could refer to the entire mountainous country, though more specifically Mount Seir is probably meant (Gn. 36:8). This deprivation will happen *in that day*, either the Day of the Lord (*cf.* v. 15) or more likely the specific day of God's judging Edom referred to earlier (v. 2; *cf.* Is. 7:18, 20; 10:20).

9. Edom will also lose her *warriors*, the élite troops, through terror (*cf.* Dt. 1:21; Is. 31:4, 9; Je. 23:4). This will result in destruction by *slaughter*. The Septuagint, Vulgate and Syriac transpose this last Hebrew word to start verse 10 due to a word there which is similar in grammatical form and meaning

---

[1] See van Dyke Parunak, 'Transitional Techniques', pp. 525–548.

(so NEB renders 'murderous violence'). While not compelling, such a minor alteration would result in the same word ('Esau') ending verses 8 and 9. For poetic variation, Edom is referred to as 'Mount Esau' (RSV) and *Teman*, the area east of Petra which is expanded in meaning to denote the entire country (*cf.* Je. 49:7, 20; Am. 1:12; Hab. 3:3).

These three oracles build toward a climax with: (1) the plunder of riches (5–6), (2) loss of wisdom and understanding (7–8), and (3) a loss of military capability (9). The very structures of society, in its constituent elements of economic well-being, wise rule and military security through armed force and international treaty, will topple.

D. Reasons for Edom's judgment (10–15)

After details of what awaits her from God's hand through the agency of other nations, Edom is faced with the factors contributing to her punishment.

i. Passive observation of pillage (10–11). 10. Punishment comes *because of the violence* – wickedness both moral and physical (Jdg. 9:24; Joel 3:19; Hab. 1:3, 9). Edom's violence was directed towards *Jacob* – that is, all of Israel (v. 18; *cf.* Nu. 20:14; Dt. 23:7; Am. 1:11). This name, and reference to *your brother*, harks back to the patriarchal account of conflict between the progenitors of these two peoples, Jacob and Esau (Gn. 25:19–34; 27:1 – 28:9; 33). This as yet unspecified violence results in Edom's *shame* (*cf.* Ps. 44:15; Je. 51:51; Mi. 7:10), resuming her being 'despised' in verse 2. Her destruction will be eternal (*cf.* Ezk. 35:9). The penalties thus summarize and structurally bracket the first three oracles.[1] Edom's afflictions are not arbitrary, but have just cause. The unexpected juxtaposition of *brother* with *violence* (*cf.* v. 7) accentuates the incongruity between expectation and realization. The description of the form of the violence is catalogued in the following verses.

11. *On the day* (or 'in the day of', see vv. 12–15) is a key term in Obadiah, especially here where it occurs eleven times (vv. 11–15; nine times in NIV), climaxing in the Day of the Lord in verse 15. 'Day' also unites this oracle with the

[1] Armerding, p. 347.

preceding one (v. 8). In this prophecy there are two distinct periods referred to, the future 'Day of the Lord' (*cf.* v. 15), and another day with a historical reference, a day of misfortune, which probably refers to the Babylonian destruction of Jerusalem (587 BC). The latter is the focus of these verses. In that time of Jacob's need of support from a brother, Edom *stood aloof* and detached (RSV, NIV; *cf.* Gn. 21:16; 2 Sa. 18:13; 2 Ki. 2:7). Rather than help, Edom watched while Jerusalem was pillaged by *strangers* and *foreigners* who *cast lots* to divide the spoil (*cf.* Ps. 22:18; Joel 3:3; Na. 3:10; Mt. 27:35). Even *you*, Edom, in your passive observation if not active involvement, are aligning yourself to be *one of them*, the enemies.

ii. Do not! (12–14). In a series of prohibitions, Edom is urged to stop opposing Judah. The verbal forms refer to future actions (so NEB, JB, NIV), reflecting the horror of the prophet at the deeds described. With less grammatical basis, these prohibitions have been translated in the past tense (so AV, RSV; *cf.* Nu. 23:25). The regularity of formal structure combined with the increasing violence and brutality of the acts described makes an emotionally powerful appeal.

12. The first step involves Edom 'gloating' at (RSV; *cf.* Pss. 22:17; 118:7; Mi. 7:8), 'rejoicing' over (AV, RSV, NIV) and ridiculing (*cf.* Ps. 35:21, 26; Is. 57:4; Ezk. 35:13 for similar idioms) Judah in its calamity. The verbs progress in involvement from an internal attitude to an outward action. These responses are related to *the day of* the *misfortune* of their brother Judah (see v. 11), explained as that of his *destruction*, 'annihilation' (*cf.* Nu. 24:24) and *trouble* (v. 14).

13. Edom is urged not to draw near to her brother's misfortune by entering their *gates* (*cf.* La. 4:12–13). This resumes verse 11, where it is the enemy who enters. This foreshadows Edom's actual position as foe rather than brother. They would enter in order to 'gloat' (see v. 12, RSV; NIV has *look down on* in vv. 12, 13), and even to 'reach' (2 Sa. 6:6; 22:17) towards their possessions (*cf.* v. 11; Joel 3:5). Another progressive process is presented (*cf.* v. 12) with Edom coming closer, first to laugh and then to loot on the day of Judah's *disaster* (Je. 18:17; Ezk. 35:5). The Hebrew of this word (*'êdām*) could be a play on the name Edom in the last passage as well as

37

here,[1] or alternatively there might be alliteration on two of the sounds in 'day' so common in this passage.[2]

14. Edom's despicable actions towards her brother climax with an attack on Judah's refugees (*cf.* v. 12; 2 Ki. 25:4–5). Not actively engaging in the conquest itself, Edom was doing something even crueller, callously handing over (*cf.* Dt. 23:15; 32:30; 1 Sa. 23:11; Am. 1:9; 6:8) *survivors* (v. 18; Jos. 10:20) caught in their demoralized flight. Edom's punishment fits her crime: they who *cut down* others will themselves be cut off (vv. 9–10).

iii. Payment in kind (15). Serving as a structural bridge, this verse joins the oracles concerning Edom (vv. 2–14) with the messages regarding Israel and the nations (vv. 16–21). The manuscript evidence and the literary structure of the book do not support a reversal of verse 15 a and b, as proposed by some (see the Introduction, pp. 24–25).

The Day of Yahweh is when God will defeat chaos and the powers in opposition to himself. Israel had seen only one aspect of this in looking forward to prosperity for herself (*cf.* vv. 17, 21) and punishment for her foes, the *nations* (*cf.* v. 16; Dt. 32:35–36; Joel 3:2; Zc. 14:1, 3). Israel will find that its own rebellion before God will also be punished (Joel 1:15, 2:1–2, 11; 3:14). Israel is at one with all people, here exemplified by Edom (see v. 16), in responsibility before God (*cf.* Am. 5:18–20). Edom's judgment is justifiable and deserved according to the talion law of tit for tat (*cf.* Lv. 24:19; Je. 50:15, 29). The statement is emphasized by repeating that what Edom has done will rebound on her head (*cf.* Pr. 12:14; 19:17; Ezk. 35:15; Ho. 4:9, Joel 3:4, 7). God shows not only his sovereignty over all people by not permitting unrequited wickedness, but also his justice by not permitting punishment to exceed crime.

The only people directly addressed elsewhere in the book as 'you' are the Edomites (vv. 2–5, 7, 9–16), so this verse again links verses 16–21 with 2–14. The representative character of Edom is explained better by seeing the verse as directed

---

[1] 'Their disaster' (*'êdām*) and 'Edom' (*'ᵉdôm*). The former suffix (*ām*) is significant in the word play, since in the next two occurrences of *'êd* in the verse the suffix is changed to 'his/its' (*'êdô*).

[2] Verse 13 could be playing on the *m* of *yôm*, '*day*', in *'amî bᵉyôm 'êdam*, with 13b and c playing on *ô*, *bᵉra'atô bᵉyôm 'êdô* and *bᵉḥêlô bᵉyôm 'edô*.

towards her, though the context of measure for measure would also fit Israel as the subject.

III. ISRAEL AND THE NATIONS (15–21)[1]

A. Tables turned (15–18)

15. The Day of Yahweh (see v. 8 and the Introduction, p. 25) as the judgment of the nations is detailed and explained.

16. Edom is presented as the paradigm of all the nations. As Edom *drank* in rejoicing at Israel's suffering, so she will *drink continually*, not this time in rejoicing, but from the cup of God's wrath (*cf.* Is. 51:17; Je. 25:15, 17–18, 28–29; 49:12; Hab. 2:15–16; Mk. 14:36). As Edom has done, so will the nations. Perpetuity of punishment is found elsewhere (*e.g.* Je. 25:9, 18), so emendation (*cf. BHS*) is not necessary. Nations will gulp down (*drink and drink*) God's punishment so that they will be completely destroyed, *and be as if they had never been*.

17. *But*, on the other hand, and in contrast to the nations in verse 16, and to Edom in particular (vv. 1–15), *on Mount Zion* the oppressor's plan will be thwarted. Instead of refugees (v. 14; *pᵉlîṭîm*), there will be *deliverance* (*pᵉlêṭâh*). God's goodness in his covenant with Israel will be realized, and the Day of Yahweh, while bringing judgment on Israel's enemies, will restore God's people to their initial position. This clause is quoted in Joel 2:32 (3:5 in the MT),[2] where it is treated as the authoritative word of God. The additional aspect of holiness could refer to Israel itself (*cf.* Is. 63:18; Je. 2:3), but Israel does not appear in the near context. A similar form is also used when referring to Jerusalem (Joel 3:17). Here the grammatical referent is masculine, so it is most probably referring to Mount Zion itself (*cf.* v. 16; Ezk. 28:14; Dn. 9:20), which is sanctified by the presence of Yahweh (*cf.* Ex. 3:5; Ps. 11:4) and set apart for his use (Is. 52:1). This mountain of blessing stands against the heights of Edom's pride (v. 3).[3]

---

[1] For the inclusion of v. 15 in two different portions, see the Introduction, p. 25.

[2] The major difference is the explanatory gloss, 'Mount Zion, that is Jerusalem'.

[3] Dick, 'A Syntactic Study', p. 14.

Israel, the *house of Jacob* (*cf.* v. 10; Is. 48:1), will also occupy her possessions or her *inheritance*, the 'promised land' (*cf.* Ex. 6:8 and more than a hundred times in Exodus). A minor textual variant, previously evident in the Septuagint and Targum, and now also found in an early Hebrew manuscript from Murabbaʿat near the Dead Sea, results in 'dispossessing the dispossessors' (*cf.* NEB, *BHS*). This reading also integrates well with verses 19–20, emphasizing the negative aspect of what is lost by other nations. Their punishment fits their crime of previously dispossessing Israel. The Massoretic reading, on the other hand, looks at the same phenomenon positively, seeing what Israel has gained. This occupation is shown in verses 19–20 to be a physical rather than a spiritual reality. Here several aspects of the Davidic covenant which had been jeopardized in 587 BC by Israel's rebellion are brought together. These are the presence of God in his holy place, and the presence of his people, or at least a remnant of them, in their promised land.

This verse is a climax of hope for God's people: their desperate state will be righted and the benefits of the covenant with God will again be enjoyed. They will be saved (*cf.* Dt. 30:3–5a). This restoration of the people took place in 537 BC under Zerubbabel (Ezr. 1–2), with the rebuilding of the 'holy place' *par excellence*, the Temple in Jerusalem, in 515 BC (Ezr. 3; 6:13–15).

18. Edom, Judah's original opponent in verses 2–15, is juxtaposed with Israel in the metaphor of *stubble* and *flame*. The traditional animosities flare, but Israel gains the upper hand. Here *Jacob* (*cf.* v. 17) could represent all Israel (*cf.* Ps. 22:23) or only Judah, with *Joseph* representing the other ten tribes (*cf.* 1 Ki. 11:28; Ps. 77:15; Am. 5:6). In either case, all of the tribes, those previously exiled by Assyria and those now taken by Babylonia, will be involved in Edom's judgment (*cf.* also Ezr. 6:17; 8:35, where all twelve tribes of Israel are represented). *Fire* and *flame* represent God's wrath (*cf.* Ps. 18:8; La. 1:13; Am. 1:4), here actualized through God's people.

As Jacob had been devoured (Je. 10:25; *cf.* Ps. 14:4; Mi. 3:3; Zc. 12:6), so will Edom be consumed. Edom had tried to eradicate Israelite refugees (v. 14, *cf.* v. 17), so she will have *no survivors* (*cf.* Jos. 8:22; Je. 42:17; 44:14; La. 2:22). What is ironic is that the instrument of Edom's destruction is the few survivors which she had sought to destroy. The remnant, the scattered residue of a defeated nation, not only symbolizes Israel's ignominy (*cf.* Is. 1:9; Am. 5:3), but also her hope. There is hope in that not all will be lost for her; a few will survive and rise again in power. For Edom, however, the judgment will be complete (see v. 16b).

Since Yahweh *has spoken*, these statements are authoritative and certain. This clause closes this prophetic section, as shown by the switch from poetry to prose in the next verses.

B. Return of the kingdom (19–21)

The prose nature of these verses has led to the suggestion that they are a gloss added by a later hand (though possibly one close to Obadiah's time[1]) to explain the previous verses. The arguments presented are not compelling, since most authors, contemporary and biblical, employ more than one literary genre, so a mixture of genres is not a sufficient reason to demand multiplicity of authors. Grammatical problems add to the difficulty of interpreting this passage.

19. Occupation is the subject of the next two verses. The first geographical reference is to the *Negev*, the wilderness south of Beersheva. This verb and noun combination brackets verses 19–20, indicating a textual sub-section. The grammatical role of the Negev people is unclear. Are they the subject of the verb, being the occupiers (RSV, JB, NIV), thus being previous Israelite inhabitants (the already mentioned house of Jacob who move into Edomite territory); or are they the object, the occupied (NEB), in which case the incoming people would again be the Israelites, replacing the Edomites who had migrated to the area (see the Introduction, p. 22)? The latter is supported by the Negev being occupied by the house of Jacob in verse 18 (*cf.* Am. 9:12). If so, the following phrase would be an explanation, defining Edom as *the mountains of Esau* (*cf.* vv. 6, 8–9, 18),[2] tying this passage to the first half of the book.[3] The Shephelah, being the low hill area between the

[1] Wolff, p. 47.
[2] See Allen, p. 170, n. 37 and references.
[3] A grammatical difficulty is the lack of a Hebrew direct object indicator for 'Negev' and its use with 'the mountains of Esau'. The marker is common in prose but rare in poetry, which could indicate that the original poetic form of this passage was made prosaic by the additions of glosses, or amplifications, which also destroy the metre. These matters are not consistent throughout the entire passage.

coastal lowlands and the central hills, is also occupied. This is amplified by indicating some of its more noteworthy inhabitants, the Philistines living on the Mediterranean coast, centring around their five major cities of Ashdod, Ashkelon, Gaza, Gath and Ekron. Even before the foundation of the Israelite state they had opposed Israel, and continued to do so, at times in alliance with Edom (Am. 1:6; *cf.* 2 Ch. 28:17–18).[1] Under the Maccabees, the territory of the Philistines and their major cities were acquired by Jews (1 Macc. 10:84–89; 11:60–62). Mention is also made of the *fields of Ephraim* in central Palestine, whose chief city is *Samaria*, the former capital of the northern kingdom (*cf.* 1 Ki. 16:24; 21:1). The latter is a gloss or explanation, as indicated by the Hebrew.[2] Judaeans gained control of part of the Samaritan territory in 153 BC (1 Macc. 10:38), and Samaria itself was taken and besieged by John Hyrcanus in 106 BC.[3] A difficulty is encountered if one suggests that *Benjamin*, a small tribe from south central Palestine (*cf.* 1 Sa. 9:21), is explained by *Gilead*, which, although directly east of Benjamin, is in Transjordan. Some have suggested emending Benjamin to 'Ammonites' (*BHS*), requiring the addition of one Hebrew letter, but there is no manuscript evidence for the proposal. Gilead was taken by the Maccabees in 164 BC (1 Macc. 5:9–54).

20. The obscurity caused by the grammatical difficulties of this verse is clarified to some extent by the parallelism of its two halves. *Exiles* are referred to in each half, using a word often associated with Judaean deportees after 587 BC (*cf.* 2 Ki. 25:27; Ezk. 1:2), supporting an exilic dating for the book. The second exiles are described as being from *Jerusalem*, but now being in *Sepharad*, possibly Sardis in Asia Minor, though locations in Spain and Media have also been suggested. These people would be early exiles who now return to resettle *the towns of the Negev* (*cf.* 2 Ch. 28:18). A number of these same elements are in the first half of the verse and can assist in its interpretation. The Jerusalemites here are substituted by *this company of Israelite exiles*. The awkwardness of the Hebrew has led to the reading of *company* as 'Halah' (RSV, with no change in Hebrew consonants), an Assyrian site where there were

[1] See *POTT*, pp. 53–78.
[2] See D. W. Baker, 'Further Examples of the *Waw Explicatiuum*', *VT* 30 (1980), pp. 129–136.
[3] Josephus, *Antiquities* 13.5.2–3.

exiles (*cf.* 2 Ki. 17:6; 18:11; 1 Ch. 5:26). The last part of the clause concerns Canaanites *as far as Zarephath*, a Mediterranean town north of Israel between Tyre and Sidon (*cf.* 1 Ki. 17:9; Lk. 4:26). The Hebrew has a relative pronoun, giving a definition of 'Israelites who are (*'šr*) in Canaan', or 'are Canaanites', which is difficult to understand. A minor textual corruption of one misread letter plus a change in letter order could have led to this from an original which spoke of Israel 'inheriting' (*yrš*) (*cf.* AV, RSV, NIV) Canaanite territory that was at the far north of their original inheritance (cf. Jos. 19:28–29), balancing the far south of the Negev.

21. Not only will there be a repossession of territorial areas, but also the capital, Jerusalem, which had been destroyed in 587 BC, will be visited by *deliverers*, or those who bring an expected or future salvation (*cf.* Ne. 9:27).

Some versions read the last word as a passive, those to whom deliverance or salvation has already come, that is, those who have been released from exile and allowed to return. This latter provides a link with the exiles in verse 20, and could refer to the returned exiles under Zerubbabel (Ezra 1–3). The problem with this interpretation is the limited success of these returnees, whose possessions never equalled those detailed in verse 20. The LXX reads 'from' *Mount Zion*, the origin of the deliverers rather than their goal, though this is not necessary, and the present form provides a link with verse 17. This salvation is better seen as eschatological, when the Messianic kingdom will be inaugurated and Israel will achieve universal dominion under its ideal King (Gn. 49:10; *cf.* Ezk. 21:25–27; Rev. 5:5–6). These deliverers will govern Edom (*the mountains of Esau*), providing salvation and rule as in the period of the judges (*cf.* Jdg. 3:9, 15). Edom will thus not be completely destroyed, but will in fact be subjugated. Here Edom is probably symbolic, representing all the nations who opposed God and his people (*cf.* vv. 19–20).

The interplay and antagonism between states is climaxed by a reminder that power is not ultimately in their hands but that dominion (*the kingdom*) will belong to Yahweh. Lest Israel or the nations consider themselves independent, they are reminded who has actual control (Ps. 22:28; *cf.* Ps. 47:7–9; Is. 52:7; Mi. 4:7). The dominant position of Yahweh is reinforced by the structure of the prophecy, since his name brackets the book in verses 1 and 21. Edom, or Esau, the recipient of God's judgment, serves the same structural function. In its final form, Obadiah is thus a unity, declaring God's punishment upon wrongdoers and his promises to his people.

JONAH

AN INTRODUCTION AND COMMENTARY

by

T. DESMOND ALEXANDER, B.A., PH.D.

Lecturer in Semitic Studies,
The Queen's University of Belfast

AUTHOR'S PREFACE

The story of Jonah being swallowed by a 'whale' has undoubtedly fascinated generations of children. Recounted by narrators eager to capture youthful imaginations, it provides all the elements necessary for a truly gripping story. Unfortunately, however, childhood memories can colour all too easily our perception of the book. The original narrative says practically nothing about the great fish; its existence is noted in only three verses.

Yet, even if we relegate the great fish to a minor role, the book need lose none of its appeal for us. We find here a most intriguing confrontation between Yahweh, the God of heaven and earth, and Jonah, his rebellious prophet. Moreover, the central message of the book remains especially relevant. *Salvation comes from the Lord.* It is not the exclusive possession of any one group, nor does it guarantee their continued existence at the expense of others. To those who appeal, on the basis of their special relationship with God, for the overthrow of their enemies, the book of Jonah voices a stern rebuke. God's mercy may extend to the most unlikely of people, and who can tell what the consequences may be?

In spite of its brevity, the book of Jonah provides more than its share of critical issues. The solutions offered in this commentary do not claim to be infallible. If, however, they lead some readers to a deeper understanding of the text, and others to consider afresh alternative approaches to the many problems raised by the book's contents, then the author will be more than satisfied.

A preface allows the opportunity to acknowledge, if but briefly and inadequately, the author's gratitude to those who have assisted him. As will be apparent from the footnotes, this commentary builds on the labours of many others. To these writers, who have stimulated and guided my thoughts, though they may not necessarily agree with my conclusions, I am deeply indebted. For inviting me to contribute to the series, I am especially grateful to Professor D. J. Wiseman. To the editors of Inter-Varsity Press I extend my sincere thanks for their encouragement and expertise in transforming a some-times untidy manuscript into a much more presentable form. Finally, to my most honest critic, my wife Anne, I am ever grateful for her support and encouragement.

Soli Deo gloria.

DESMOND ALEXANDER

LOCATION OF TARSHISH

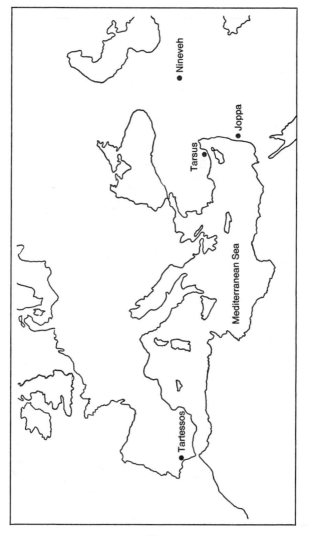

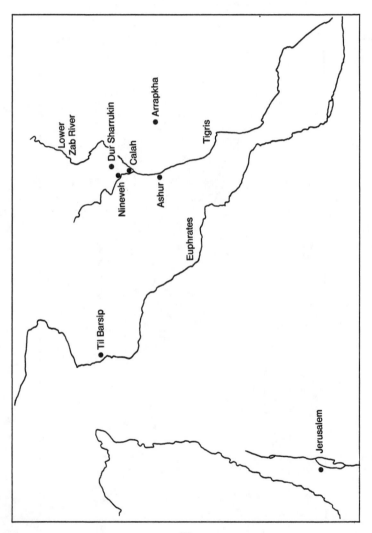

INTRODUCTION

The book of Jonah is undoubtedly one of the masterpieces of biblical literature. The account of Jonah's dramatic attempt to escape from God's presence by boarding a ship bound for Tarshish, only to be thwarted by a raging storm and returned to land incarcerated within a great fish, is possibly one of the best-known stories in the Bible. With its unexpected twists and turns the plot successfully retains our attention throughout. Superfluous details are omitted, and the text abounds in word-plays and other compositional techniques. Everything indicates that it has been composed by an author who has used his literary skills to the full.

I. AUTHORSHIP AND DATE

In common with a number of other books in the Minor Prophets (*e.g.* Obadiah, Nahum, Habakkuk), Jonah contains no precise statement as to when the events recorded actually occurred. An important clue to the timing of these, however, is the name 'Jonah son of Amittai' (1:1). Significantly, 2 Kings 14:25 refers to a prophet of the same name, who prophesied during the reign of Jeroboam II (782/81–753 BC),[1] and it is reasonable to suppose that these two passages refer to the same person. This being so, we may date the events underlying the book to the eighth century BC.

Although we can place Jonah's mission to Nineveh within the historical context of the eighth century BC, we are still a long way from determining the date and authorship of the book. Two difficulties confront us. Firstly, the Old Testament itself contains no specific details regarding the book's author or

[1] Throughout this commentary on Jonah, the dates of the kings of Israel and Assyria are those adopted in the *IBD*. These reflect but one of a number of possible chronologies. For a similar, but not quite identical approach, see N. Na'aman, 'Historical and Chronological Notes on the Kingdoms of Israel and Judah in the Eighth Century B.C.', *VT* 36 (1986), pp. 71–92.

date of writing. As it stands the book of Jonah is a completely anonymous and undated work. Secondly, although the events described pertain to the eighth century BC, it is quite possible that the book itself may have been composed much later. Indeed some scholars have even suggested a date of composition as late as the third century BC. This represents the very latest possible date, because the book's existence is clearly presupposed by a statement in Ecclesiasticus 49:10, written shortly after 200 BC, which refers to 'the twelve prophets', that is, the twelve Minor Prophets, of whom Jonah is one.[1] Proposals for dating the composition of Jonah have ranged across the entire period 800 to 200 BC. However, the majority of recent writers now favour a date after the exile, in the fifth or fourth centuries BC, on the basis of two main arguments.

A. *Linguistic features*

Of the various criteria for dating Jonah the linguistic features of the text are generally thought to be the most reliable and accurate guide to the book's age. The present text of Jonah, it is argued, not only has expressions which are more typical of late biblical Hebrew, but it also contains lexical and grammatical forms of Aramaic origin. Together these factors support strongly a post-exilic date, a time when the Hebrew language was heavily influenced by Aramaic.

The whole question of recognizing different stages in the development of biblical Hebrew and of identifying Aramaic influence is extremely complex.[2] Also our knowledge of ancient Near Eastern languages and dialects is ever increasing, especially as new textual evidence is constantly being brought

[1] Whether or not the fourth/third century BC book of Tobit originally referred to Jonah is uncertain. One important ancient manuscript, Codex S (Sinaiticus), reads 'Jonah' in Tobit 14:4, 8 (*cf.* RSV Apocrypha). However, another equally important manuscript, Codex B (Vaticanus), contains no reference to Jonah; rather the prophet Nahum is mentioned in 14:4 (*cf.* JB).

[2] For the benefit of general readers, the presentation of the linguistic arguments has been greatly simplified. For those wishing to pursue the matter in detail, the following works may be consulted: E. Kautzsch, *Die Aramaismen im Alten Testament* (Niemeyer, Halle, 1902); M. Wagner, *Die lexikalischen und grammatikalischen Aramaismen im alttestamentlichen Hebräisch, BZAW* 96 (Töpelmann, 1966); R. Polzin, *Late Biblical Hebrew: Toward an Historical Typology of Biblical Hebrew Prose,* Harvard Semitic Monographs 12 (Scholars Press, 1976). On the problem of using Aramaisms for dating biblical Hebrew, see A. Hurvitz, 'The Chronological Significance of "Aramaisms" in Biblical Hebrew', *IEJ* 18 (1968), pp. 234–240.

to light through the activities of archaeologists. Consequently the results of older studies are continually being modified and sometimes corrected.

Among recent writers on Jonah, O. Loretz pioneered the idea that certain features of the book normally designated as Aramaisms may in fact reflect Canaanite-Phoenician influence, and hence need not indicate a post-exilic date.[1] To Loretz it seemed likely that the nouns *mallāḥ*, 'sailor' (1:5), *sᵉp̄înāh*, 'ship' (1:5), and *ribbô*, 'ten thousand' (4:11), and the particle *še*, 'which' (1:7; 4:10), found their way into Hebrew via Phoenician, rather than through Aramaic. Although Loretz accounted for only some of the Aramaisms in Jonah, his article prompted further investigations.

By far the fullest and most detailed study on the dating of the language of Jonah is that of G. M. Landes.[2] In this Landes considers not only supposed Aramaisms but also other datable linguistic features. He agrees with Loretz that the terms *mallāḥ*, *še*, *ribbô*, and possibly also *sᵉp̄înāh*, may have been borrowed from Phoenician. Of the remaining Aramaisms Landes concludes that, with the exception of *yitʿaššēt*, 'he will consider' (1:6), not one belongs exclusively to the post-exilic age.[3] However, the fact that Jonah 1:6 is the sole biblical occurrence of the verb *yitʿaššēt* raises doubts as to its significance for dating purposes.

Landes also examines a number of special word usages thought to be characteristic of late biblical Hebrew.[4] However, of these only one actually supports a late date. Following A.

---

[1] O. Loretz, 'Herkunft und Sinn der Jonah-Erzählung', *BZ* 5 (1961), pp. 18–29.

[2] G. M. Landes, 'Linguistic Criteria and the Date of the Book of Jonah', *Eretz Israel* 16 (1982), pp. 147–170.

[3] In this category Landes places the following words and expressions: *štq*, 'to be calm' (1:11–12); *zʿp̄*, 'to rage' (1:15); the Pi'el of *mnh*, 'to appoint' (2:1 Heb., 1:17 EVV; 4:6–8); *mr*, with the specific meaning 'to command' (2:11 Heb., 2:10 EVV); *qdm*, 'to do for the first time' (4:2); *ḥws*, 'to have pity' (4:10–11); *qryʾh*, 'proclamation' (3:2); *ʾlhy hšmym*, 'God of heaven' (1:9); *ṭʿm*, 'decree' (3:7); the use of the preposition *lᵉ*, 'to', as a *nota accusativa* particle (2:11 Heb., 2:10 EVV; 4:6). On the expression 'God of heaven', see B. Porten, 'Baalshamem and the Date of the Book of Jonah', in M. Carrez, J. Doré, P. Grelot (eds.), *De la Tôrah au Messie* (Desclée, 1981), pp. 237–244.

[4] He lists seven in all: *qr' ʾl*, 'to proclaim against', and *qr' ʾl*, 'to proclaim to' (1:2; 3:2); the hiph'il of the root *ṭwl*, 'to cast' (1:4–5,12,15); *rb ḥḇl*, 'captain' (1:6); *mhlk*, 'journey' (3:3–4); two instances of 'diachronic chiasmus': *mgdwlm wʿd qṭnm*, 'from the greatest to the least' (3:5) and *ḥnwn wrḥwm*, 'gracious and compassionate' (4:2); *wyrʿ ʾl*, 'to displease' (4:1); *lmḥrt*, 'the next day' (4:7).

Brenner,[1] Landes accepts that the word order in the expression *ḥannûn wᵉraḥûm*, 'gracious and compassionate' (4:2), reflects a later usage; early Hebrew is characterized by the reverse order.[2] However, even if one accepts that the sequence in Jonah represents a later development, we should note that there is no compelling reason to date the transition from one format to the other to the fifth century BC. A sixth- or seventh-century date would also be feasible.

Finally, Landes evaluates the text of Jonah against an index, compiled by R. Polzin, of grammatical syntactic features distinctive of late biblical Hebrew.[3] As a result, two additional features are reckoned by Landes to indicate a late date: (1) the attaching of the direct object pronoun as a suffix to the verb, and (2) the use of a plural noun where in pre-exilic Hebrew the singular would have been used. Of these, however, we should observe that the latter, which relies solely upon the use of the plural term *gôrālôt*, 'lots' (1:7), is hardly decisive for determining the date of Jonah. Apart from Jonah 1:7 and Leviticus 16:8 the plural form *gôrālôt* is found elsewhere only in post-exilic writings (*e.g.* 1 Ch. 24:5; Ne. 11:1). To explain the use of the plural in Leviticus 16:8 Landes notes that the passage refers specifically to *two* lots. Yet, given that Jonah 1:7 describes the casting of lots by foreign sailors, and not by Hebrews, as is the case elsewhere in the pre-exilic literature, is it not possible that the present use of *gôrālôt* is determined by pagan rather than post-exilic practice? Unfortunately Landes overlooks this possibility.

Whereas Landes finds little to support a post-exilic date for Jonah, he observes that other features of the language indicate a pre-exilic date. One of these is the form of the Hebrew preposition *min*, 'from', before anarthrous nouns (*i.e.* nouns without the definite article). Whereas in post-exilic Hebrew the preposition normally takes the shorter form *mi*, all ten occurrences in Jonah have *min*. Another possible indication of a pre-exilic date is the combination of the particle *še*, 'which', with the noun *bin*, 'son', in 4:11. Landes believes that this particular expression is not only another example of Phoeni-

---

[1] A. Brenner, 'The Language of Jonah as an Index to its Date', *Beth Mikra* 79 (1979), pp. 396–405 (in Hebrew). However, note also the response of E. Qimron, 'The Language of Jonah', *Beth Mikra* 81 (1980), pp. 181–182 (in Hebrew).

[2] *Cf.* Ex. 34:6; Pss. 86:15; 103:8.   [3] Polzin, *Late Biblical Hebrew*.

cian influence, but 'could well represent a North Israelite-Ephraimite dialect feature'.[1] Indeed, although our present knowledge of Hebrew dialects is very limited, it may well be that the linguistic peculiarities of Jonah are indicative not of a late date but of a north Israelite dialect which in various respects differed from the classical Hebrew of Jerusalem.[2]

Because the linguistic criteria for dating Jonah to the post-exilic period are inconclusive, and certain features of the text suggest a pre-exilic Phoenician influence, Landes inclines towards a sixth-century date for the composition of Jonah.[3] Our analysis of the evidence, however, indicates that there are fewer reasons for maintaining a late date than even Landes allows. It is, therefore, not inconceivable that the book of Jonah could have been written prior to the sixth century, possibly even in the eighth century BC, especially if one envisages a north Israelite provenance.[4]

B. Legendary descriptions

A second argument for the late dating of Jonah arises from the fact that the narrative is deemed to contain a number of elements which are historically inaccurate. On two separate counts these suggest a late date of composition. First, the author of Jonah must have penned his material well after the destruction of Nineveh in 612 BC, at a time when knowledge of the city was influenced largely by legendary descriptions. Thus it is maintained that the exaggerated size of the city ('a visit required three days', 3:3) and of its population ('a hundred and twenty thousand people', 4:11) is the product of

[1] Landes, 'Linguistic Criteria', p. 153.
[2] Various writers have indicated the possibility that the language of Jonah represents a northern dialect: C. F. Keil, p. 381; S. R. Driver, *An Introduction to the Literature of the Old Testament* (T. & T. Clark, ⁹1913), p. 322; I. H. Eybers, 'The Purpose of the Book of Jonah', *Theologica Evangelica* 4 (1971), pp. 216–217, 219, n. 26. For a recent study on dialects in Syria-Palestine, see W. R. Garr, *Dialect Geography of Syria-Palestine 1000–586 B.C.E.* (University of Pennsylvania Press, 1985). No attempt is made, however, to identify different dialects within the Hebrew Bible.
[3] Brenner, 'The language of Jonah', reaches a similar conclusion.
[4] With the capture of Samaria in 723/2 BC by the Assyrian king Sargon II, the northern kingdom of Israel became an Assyrian province. Most of the population were deported to Assyria and replaced by peoples from elsewhere (*cf.* 2 Ki. 17:23–24). Thus if the book of Jonah originated in the north, it would seem necessary to assume that it was composed prior to 723/2 BC, or soon after.

later popular tradition rather than historical fact. A similar position is adopted concerning the title 'king of Nineveh' (3:6), which never occurs in Assyrian annals. Also the comment in 3:3 that 'Nineveh *was* a very important city' is said to carry the implication that at the time of writing it was no longer so. Second, the narrative itself records several customs typical of the Persian period (late sixth century to fourth century BC), but apparently unknown in eighth-century Assyria: (1) the issuing of a decree by both the king and his nobles (3:7) and (2) the participation of animals in a religious fast (3:7–8). On the basis of these observations recent writers tend to favour a post-exilic date of composition.

a. The size of Nineveh. The description of Nineveh as a city of 'three days' journey' (RSV) *mahᵃlak šᵉlošet yāmîn* (3:3), has been viewed by many commentators as a gross exaggeration of its size. On the assumption that a day's journey was approximately twenty miles, this would make Nineveh either sixty miles wide, or possibly sixty miles in circumference.[1] We know, however, from a contemporary document that the early seventh-century Assyrian king Sennacherib (704–681 BC) enlarged the circumference of the city of Nineveh from 9300 cubits (approximately three miles) to 21,815 cubits (approximately seven miles),[2] and modern archaeological surveys confirm the basic accuracy of this report.[3] Thus prior to the end of the eighth century Nineveh was probably no more than a mile across at its widest part. On this reckoning, one would hardly have required three days either to traverse the city or to circumambulate its walls.

Various proposals have been made to overcome this difficulty. It has been suggested that the expression 'three days' journey' refers not to the *length* of Jonah's journey, but rather to the *time* required to undertake it. If Jonah was to declare God's message to the Ninevites, he must have gone from

[1] There is no indication in ancient documents, however, of the size of any city being determined by its circumference: 'I do not know of any description of the size of an ancient city by the circuit of its walls,' D. J. Wiseman, 'Jonah's Nineveh', *TynB* 30 (1979), p. 37.

[2] Taking one cubit to equal approximately 50 cms or 19.6 ins.

[3] F. Jones, 'The Topography of Nineveh', *JRAS* 15 (1855), p. 324, gives a circumference of 7.5 miles; T. Madhloum, 'Excavations at Nineveh', *Sumer* 23 (1967), p. 77, estimates the circumference of the city to be 12 km. (7.4 miles).

street corner to street corner and from city gate to city gate. Naturally, such a task would require several days to complete. Alternatively, D. J. Wiseman has suggested that, in accordance with the ancient Near Eastern practice of hospitality, 'the "three day" journey' could refer to the day of arrival in the city, followed by the customary day of visiting, business and rest, then the day of departure.'[1] One factor weighs against both of these proposals, however: the expression 'three days' journey' clearly refers in 3:3 to the size of Nineveh, and not to the time allotted for Jonah's mission.[2] A third solution has been to view the reference to three days as merely symbolic, signifying a city of gigantic proportions.[3] The comment, however, that 'Jonah began to go into the city, going a day's journey' (3:4, RSV) favours a literal interpretation of the phrase 'three days' journey'.

A quite different approach is to understand the name Nineveh as applying to a much larger district. According to A. Parrot, Nineveh designates the 'Assyrian triangle', the region between the rivers Tigris, Zabu and Ghazir, extending from Dur-Sharrukin (Khorsabad) in the north to Calah (Nimrud) in the south.[4] Yet although this approach resolves the problem of the 'three days' journey', the text of Jonah describes Nineveh as a 'city', *ʿîr*, and Jonah is portrayed as going and sitting down outside it (4:5). For these reasons it is objected that there are insufficient grounds for believing that the name 'Nineveh' actually designated a much wider area.

The narrative, however, contains one other element which favours the suggestion that the term Nineveh covers a broader region than just the city itself. This is the phrase 'the great city', *hāʿîr haggᵉdôlāh* (1:2; 3:2; 4:11). Significantly, this very same expression occurs in connection with Nineveh in Genesis

---

[1] Wiseman, 'Jonah's Nineveh', p. 38; *cf.* NIV, 'a very important city – a visit required three days'.

[2] Wiseman's reference to the use of *mahᵃlāk* in Ne. 2:6 (p. 36) is hardly sufficient to overcome this objection; *cf.* Rudolph, p. 355, n. 2.

[3] Cohn, p. 58; Wolff (1975), p. 50.

[4] A. Parrot, *Nineveh and the Old Testament*, Studies in Biblical Archaeology 3 (SCM Press, 1955) pp. 85–86; translated by B. E. Hooke from *Ninive et l'Ancien Testament* (Delachaux et Niestlé, ²1955); *cf.* C. F. Keil, pp. 390–391; Trible, pp. 175–176; D. W. B. Robinson, 'Jonah', in *NBC*, p. 750; Maier, p. 62. Wiseman, 'Jonah's Nineveh', p. 38, extends this area to include the city of Assur to the south of Calah.

10:11–12: 'From that land he [Nimrod] went to Assyria, where he built Nineveh, Rehoboth Ir, Calah and Resen, which is between Nineveh and Calah; that is the great city [*hā'îr hagg^edôlāh*]'. Commenting on this passage C. F. Keil remarks,

> it follows that the four places formed a large composite city, a large range of towns, to which the name of the (well-known) great city of *Nineveh* was applied, in distinction from Nineveh in the more restricted sense, with which Nimrod probably connected the other three places so as to form one great capital, possibly also the chief fortress of his kingdom on the Tigris.[1]

If Keil's interpretation of Genesis 10:11–12 is accurate, then the expression 'the great city of Nineveh' may well designate not only the walled city of Nineveh, but also the surrounding region. Indeed, the phrase may even have been understood in a semi-technical sense, meaning 'Greater Nineveh'.[2] Jonah was thus sent not merely to the walled city of Nineveh, but rather to 'Greater Nineveh'.[3]

b. The population of Nineveh. The precise size of the population of Nineveh is a matter of some dispute, in spite of the statement in 4:11 that Nineveh had 'more than a hundred and twenty thousand people'. Some commentators take this number to include only children because of the expression of an inability to distinguish 'their right hand from their left'. Consequently the total population of Nineveh is estimated to be about 600,000.[4] This, however, represents a population well in excess of that which could have lived within the walled city of Nineveh. Other scholars argue that the expression 'who cannot tell their right hand from their left' does not denote infants, but rather highlights figuratively the inability of all the inhabitants of Nineveh to distinguish between right and

---

[1] C. F. Keil, *The Pentateuch*, 1 (T. & T. Clark, 1864), p. 167; *cf.* J. J. Davis, *A Dictionary of the Bible* (Collins, ⁴1924), p. 543; G. Ch. Aalders, *Genesis*, 1 (Zondervan, 1981), p. 227. The description 'great city' is used of Nineveh only in Genesis and Jonah.

[2] Compare the contemporary designations 'London' and 'Greater London'.

[3] Wiseman, 'Jonah's Nineveh', pp. 38–39, notes that the Hebrew name for Nineveh, unlike the Assyrian, does not allow one to distinguish between the metropolis proper and a larger district.

[4] Bewer, p. 64.

wrong.[1] This gives a total population of 120,000 inhabitants, which, according to L. C. Allen, 'is a reasonable figure for the historical city 3 miles wide'.[2] Allen, however, bases his argument on the fact that the population of nearby Calah, which was about half the size of Nineveh, was estimated initially by Mallowan and Wiseman to be about 65,000.[3] More recently, however, Wiseman has revised substantially this estimate in favour of a much lower figure of about 18,000 persons.[4] As a consequence of this, 120,000 inhabitants would now appear to be an overly high estimate for the total population of the walled city of Nineveh. It would, however, be quite appropriate for the population of 'Greater Nineveh'.

c. 'Nineveh was a very important city'. A further possible indication of a late date of composition is the remark that 'Nineveh *was* a very important city'. Many writers take this to imply that the time of writing was after the city's destruction in 612 BC. Given, however, that the entire report of Jonah's mission to Nineveh is recorded in the past tense, there is no reason why the comment about Nineveh should be couched differently.[5]

d. The king of Nineveh. Another feature thought to be indicative of a late date is the expression 'king of Nineveh'. Two factors are held to suggest that this title was invented at a time when knowledge of the Assyrian Empire was very limited and remote. Firstly, the actual designation 'king of Nineveh' is unattested in the Mesopotamian documents so far uncovered and examined. Secondly, the Assyrian ruler is usually referred to as the 'king of Assyria'. Although both of these factors point towards a late date of composition, this raises further questions. Even if by the time of the Exile the

[1] R. B. Y. Scott, 'The Sign of Jonah', *Int* 19 (1965), p. 24; Walton, p. 61. Wiseman, 'Jonah's Nineveh', pp. 39–40, notes that in Babylonian texts the phrase 'right hand and left hand' is a synonym for 'truth and justice' or 'law and order'.
[2] Allen, p. 222; *cf.* J. Simons, *The Geographical and Topographical Texts of the Old Testament* (E. J. Brill, 1959), p. 527.
[3] Allen, p. 234; *cf.* M. E. L. Mallowan, 'The Excavations at Nimrud (Kalhu), 1951', *Iraq* 14 (1952), pp. 20–22; D. J. Wiseman, 'A New Stela of Assur-naṣir-pal II', *Iraq* 14 (1952), p. 28.
[4] Wiseman, 'Jonah's Nineveh', pp. 41–42.
[5] Compare Gn. 3:1, 'Now the serpent was more crafty than any of the wild animals . . .'

Assyrian Empire no longer existed, there still remained within the Hebrew traditions various references to it, in particular 2 Kings 19 – 20, paralleled in Isaiah 37 – 39, and the book of Nahum. Significantly, in these passages the Assyrian ruler always receives the title 'king of Assyria', even when he is directly associated with Nineveh (2 Ki. 19:36; Is. 37:37). Thus, apart from the book of Jonah, the expression 'king of Nineveh' is never used in the Old Testament. If, assuming a late date of composition, the author of Jonah drew upon the book of Kings for his choice of prophet (*cf.* 2 Ki. 14:15), is it not strange that he did not likewise draw upon this same work for information concerning the Assyrians (*i.e.* 2 Ki. 15 – 20)? Alternatively, however, the designation 'king of Nineveh' may reflect accurately the political situation which existed at the time of Jonah's mission: at this stage the Assyrian king exercised absolute control over a very limited region centred on Nineveh – hence the designation 'king of Nineveh'.[1] It was only towards the end of the eighth century BC that the Assyrian Empire re-emerged as a major world power.

e. Late customs. The book of Jonah, it is suggested, records several customs typical of the later Persian period but unknown in eighth-century Assyria: the giving of a decree by both the king and his nobles (3:7),[2] and the wearing of sackcloth by animals as a sign of mourning (3:8).[3] Two factors, however, should caution us against relying solely on these customs for deciding the date of composition of Jonah: (1) the limited nature of the documentary evidence from Assyria in the early eighth century, and (2) the problems associated with using ancient Near Eastern customs for dating purposes.[4]

As regards the issuing of a decree by both the king and his nobles, several explanations have been offered to account for

[1] See the Additional Note, 'Eighth-century Assyria', pp. 77–81; *cf.* A. K. Grayson, 'Assyria: Ashur-dan II to Ashur-Nirari V (934–745 B.C.)' in *CAH* III/I, pp. 271–281; P. J. N. Lawrence, 'Assyrian Nobles and the Book of Jonah', *TynB* 37 (1986), pp. 121–132.

[2] For a list of references, see E. J. Bickerman, 'Les deux erreurs du prophète Jonas', *RHPR* 45 (1965), p. 250, n. 67.

[3] *Cf.* Judith 4:10; Herodotus 9.24; Plutarch, *Alexander* 72.

[4] *Cf.* M. Selman, 'Comparative Customs and the Patriarchal Age', in A. R. Millard and D. J. Wiseman (eds.), *Essays on the Patriarchal Narratives* (IVP, 1980), pp. 93–138. Although Selman discusses the use of customs for dating the patriarchal period his observations are applicable to later periods.

this within an Assyrian context. According to Wiseman,[1] during a time of extreme crisis (*e.g.* a solar eclipse) it was not unknown for a king to descend from his throne and be replaced by a substitute king until the time of danger had passed. The actions of the king in Jonah 3:6 possibly reflect such a *šar puhi* ritual, and this might account for the king and his nobles being associated in the issuing of the decree. Alternatively, P. J. N. Lawrence believes that the joint issuing of the decree is a consequence of the political situation which existed in Assyria during the early part of the eighth century.[2] At this time Assyria was controlled by weak kings surrounded by powerful provincial governors. Consequently the head of the Assyrian dynasty found it necessary to issue a decree in conjunction with his nobles.

From our investigation of the supposed historical inaccuracies in Jonah it is evident that there is no compelling reason to believe that the author of Jonah wrote at a time when eighth-century Assyria belonged to the dim and distant past. On the contrary, there are various indications that the story of Jonah accurately reflects the situation which existed in Assyria during the middle of the eighth century BC. Given, however, our very limited knowledge of this particular period of Assyrian history, any conclusions reached regarding the historical background of the book of Jonah must remain tentative. Nevertheless, in the light of the evidence just considered there is no reason why the date of composition of the book of Jonah should be placed in the post-exilic era.

C. *Further considerations*

As well as the linguistic features of the text and the supposed presence of legendary descriptions, several other factors have been taken into account by scholars seeking to determine the date of composition: (1) literary dependency; (2) audience. However, at the outset it must be stressed that these criteria tend to be less objective than those just considered. At best they are really only suitable for confirming a date which has already been reached on the basis of other considerations.

---

[1] Wiseman, 'Jonah's Nineveh', pp. 47, 51.
[2] Lawrence, 'Assyrian Nobles', pp. 121–132.

JONAH

a. Literary dependency. It has long been recognized that various elements in the book of Jonah bear a close resemblance to material found in other Old Testament books.[1] To account for this it is argued that the author of Jonah was familiar with these other works, and since some of this source material is dated to the time of the Babylonian exile the book of Jonah must have been composed subsequently.[2] This argument for a post-exilic date rests, however, on a very insecure foundation: there is no way of determining with certainty the direction of borrowing. Other considerations aside, it could equally well be argued that these works were dependent on Jonah.

b. Audience. On the assumption that Jonah must have been penned to meet a particular need, scholars have sought to identify the situation which gave rise to the writing of the book.[3] Although this approach is methodologically valid, the task of identifying the book's audience is fraught with complications. Various attempts to do so have subsequently been shown to be quite inadequate. Thus, for example, it used to be popular to suggest that the book was directed at Jews who adopted a bigoted attitude towards Gentiles in the time of Ezra and Nehemiah. However, as R. E. Clements has demonstrated, the actual evidence does not support the opinion that the book was composed against such a background.[4] Experience shows that any attempt to identify the audience of the book is likely to be too subjective to be of lasting value in determining its date of composition.

Although the majority of recent writers on Jonah favour an exilic or post-exilic date for the composition of the book, the linguistic evidence examined above does not exclude an earlier date, possibly as early as the eighth century, especially if the book was composed in the northern kingdom of Israel. Nor

[1] Similarities have been noted with the following passages: Gn. 6:11, 13; 19:25, 29; 1 Ki. 19:4–5; Pss. 18:6; 69:1; 88:6–7; 118:5; 120:1; Je. 18:11; 26:3, 15; Ezk. 24:16; 27:8–9, 25–29; Joel 1:13; 2:13–14.

[2] *Cf.* A. Feuillet, 'Les sources du livre de Jonas', *RB* 54 (1947), pp. 161–186. Feuillet also argues that this dependence upon other works indicates that the book of Jonah is a fictitious narrative. This, however, is rejected by B. Trépanier, 'The Story of Jonas', *CBQ* 13 (1951), pp. 8–16.

[3] *Cf.* D. F. Payne, 'Jonah from the Perspective of its Audience', *JSOT* 13 (1979), pp. 3–12.

[4] R. E. Clements, 'The Purpose of the Book of Jonah', *VTS* 28 (1975), pp. 18–19.

is the possibility of such an early date ruled out by other considerations. As our investigation of the other relevant criteria has revealed, there is nothing which is totally incompatible with a pre-exilic date of composition.

Closely related to the issue of authorship and date is the question of unity of composition. Was the book of Jonah produced by a single individual, or did various writers contribute to its present form?

During the nineteenth century Jonah, in common with other Old Testament books, was subjected to rigorous and exacting scrutiny by scholars interested in uncovering its redactional history. As a result the text was severely dissected, with some scholars uncovering as many as four different writers contributing to the final form of the book.[1] From the vantage point of the present day the excesses of this approach are all too apparent. However, although twentieth-century scholars have rejected, as far as Jonah is concerned, the source-critical conclusions of their nineteenth-century counterparts, one aspect of the book has continued to figure prominently in discussions regarding its unity: this concerns the authenticity of the poetic section in Jonah 2:2–9.

As early as 1786 Ch. G. Hensler suggested that there were incongruities between the psalm of chapter 2 and the rest of the book.[2] A few years later J. G. A. Müller speculated that whereas the psalm was composed in the eighth century BC by Jonah himself, the rest of the book was the product of an exilic author.[3] This position, however, was overturned by W. M. L. DeWette, who argued for the priority of the prose narrative,

---

[1] For an outline and critique of nineteenth-century approaches, see Bewer, pp. 13–21. On the distribution and use of the divine names, Yahweh and Elohim, see F. D. Kidner, 'The Distribution of Divine Names in Jonah', *TynB* 21 (1970), pp. 77–87; Magonet, pp. 34–38.

[2] Ch. G. Hensler, *Animadversiones in quaedam duodecim prophetarum minorum loca* (1786); see G. M. Landes, 'The Kerygma of the Book of Jonah', *Int* 21 (1967), p. 3.

[3] J. G. A. Müller, 'Jona, eine moralische Erzählung', in Paulus' *Memorabilien*, 6 (1794), pp. 142–143.

with the psalm being a later insertion.[1] If incongruities exist between the psalm and the surrounding narrative, there can be only one explanation for this: the author of the prose account had no detailed knowledge of the psalm's contents. The psalm must therefore have been incorporated into the text of Jonah at a later stage. This position was to form the critical consensus for the next one hundred and fifty years.

The last twenty years, however, have witnessed a significant transformation in attitudes towards the compositional unity of Jonah. A substantial number of recent writers now dismiss as quite inadequate the evidence *against* viewing 2:2–9 as an integral part of the book.[2] The reasons for doing so are outlined below. Before considering these, however, it is necessary to summarize briefly those arguments which favour the suggestion that the psalm in chapter 2 was a later interpolation into the prose narrative.[3]

1. On the basis of form and content 2:2–9 is usually classified as a psalm of individual thanksgiving. It is argued, however, that a psalm of thanksgiving is quite inappropriate in the present context. Given his incarceration within the belly of the great fish, Jonah, it is suggested, is hardly likely to have expressed gratitude to God.

2. Jonah's character as revealed in the psalm is at odds with the author's portrayal of him elsewhere in the book. For example, the picture of Jonah gratefully praising God is hardly in keeping with the prose section which portrays him as rebellious, sullen and unappreciative. Similarly, whereas in 1:12 he apparently greets the prospect of dying with little apprehension, his words in 2:2 reveal tremendous anxiety in the face of imminent death.

3. Certain comments in the psalm are at variance with statements found in the prose narrative. For example, in 1:15 it is stated that the sailors were responsible for hurling Jonah into the sea. Yet Jonah claims in 2:3 that Yahweh cast him into the deep. In chapter 1 Jonah flees from God of his own

---

[1] W. M. L. DeWette, *Lehrbuch der historisch-kritischen Einleitung in kanonischen und apocryphischen Bücher des A.T.* (Reiner, 1817), p. 298.

[2] For a comprehensive list of recent writers who question the later addition of the psalm, see D. L. Christensen, 'The Song of Jonah: A Metrical Analysis', *JBL* 104 (1985), p. 217, n. 3.

[3] *Cf.* Trible, pp. 75–80; P. Weimar, 'Jon 2,1–11. Jonapsalm und Jonaerzählung', *BZ* 28 (1984), pp. 46–50.

accord, while it is emphasized in 2:4 that he was actually banished from the divine presence. The derogatory remarks about pagans in 2:8 seem strange in view of the positive portrayal of the sailors and the Ninevites in chapters 1 and 3 respectively. Finally, whereas the psalm expresses gratitude for deliverance from drowning, the narrative in chapter 1 conveys the impression that Jonah, after being thrown overboard, was immediately swallowed by the fish.

4. There are linguistic discrepancies between 2:2–9 and the rest of the book which cannot be accounted for purely on the basis of a distinction between prose and poetry. A different term is used for 'throw' in 2:3 from that found in 1:12, 15. Whereas in chapter 1 the singular 'sea' is consistently employed (vv. 4, 5, 9, 11, 12, 13, 15), in 2:3 the plural word 'seas' occurs. The expression 'from the face of' in 1:3, 10 is replaced in 2:4 by 'from before the eyes of'. Furthermore, certain words which are common in the prose are totally absent from the psalm. For example, although 'great' comes fourteen times in the prose narrative, it never occurs in the psalm.[1] The term $r\bar{a}^{\varsigma}\bar{a}h$, 'evil', does not figure in the psalm, yet appears seven times in the rest of the book.[2]

5. By excising 2:2–9 the original structure of the book is restored. According to N. Lohfink, verses 1:17, 2:1 and 2:10, taken together, form a well-defined chiasmus:[3]

A   God appointed a fish to swallow Jonah (1:17a)
B   Jonah was within the fish (1:17b)
B¹   Jonah prayed from within the fish (2:1)
A¹ God commanded the fish to vomit up Jonah (2:10).

With the inclusion of 2:2–9 this pattern is destroyed. From a different perspective P. L. Trible concludes that the entire book of Jonah consists of two parallel sections: chapters 1 and 2 are paralleled by chapters 3 and 4. However, to achieve the best correspondence between the two sections it is necessary to delete 2:2–9.[4]

---

[1] 1:2, 4 (twice), 10, 13, 15; 2:1; 3:2, 3, 5, 7; 4:1, 7, 11; *cf.* Wolff (1975), p. 61, n. 82; Fretheim, pp. 43–44.

[2] 1:2, 7, 8; 3:10; 4:1, 2, 6. The same term comes as an adjective in 3:8, 10.

[3] N. Lohfink, 'Jona ging zur Stadt hinaus (Jon 4,5)', *BZ* 5 (1962), p. 196, n. 37.

[4] Trible, pp. 76, 184–202. According to Trible, the prayer in 4:2 parallels the sailors' prayer in 1:14, and not Jonah's prayer in 2:2–9.

JONAH

Although there appear to be substantial grounds for believing that 2:2–9 is not an authentic part of the book of Jonah, these arguments are not wholly convincing.

1. Recent studies confirm that the psalm in chapter 2 expresses gratitude not for deliverance from within the great fish, as many older commentators supposed, but rather for deliverance from drowning.[1] The fish, like the gourd in 4:6, is divinely appointed to rescue, not punish.[2] The psalm is therefore quite appropriate in its present context. From within the great fish Jonah reflects on his near death by drowning and praises God for answering his cry for help.

2. The character of Jonah as presented in the psalm need not be viewed as incompatible with what we know of him elsewhere in the book. The picture of Jonah praising God for saving him from drowning finds a parallel in his attitude immediately following the divine provision of the gourd: 'Jonah was exceedingly glad' (4:6, RSV). On the supposed lack of harmony between chapters 1 and 2 regarding Jonah's attitude to death, Landes comments:

> he [Jonah] is willing to risk the possibility of death, but he does not yearn to die or welcome annihilation with open arms. The difference in language at 1:12 and 4:3, 8 underlines this. In Chapter 4 Jonah's wish for death is heavily stressed by reiteration, while in Chapter 1 neither the noun 'death' nor any synonym for 'to die' is introduced . . . Thus when Jonah finds himself in the watery Deep, he joins that company of Israelites who have experienced the threat and terror of an untimely death and cried to Yahweh for deliverance.[3]

Thus chapters 1 and 2 are not inconsistent regarding Jonah's disposition towards death. Furthermore, without the psalm of thanksgiving there is no reason to suppose that Jonah's initial attitude to God's call has changed following his expulsion from the ship. Yet the book's plot requires an

[1] *Cf.* Allen, p. 184; J. T. Walsh, 'Jonah 2,3–10: A Rhetorical Critical Study', *Bib* 63 (1982), pp. 219–229; Christensen, 'The Song of Jonah', pp. 226–227.

[2] See Landes, 'The Kerygma', pp. 12–13. The allegorical interpretation that the swallowing of Jonah by the fish represents Judah being swallowed up into captivity by the Babylonians must be rejected. The fish is an instrument of salvation, not punishment.

[3] *Ibid.*, p. 23.

explanation as to why Jonah should be willing to go to Nineveh in chapter 3. The statement of Jonah's gratitude to God for deliverance from death is an essential link between chapters 1 and 3.

3. Supposed contradictions between the psalm and the rest of the book present no real problem. Throughout the psalm Jonah readily acknowledges the absolute sovereignty of God. Thus, although the sailors cast him overboard, in Jonah's eyes it was God who engineered the entire situation; the sailors are merely the means by which God punishes him. No contradiction, therefore, exists between 1:15 and 2:3. Similarly, the reference to banishment in 2:4 is not at odds with the earlier statement about Jonah's desire to abscond from God's presence (1:3). Although Jonah seeks to evade his commission by fleeing to Tarshish, he becomes conscious of being divinely banished only after his ejection from the ship. Jonah's banishment is a consequence of his attempt to evade his commission. The comment about idolators in 2:8 is hardly incompatible with the rest of the book. The episodes involving the sailors and the Ninevites both reveal that it is only those who turn to Yahweh who can expect to find grace. Finally, although chapter 1 may give the impression that Jonah was instantly swallowed by the fish and therefore did not come close to drowning, the text gives no indication as to how long Jonah remained in the water. In any case, since Jonah could not have survived long underwater, he must have been rescued quickly.

4. Linguistic discrepancies between the prose and poetry need not necessarily mean that the psalm is a secondary addition. Alternative explanations are possible. The fact that the psalm draws upon traditional cultic language could account for such differences.[1] Moreover, the psalm and the narrative framework may have been composed by separate individuals. This, however, need not require, as is generally supposed, that the psalm is later.

Furthermore, it ought not to be overlooked that there is some correspondence in themes and terminology between the prose and poetry. For example, the theme of *going down*, as

[1] Considerable attention has been given to the affinities between this and other psalms; *cf.* A. R. Johnson, 'Jonah 2,3–10. A Study in Cultic Phantasy', in H. H. Rowley (ed.), *Studies in Old Testament Prophecy presented to T. H. Robinson* (T. & T. Clark, 1950), pp. 82–102; Magonet, pp. 44–54.

various writers observe, is significant in chapters 1 and 2:[1] Jonah goes down to Joppa (1:3), to the ship (1:3), below deck (1:5), and, eventually, to the roots of the mountains (2:6). This downward movement is only reversed in 2:6, where Jonah states, 'You brought my life up from the pit.' Another link between the initial two chapters is the fact that the sailors (1:16) and Jonah (2:9) respond to God's mercy by offering sacrifices and making vows.[2]

5. The study of literary structures in the book of Jonah is a relatively recent innovation, and the observations of Lohfink and Trible, noted above, were significant in the initial development of such an approach. Since then, however, further studies have tended to favour the retention of 2:2–9 as an integral part of the book of Jonah.

It has long been recognized that the initial call of Jonah (1:1–3) is closely paralleled by his second summons in 3:1–3a. This observation has prompted various writers to suggest that the second half of the book parallels the first. J. Magonet, for example, outlines the overall structure of the book as follows:[3]

A   1:1–16   The first call – flight. Sailors.
B   2:1   Transition.
C   2:2–11   Prayer – 'discussion' with God.
A[1]   3:1–10   The second call – obedience. Nineveh.
B[1]   4:1   Transition.
C[1]   4:2–11   Prayer – 'discussion' with God.

Apart from having similar introductions, sections A and A[1] correspond by portraying favourably the actions of the pagan sailors and the Ninevites. Sections C and C[1], however, focus entirely on Jonah, highlighting his reactions to the events of the preceding episodes. The gratitude which he expresses for his own deliverance in chapter 2 contrasts sharply with the abhorrence which he feels in chapter 4 as a result of God's willingness to forgive Nineveh. Unlike Trible, however, Magonet argues for the retention of the psalm in chapter 2

[1] *Cf.* J. S. Ackerman, 'Satire and Symbolism in the Song of Jonah', in B. Halpern and J. D. Levenson (eds.), *Traditions in Transformation. Turning Points in Biblical Faith* (Eisenbrauns, 1981), pp. 223–224, 229–235; Christensen, 'The Song of Jonah', p. 226.

[2] Allen, p. 184, n. 47, notes also the following similarities in terminology between the prose and poetry: *qr'*, 'call', 1:6, 14; 2:2; *nepeš*, 'life', 1:14; 2:5, 7; 'Yahweh his/my God', 2:1, 6.

[3] Magonet, p. 55; *cf.* Rudolph, p. 326; Fretheim, p. 55.

on the basis that it finds a counterpart in 4:1–3. Not only are both prayers introduced by similar statements, 'and he [Jonah] prayed to Yahweh . . . and said', but as Allen comments, 'The themes that drew forth Jonah's praise in the psalm are ironically the very ones that cause him grief in his second prayer.'[1] By removing chapter 2 the balanced structure of the book is destroyed.

In the preceding paragraphs we have sought to evaluate the arguments for and against excising the psalm in chapter 2 as a later interpolation. The weight of evidence clearly favours the retention of 2:2–9 as part of the author's original draft. It is an essential element in the plot of the book, providing a very necessary bridge between the events of chapters 1 and 3. We concur, therefore, with the majority of recent writers that the book of Jonah, as it now stands, is a literary unity.

III. GENRE

Considerable time and effort have been expended by modern writers on the question of the genre[2] of the book of Jonah. What type of work did the author intend to produce? Under what literary category should the book be classified?

The importance of these questions should not be underestimated. It has long been noted that the book of Jonah is markedly different from the other works which comprise the Minor Prophets. Whereas they focus primarily on the sayings of the prophets, the book of Jonah concentrates rather on the events surrounding the prophet's mission and contains but the briefest record of his pronouncements.

More significantly, however, the identification of the book's genre is of importance for our interpretation of the text. If we are to grasp correctly what the author sought to communicate, we must identify the literary category to which his work belongs. It is essential, therefore, to determine what kind of literature the author intended to write. Did he wish the book to be regarded as in some sense a work of fiction, or as history?

---

[1] Allen, p. 199; *cf.* Ackerman, 'Satire and Symbolism', pp. 224–225.

[2] For a fuller treatment of this issue, see my essay 'Jonah and Genre', *TynB* 36 (1985), pp. 35–59.

JONAH

A. Fiction

Recent efforts to classify the book of Jonah as fiction have produced a wide range of suggestions: allegory;[1] midrash;[2] parable;[3] prophetic parable;[4] legend;[5] prophetic legend;[6] novelle;[7] satire;[8] didactic fiction;[9] satirical, didactic, short story.[10] Such a list of proposals suggests that there is a considerable lack of agreement among scholars regarding the genre of Jonah. This, however, is not really so. Differences of opinion over the choice of some of these terms are of a relatively minor nature. The large number of suggestions reflects rather the difficulty of finding a single label which commands widespread support. Thus, for example, there is little to distinguish in practice between the designations parable and didactic fiction, although, as we have argued elsewhere, the term parable is not particularly apt, especially if one thinks in terms of the New Testament use of the word.[11]

The majority of scholars now reject as unlikely the possib-

---

[1] G. A. Smith, *The Book of the Twelve Prophets*, Expositor's Bible (Hodder and Stoughton, ²1898); Martin; Johnson, 'Cultic Phantasy', pp. 82–102; Knight.

[2] K. Budde, 'Vermutungen zum "Midrasch des Buches der Könige" ', *ZAW* 12 (1892), pp. 37–51 (a midrash on 2 Ki. 14:25); L. H. Brockington, 'Jonah', in M. Black, H. H. Rowley (eds.), *Peake's Commentary on the Bible* (Nelson, 1962), pp. 627–629 (a midrash on Je. 18:8); Trible (a midrash on Ex. 34:6).

[3] Bewer; J. Smart, 'The Book of Jonah', *The Interpreter's Bible*, 6 (Abingdon, 1956), pp. 871–894; Watts; Allen; P. C. Craigie, *The Twelve Prophets*, 1, The Daily Study Bible (Saint Andrew Press, 1984).

[4] A. Rofé, 'Classes in the Prophetical Stories: Didactic Legenda and Parable', *VTS* 26 (1974), pp. 143–164.

[5] O. Eissfeldt, *The Old Testament. An Introduction* (Basil Blackwell, 1965), pp. 403–406; A. Jepsen, 'Anmerkungen zum Buch Jona', *Wort-Gebot-Glaube. Beiträge zur Theologie des Alten Testaments. Walter Eichrodt zum 80 Geburtstag, Abhandlungen zur Theologie des Alten und Neuen Testaments* 59 (1970), pp. 297–305.

[6] Haller; Keller.

[7] Wolff (1975); O. Kaiser, *Introduction to the Old Testament*, trans. J. Sturdy (Basil Blackwell, 1975), pp. 194–198; G. M. Landes, 'Jonah, Book of', *IDBS*, pp. 488–491.

[8] M. Burrows, 'The Literary Category of the Book of Jonah', in H. T. Frank, W. L. Reed (eds.), *Translating and Understanding the Old Testament* (Abingdon, 1970), pp. 80–107; Allen.

[9] Weiser; Wolff, 'Jonabuch', in *Die Religion in Geschichte und Gegenwart*, (Tübingen, ³1959), pp. 853–856; Rudolph.

[10] Fretheim; Wolff (1977).

[11] Alexander, 'Jonah and Genre', pp. 38–40.

ility that the book of Jonah is either allegory or midrash.[1] Allegorical interpretations of the text have not proved particularly convincing. Although a few recent writers still maintain that the name Jonah, meaning 'dove', is symbolic, the majority of modern commentators now dismiss this idea completely.[2] The suggestion that Jonah's imprisonment in the fish represents the Babylonian captivity is also less than convincing, especially when it is recognized that the fish is portrayed as an instrument of deliverance, not punishment. As regards Jonah being a midrash (*i.e.* an exposition of a biblical text), no agreement has been reached as to what passage the book of Jonah expounds. Moreover, Jewish midrash is a post-exilic phenomenon, whereas, as we have argued above, the book of Jonah belongs to the pre-exilic period.

As is evident from many of the proposed classifications of Jonah, the question of the historical nature of the book is of considerable importance. Many of the terms used are deliberately chosen because they designate non-historical writings (*e.g.* parable, legend, novelle). This tendency to view the book as fiction rather than fact is a relatively modern development and is proposed mainly on the basis of the following arguments.

a. Historical improbability. A major difficulty confronting many modern readers is the number of extraordinary events which are recorded. Jonah's rescue by the great fish, the repentance of the entire city of Nineveh, the remarkable growth of the plant and its equally swift destruction are hardly everyday events. Since, so it is argued, it is highly improbable that these ever occurred, they must be the creation of the author's mind; the book of Jonah cannot possibly be based on actual happenings.

However, while many modern readers may view these events with considerable scepticism, it is surely more important to ask how the author of Jonah viewed them.

---

[1] *Cf.* Aalders, *Problem*, pp. 15–16; Burrows, 'Literary Category', pp. 88–90; Eybers, 'The Purpose of the Book of Jonah', pp. 212–213; however, Allen, p. 181, maintains that the book contains 'certain allegorical features'.

[2] The most recent writer to suggest that the name Jonah is significant is A. J. Hauser, 'Jonah: In Pursuit of the Dove', *JBL* 104 (1985), pp. 21–37. His proposal that the dove was associated in the Old Testament with 'flight' and 'passivity' is suggestive, but not completely convincing.

Although he may have thought them extremely unusual, he need not necessarily have dismissed them as completely improbable. After all, the author of the biblical book of Kings incorporates into his historically based account events which are no less incredible than those found in Jonah (*e.g.* Elijah's ascent into heaven, 2 Ki. 2:1–18), and clearly, he was quite prepared to accept these as having actually occurred. In view of this, it is surely mistaken to expect an ancient writer to abide by modern standards of historical probability and improbability. Furthermore, even if it could be clearly demonstrated, as some modern writers suggest, that some of these events did not take place, this does not automatically indicate that the author of Jonah did not view them as historical. What is all important is the author's perception of what he was writing. In the present instance, weighing historical probability and improbability does not answer this issue. To determine the author's intention we must look elsewhere.

b. Hyperbole. A second feature of the book of Jonah which is thought to indicate its non-historical character is hyperbole. Everything, from the fish to the population of Nineveh, is presented in an exaggerated manner.[1] This, it is suggested, is no sober account of reality, but rather a flight of fancy on the part of the author, who never intended his work to be treated as a serious piece of historical narrative; it was composed primarily to entertain and amuse the reader. Consequently various writers have stressed the ironical or satirical tone of the entire book.[2]

That the author of Jonah actually portrays everything as

[1] Attention is drawn to the repeated use of the adjective *gādôl*, which occurs fourteen times in the book.

[2] Burrows, 'Literary Category', pp. 95–96, develops the idea that everything is exaggerated and suggests that the book was composed as a satire. Similarly, Fretheim, pp. 51–55, sees these exaggerations as ironical; *cf.* E. M. Good, *Irony in the Old Testament* (SPCK, 1965), pp. 39–55; Ackerman, 'Satire and Symbolism', pp. 213–246; M. West, 'Irony in the Book of Jonah: Audience Identification with the Hero', *Perspectives in Religious Studies* 11 (1984), pp. 232–242. S. D. Goitein, 'Some Observations on Jonah', *JPOS* 17 (1937), p. 74, rejects the view that the book of Jonah is a satire: 'The whole tenor of the story is much too earnest for a satire; Jonah is not painted with the brush of mockery or disdain, but drawn with the pencil of deep and sympathetic insight into human weakness' (quoted by Magonet, p. 86); *cf.* C. A. Keller, 'Le portrait d'un prophète', *Theologische Zeitschrift* 21 (1965), p. 329; A. D. Cohen, 'The Tragedy of Jonah', *Judaism* 21 (1972), pp. 170–172.

larger than life is highly questionable. A careful analysis of the text suggests that events are not exaggerated but rather reflect accurately the situation described. For example, it is only to be expected that a fish capable of swallowing a man should be designated 'big' (1:17). Moreover, the author, if anything, actually plays down the miraculous nature of the various extraordinary events recorded in the narrative. Thus his description of Jonah being swallowed by the great fish is told in a very matter-of-fact manner, with no attempt being made to embellish the account with extravagant details. This seems remarkable, especially when we are asked to believe that the author is fond of hyperbole. Whereas many modern expositions of Jonah tend to dramatize the events in a most unrealistic manner, the same is not true of the Hebrew original.

c. Symmetrical structure. Modern studies of Jonah have revealed that the entire book shows signs of careful composition. The presence of symmetrical structures underlying the text, however, has led some scholars to suggest that this is a further indication that the book is fictional. As T. E. Fretheim comments, 'The carefully worked out structures in the book . . . suggest a non-historical intention on the author's part. Such a concern for structure and symmetry is not as characteristic of straightforward historical writing and is more suggestive of an imaginative product'.[1]

However, although the author of Jonah makes use of literary structures, this need not automatically imply that his work is fictional. A distinction needs to be drawn between form of presentation and content. The fact that the author of Jonah employs particular literary devices tells us more about his skill as an author than about the historicity or non-historicity of his account. Furthermore, although the book of Jonah exhibits certain literary structures and patterns, these are in no way as restrictive and limiting as Fretheim implies. There is no reason why a skilful author could not use these and still present an accurate account of what took place.

d. Didactic nature. A further reason why many scholars assume the book of Jonah to be non-historical is its didactic

[1] Fretheim, p. 66.

nature. It is argued that the book was not written with the intention of recording actual events, but rather was designed to convey particular ideas. Some writers would even go so far as to say that the didactic nature of the book is perhaps the most compelling reason for viewing it as fictional.[1] Because Jonah is didactic, it cannot be historical.

This conclusion, however, does not follow. Writers who adopt this argument unfortunately create a quite unnecessary distinction between 'historical' and 'didactic' works. There is no reason why the book of Jonah may not be both didactic and historical. The fact that the author of Jonah communicates to his readers a particular message does not exclude the possibility that his account is based on historical happenings. Indeed, it is the very reality of these events which adds significance to the teaching of the book.

In spite of their popular appeal, these arguments for the fictional nature of the book of Jonah are not as decisive as they may at first appear.

B. History
On the other hand several factors favour the view that the author of Jonah consciously wrote about these events believing them to have actually occurred.

a. Traditional understanding. Although the majority of modern scholars prefer to view Jonah as fictional, this is a relatively recent development. Only in the past one hundred years has there been a marked departure from what was once the almost unanimous opinion that the events described actually occurred.[2] Although traditional positions are not necessarily correct, it is surely significant that such unanimity existed regarding the nature of the book of Jonah:

> The fact that generations of scholars and writers were convinced that the author of Jonah did not intend to write fiction argues against the modern view that the form or

[1] *Cf.* J. Licht, *Storytelling in the Bible* (Magnes, 1978), p. 124.
[2] The historicity of Jonah is accepted by the following writers: G. Ch. Aalders, *The Problems of the Book of Jonah* (Tyndale Press, 1948); Trépanier, 'The Story of Jonas', pp. 8–16; E. F. Sutcliffe, 'Jonas', in B. Orchard, E. F. Sutcliffe, R. C. Fuller, R. Russell (eds.), *A Catholic Commentary on Holy Scripture* (Thomas Nelson and Son, 1953), pp. 669–671; Robinson, 'Jonah', pp. 746–751; Maier; Walton.

style of the narrative conveys this very impression. Were these earlier generations completely blind to features which we are asked to believe are immediately apparent? Did these earlier writers not live and study in an environment much closer to that of the author of Jonah than we do? And if so, would they not have been more attuned to the generic signals of an ancient narrative? With these factors in mind, we must surely expect good reasons for ignoring or rejecting the traditional appraisal of Jonah.[1]

Thus, for example, the first-century AD Jewish historian Flavius Josephus incorporates the story of Jonah into his history of the Jewish people (*Antiquities* 9.206–214). He justifies his inclusion of this material by making the following remark, 'But, since I have promised to give an exact account of our history, I have thought it necessary to recount what I have found written in the Hebrew books concerning this prophet'.[2]

This traditional understanding of the book ought not to be dismissed lightly. It is perhaps a better guide to the book's genre than the opinions of modern scholars who are perhaps insufficiently critical of their own presuppositions regarding supernatural occurrences. We must never forget that the author of Jonah lived in a culture whose ethos was very different from that of modern Western society.

b. Historical introduction. Another feature which suggests that the book of Jonah was intended by its author to be understood as historical is the way in which it begins. Two points are worth emphasizing here.

1. The main character of the book is identified as Jonah ben (son of) Amittai. 2 Kings 14:25 mentions a prophet of the same name, who during the reign of Jeroboam II (782/81–753 BC) predicted the expansion of Israel's territory. This naturally raises the question, why, if they never actually occurred, did the author apparently associate the events recorded in the book of Jonah with a known prophet? Is it not strange that having invented the entire plot the author did not likewise invent his central character?

[1] Alexander, 'Jonah and Genre', p. 58
[2] From the translation by R. Marcus, *Josephus*, VI (Heinemann, 1937), pp. 109–111.

2. The style of introduction is similar to that found in other historical works. The opening words are very reminiscent of 1 Kings 17:8–9, 'The word of the Lord came to him [Elijah], "Arise, go to Zarephath . . ." ' To anyone familiar with Hebrew narrative, such an introduction must surely have suggested that what followed was intended by the author to be treated as fact. Thus the very first impression created by the introductory words of the book is that the account is meant to be taken as fact, not fiction.

c. Other considerations. Finally, two other considerations which have a bearing on the historicity of the book of Jonah must be mentioned briefly.

1. Many scholars are inclined to view the book as fictional because of the supposed legendary features of the text. The author, it is argued, is far removed from the period and situation about which he writes and therefore merely imagines how things may once have been. However, it is highly questionable whether the text contains legendary details. We have already examined them in considering the date of composition and concluded that they are by no means as certain as some scholars suppose. Indeed a mid-eighth century BC setting seems particularly suitable for Jonah's mission, especially in the light of events taking place then in Assyria.[1] While this does not prove that the book is an accurate record of actual happenings, it does lend weight to a historical interpretation of the text.

2. The closest literary parallel to the book of Jonah is probably the account found in 1 Kings 17 – 19 concerning the prophet Elijah. Various links with this material are noted in the commentary, especially in chapter 4.[2] Although many scholars raise questions about the actual nature of the events described in 1 Kings 17 – 19, few would go so far as to say that they have no historical basis. There would seem to be good grounds for adopting a similar approach towards the book of Jonah.

[1] See the Additional Note, 'Eighth-century Assyria', pp. 77–81.
[2] Porten, 'Baalshamem and the Date of Jonah', pp. 238–239, draws attention to the following parallels which exist between the book of Jonah and the prophetic tales which relate to the Omri dynasty (1 Ki. 18 – 2 Ki. 8): (1) the occurrence of extraordinary happenings; (2) events which range beyond the borders of Israel.

Conclusion

Hebrew authors no doubt had their own literary conventions and classifications. For this reason modern labels may not be altogether appropriate. Nevertheless, in the light of the above discussion the following conclusions may be drawn regarding the genre of the book of Jonah. On the one hand, in agreement with the consensus of modern scholarship, we would wish to emphasize the didactic nature of the text. Whatever else our author intended, he clearly sought to impart a theological lesson to his readers. On the other hand, however, against the current of modern thought on Jonah, we would suggest that the author's message derives from actual historical events and that these form the basis of his account. Consequently the most appropriate designation for the book's genre would appear to be didactic history.

Note on eighth-century Assyria

Although no specific date is given within the book itself, it is generally accepted that the account of Jonah's mission to Nineveh ought to be placed within the first three-quarters of the eighth century BC; this seems to be clearly indicated by the fact that 2 Kings 14:15 connects Jonah ben Amittai with the reign of the Israelite king Jeroboam II (782/81–753 BC). With this dating in mind, let us consider briefly the history of eighth-century BC Assyria.

To appreciate the situation which developed within Assyria in the first half of the eighth century it is necessary to begin some time earlier. Under the leadership of Ashurnaṣirpal II (883–859) and Shalmaneser III (859/58–824/23), Assyria experienced remarkable growth and prosperity; according to A. K. Grayson, this was one of the golden ages of Mesopotamian history.[1] However, things were not to remain like this for long, and even before his death Shalmaneser began to witness the break-up of his mighty kingdom. In 826 a major rebellion broke out within Assyria itself, led by the eldest of Shalmaneser's sons, Ashur-da'in-apla. One of the factors prompting this crisis was Shalmaneser's inability to restrict the authority of provincial governors who 'assumed powers

[1] Grayson, 'Assyria', p. 259.

KINGS OF ISRAEL AND ASSYRIA

Israel		Assyria	
Omri	*885/84–874/73*		
		Ashurnasirpal II	*883–859*
Ahab	*874/73–853*		
		Shalmaneser III	*859/58–824/23*
Ahaziah	*853–852*		
Joram	*852–841*		
Jehu	*841–814/13*		
		Shamshi-Adad V	*823–811/10*
Jehoahaz	*814/13–798*		
		Adad-nirari III	*810–783/82*
Jehoash	*798–782/81*		
Jeroboam II (co-regent from	*782/81–753 793/92*)		
		Shalmaneser IV	*783/82–773/72*
		Ashur-dan III	*772/71–755/54*
		Ashur-nirari V	*754/53–746/45*
Zechariah	*753–752*		
Shallum	*752*		
Menahem	*752–742/41*		
		Tiglath-pileser III	*745/44–727/26*
Pekahiah	*742/41–740/39*		
Pekah	*740/39–732/31*		
Hoshea	*732/31–723/22*		
		Shalmaneser V	*727/26–722*
		Sargon II	*722/21–705/4*

out of proportion to the real nature of their duties'.[1] The revolt was not quelled until 820, when another of the king's sons, Shamshi-Adad V (823–811/10), following the death of his father, finally defeated the rebels. However, the preceding seven years of internal strife and disruption had taken their toll and they marked the beginning of a period of significant decline for Assyria. Although Shamshi-Adad V took steps to

[1] Grayson, 'Assyria', p. 273.

re-establish Assyria's position as the leading world power, and not without some success, his reign was far too brief to permit the restoration of the nation to its former glory. Over the next seventy years Assyria was to experience a period of marked decline and eclipse. Not until the reign of Tiglath-pileser III (745/44–727/26) would the nation's fortune take a decisive turn once more for the better.

After his father's death, Adad-nirari III (810–783/82) succeeded to the throne. Unfortunately, our knowledge of his twenty-seven year reign is very limited; only one major royal inscription has so far been discovered. Other texts from this time, concerning provincial rulers, convey the impression that the king's power was severely curtailed. As Grayson remarks, 'A prominent phenomenon in this dark age . . . is the emergence of powerful provincial governors who act as virtual monarchs in their own districts, although most profess allegiance to the Assyrian crown.'[1] The earlier revolt had done little to restrict the authority of the provincial governors.

One of the most important of these officials, Shamshi-ilu, seems to have enjoyed a particularly long and successful career (possibly from at least 792 to 752). During the reign of Shalmaneser IV (783/82–773/72), Shamshi-ilu records on two stone lions at the Syrian city of Til Barsip (Tell Ahmar) his victory over Argishtish, king of Urarṭu, without making any mention of the Assyrian king; according to G. Roux this was 'unprecedented in Assyrian records'.[2] Nor is Shamshi-ilu an exception. It is possible to identify a number of other important officials who, although paying nominal allegiance to the Assyrian king, appear to have exercised considerable independence during the first half of the eighth century.[3]

In contrast to provincial rulers like Shamshi-ilu, the Assyrian kings of this period seem particularly impotent. This is especially the case with Shalmaneser IV (783/82–773/72), Ashur-dan III (772/71–755/54) and Ashur-nirari V (754/

---

[1] Grayson, 'Assyria', p. 273.

[2] Roux, *Ancient Iraq*, p. 280; *cf.* F. Thureau-Dangin, 'L'inscription des lions de Til-Barsip', *Revue d'Assyriologie et d'Archéologie orientale* 27 (1930), pp. 15–19; Grayson, 'Assyria', pp. 278–279; Lawrence, 'Assyrian Nobles', pp. 127–129.

[3] Lawrence, 'Assyrian Nobles', pp. 123–126, discusses briefly the careers of two other provincial governors, Bēl-tarṣi-iluma and Nergal-eresh; Grayson, 'Assyria', pp. 273–274, mentions Nergal-eresh, and elsewhere (p. 279) refers to several other important officials, Bel-kharran-beli-uṣur and Shamash-resha-uṣur.

53–746/745). Unfortunately what we know of the reigns of these three kings, all sons of Adad-nirari III, is meagre. Possibly this reflects the troubled times in which they lived.

Several features are worth noting about this period of Assyrian history. Firstly, there was a marked decrease in the number of campaigns against foreign nations. According to the Assyrian Eponym Chronicle, Ashur-dan III remained 'in the land' (*i.e.* did not embark on an external military campaign) for four years of his reign (768, 764, 757, 756), and Ashur-nirari V did likewise for five years (753, 752, 751, 750, 747). Furthermore, there were domestic rebellions in Ashur (763–762), Arrapkha (761–760) and Calah (746). These factors clearly indicate the increasing impotence of the Assyrian monarchs towards the middle of the eighth century BC. Secondly, during the reign of Ashur-dan III there occurred two events which would have been viewed as particularly ominous: (1) a famine and (2) a solar eclipse. Famine came to the land in the year 765 and either recurred in 759, or possibly continued for the entire seven year period. At the same time there occurred a total solar eclipse, now reckoned to have taken place on 15 June 763. Such happenings would certainly have been viewed with considerable apprehension and fear. As Wiseman suggests, had Jonah appeared in Nineveh about this time, his message might well have evoked the kind of response recorded in chapter three.[1]

In the light of the authority exercised by the provincial governors and the weakness of the Assyrian kings, it is possible that two features of the book of Jonah which have long been considered inappropriate to an Assyrian setting may in fact reflect accurately events which occurred during the first half of the eighth century. Thus the issuing of a decree by the king and his nobles (3:7) would seem highly possible given the factors observed above. Similarly, in view of the unstable political situation of this period, the designation 'king of Nineveh', in contrast to the more usual title 'king of Assyria', may not be wholly inappropriate.

Assyria's decline was eventually arrested when Tiglath-pileser III (745/44–727/26) seized control of the throne from Ashur-nirari V. Under his firm leadership the nation once more established itself as the major power in the ancient Near

---

[1] Wiseman, 'Jonah's Nineveh', pp. 42–51.

East. Significantly, he adopted a new policy towards those nations who opposed Assyria: 'total conquest, accompanied by the deportation of the populations and the establishment of Assyrian provinces under an Assyrian administration'.[1] It was as a result of these measures that the northern kingdom of Israel was eventually to suffer the destruction of its capital, Samaria, and the deportation of its population. Although the siege of the city commenced in 724, during the reign of Shalmaneser V (727/26–722), it is Sargon II (722/21–705/4) who claims its capture:

> At the beginning of my royal rule . . . I besieged and conquered Samaria, led away as booty 27,290 inhabitants of it. I formed from among them a contingent of 50 chariots and made remaining (inhabitants) assume their (social) positions. I installed over them an officer of mine and imposed upon them the tribute of the former king.[2]

Thus the nation of Assyria, to whom the prophet Jonah had been divinely sent, was subsequently responsible for the total destruction of his homeland. The early readers of the book could hardly have failed to notice the irony.

IV. PURPOSE

Jonah is first and foremost a didactic work. As the majority of modern commentators emphasize, the author of this remarkable book was intent on educating his audience, and not merely on entertaining them. Consequently, it is important to ask, What lesson (or lessons) does he wish to teach?

To answer this it is best to begin by surveying how others have understood the 'message' of the book. Although an amazing variety of opinions exist, these fall into four broad categories. By examining each in turn we may be in a better position to appreciate the purpose of Jonah.

A. Repentance
Writers from all ages have noted the importance of repentance in the book of Jonah. Indeed in Jewish tradition, Jonah, together with the final three verses of Micah, forms part of the ritual on the Day of Atonement when Jews in repentance

---

[1] Grayson, 'Assyria', p. 409.   [2] *ANET*, pp. 284–285.

confess their sins to God. Yet even among those who agree that repentance is the main theme of Jonah, there is a wide range of opinion as to the precise purpose of the book.

Jerome suggested that Jonah was composed to *encourage* Jews to repent.[1] If pagan sailors and wicked Ninevites could respond with repentance to prophetic preaching, Jewish hearers ought to do likewise. Kimchi, the twelfth-century Jewish commentator, adopted this view, and more recently C. A. Keller, Landes and H. Gevaryahu have each advocated a similar approach.[2] On the other hand, Clements has argued that the book of Jonah was intended to *show the possibility* of human repentance leading to a subsequent change in divine plans; both man and God may experience a similar change of heart.[3] Jonah, for his part, represents those who reject the view that God may alter a decree which has already been announced.

According to Y. Kaufmann, Jonah originated in the middle of the eighth century BC as the *classical formulation* of the Israelite concept of repentance.[4] With Jonah a major innovation occurred, for previously repentance had played no part in the religious thought of Israel. Jonah, typifying those who believed that all sin must be punished, is unable to accept God's willingness to forgive those who repent. A somewhat similar position is adopted by J. Walton, who suggests that the book of Jonah formed a *bridge* between the pre-classical (*e.g.* Elijah, Elisha) and classical prophets (*e.g.* Amos, Hosea).[5] Jonah sees himself as standing in the tradition of the pre-classical prophets, whose pronouncements were viewed as irrevocable, and is unwilling to readjust when called to act as a classical prophet whose pronouncement would be set aside if repentance was forthcoming. By highlighting Jonah's dilemma the author indicates that repentance is the correct response to the pronouncements of the classical prophets.

Repentance also figures prominently in the view of E. J.

[1] Jerome, 'Commentariorum in Ionam Prophetam', *Corpus Christianoru.* (Series Latina) 76 (1969), pp. 376–419.
[2] C. A. Keller, *Joel, Abdias, Jonas*; Landes, 'Jonah, Book of', pp. 488–491; H. Gevaryahu, 'The Universalism of the Book of Jonah', *Dor le Dor* 10 (1981), pp. 20–27.
[3] Clements, 'The Purpose of the Book of Jonah', pp. 16–28.
[4] Y. Kaufmann, *The Religion of Israel*, trans. and abridged M. Greenberg (University of Chicago, 1960), pp. 282–286.
[5] Walton; *cf.* Porten, 'Baalshamem and the Date of Jonah', pp. 237–244.

Bickerman that Jonah was composed to *counter* the belief, popular in post-exilic Judaism, that repentance guaranteed divine forgiveness.[1] The book of Jonah underlines the fact that God shows mercy because he is a compassionate sovereign Creator; forgiveness is not automatically merited by repentance.

Although repentance is indeed a major theme in Jonah, a variety of considerations suggest that we must look elsewhere for the purpose of the book. The traditional view, that Jonah was composed to encourage Jews to repent, fails to account for the inclusion of chapter 4 within the account: had the book been designed to promote repentance, it would surely have been more appropriate to conclude the narrative at 3:10. Clements, Kaufmann and Walton explain the inclusion of chapter 4 by arguing that this episode brings to a climax Jonah's outright rejection of the doctrine of repentance on the part of man or God. Yet the assumption of these scholars that Jonah was quite unfamiliar with the concept of repentance must surely be questioned in view of Jonah's confession in 4:2, 'I knew that you are a gracious and compassionate God, slow to anger and abounding in love, a God who relents from sending calamity.' Citing Exodus 34:6, Jonah clearly acknowledges the divine privilege to forgive sins and relent from sending punishment. Jonah does not object to the doctrine of repentance *per se*, rather, as we shall argue below, he objects to the Ninevites being the recipients of divine forgiveness.

Nor is the alternative proposal of Bickerman less problematic. If the book was directed against those who thought divine forgiveness an automatic consequence of repentance, we would surely have expected the author to portray Jonah as adopting this very position. As it is, the book actually criticizes Jonah for opposing God's gracious response to the repentance of the Ninevites. Bickerman's interpretation is much too elusive.

B. Unfulfilled prophecy
G. Emmerson and J. Licht have suggested that the book examines the problem of a prophet who *lacks authentication* due

---

[1] E. J. Bickerman, *Four Strange Books of the Bible* (Schocken Books, 1967), pp. 3–49; trans. from his 'Les deux erreurs du prophète Jonas', pp. 232–264.

to the non-fulfilment of his prophecy.[1] Jonah fears that he will be termed a false prophet because his pronouncement against Nineveh remains unfulfilled (*cf.* Dt. 18:22, 'If that which a prophet speaks in the name of the LORD does not take place or come true, his message is not from the LORD'). Thus the narrative emphasizes the conditional nature of prophetic pronouncements.

Towards the end of the last century, F. Hitzig proposed that Jonah was meant to *justify the non-fulfilment* of divine prophecies.[2] Jonah illustrates how God could indeed revoke an already pronounced judgment. Refining this proposal, A. Feuillet limited the scope of such unfulfilled prophecies to those addressed against Gentile nations.[3] The narrative was intended to explain why some prophecies against foreign nations had remained unfulfilled; such pronouncements were not, as had been assumed, absolute in nature, but rather conditional.

According to A. Rofé, Jonah examines the relationship between conditional and unconditional prophecy, and, in so doing, reflects a debate, which occurred during the exilic period, between those who maintained the traditional view that every divine decree was absolute and those who advocated the more modern suggestion that all prophecy was ultimately conditional.[4]

These proposals, however, are not without objection. On the issue of 'lack of authentication', one might ask if this suggestion does full justice to the character of Jonah as portrayed in the book; is he merely worried about being viewed as a false prophet? Does the response of the Ninevites to Jonah's message not indicate beyond doubt that he is indeed a true prophet? And are we not to see the hand of God in such remarkable events, suggesting again that Jonah is divinely commissioned? Could it not also be argued, as E. M. Good suggests, that in one sense the prophecy of Jonah actually was fulfilled: Yet forty days and Nineveh

[1] G. I. Emmerson, 'Another look at the Book of Jonah', *ET* 88 (1976), pp. 86–88; Licht, *Storytelling in the Bible*, pp. 121–124; this approach was also suggested by some earlier commentators; *e.g.* Rashi and Calvin.

[2] F. Hitzig, *Die zwölf kleinen Propheten*, Kurzgefasstes exegetisches Handbuch zum AT (Hirzel, ³1863).

[3] Feuillet, 'Les sources', pp. 161–186; *idem*, 'Le sens du livre de Jonas', *RB* 54 (1947), pp. 340–361.

[4] Rofé, 'Classes in the Prophetical Stories', pp. 143–164.

will be turned upside down.[1]

If the book of Jonah was intended to justify the non-fulfilment of divine prophecies, various questions arise. Is it not strange that the term 'prophet' is never applied to Jonah? And could it not be argued that Jonah was quite unworthy of his calling, and therefore what befell him is most untypical? And what if the book is dated, as many suppose, after the destruction of Nineveh in 612 BC? Would this not suggest to a later audience that the divine threat had indeed been carried out (even if somewhat belatedly)?

As for the suggestion that Jonah examines the relationship between conditional and unconditional prophecy, it is apparent from 4:2, as we have observed above, that Jonah himself recognizes that all prophecy is conditional; indeed the entire story presupposes this possibility.

These considerations suggest that the purpose of Jonah cannot be limited to the issue of unfulfilled prophecy. While the lack of fulfilment is a very real problem for Jonah, it is important to decide whether this is on account of his belief that *all* prophecy should be fulfilled, or due, in this instance, to the non-fulfilment of the prophecy against Nineveh. In the light of factors still to be considered, this latter possibility seems the more likely.

C. *Jewish attitudes towards Gentiles*
The relationship between Jews and Gentiles lies at the heart of two of the most popular interpretations of the book of Jonah. For Augustine, Luther and many modern writers, the narrative emphasizes the *missionary* concern of God, whose love and mercy was not limited to the Jews.[2] Through Jonah, God not only rebukes those who would confine his saving grace to the Jewish people, but he also forcefully demonstrates his real interest in the salvation of ignorant, sinful pagans. Alternatively, many nineteenth- and twentieth-century scholars have suggested that the book of Jonah was an attack on the Jewish

[1] Good, *Irony in the Old Testament*, p. 48; *cf.* Wiseman, 'Jonah's Nineveh', pp. 48–49; see Commentary, p. 121.
[2] Augustine, *Epistularum*, CII, 6, 30–38; Luther, 'Lectures on Jonah', in H. C. Oswald (ed.), *Luther's Works*, 19 (Concordia, 1974), pp. 3–104; H. H. Rowley, *The Missionary Message of the Old Testament* (Carey, 1945), p. 69; E. Haller *Die Erzählung von dem Propheten Jona*; Eybers, 'The Purpose of the Book of Jonah', pp. 211–222.

bigotry against Gentiles which surfaced in the religious reforms of Ezra and Nehemiah.[1] Thus the author of Jonah portrays the pagan sailors and Ninevites in a favourable light in order to counter the negative attitude adopted by many of his contemporaries. M. Burrows, refining this approach, suggests that the book was directed primarily against a relatively small group of returning exiles who were extreme fanatics.[2]

In the opinion of S. Goldman and G. von Rad, the book was designed to rebuke the *grudging attitude* of some Jews concerning God's willingness to forgive Gentiles.[3] Jonah, typifying those who adopt this stance, is condemned because he callously begrudges the Ninevites divine mercy and forgiveness. M. Delcor, on the other hand, suggests that the book addressed those who eagerly *anticipated the destruction* of the Gentile nations through the fulfilment of prophecies of doom.[4]

Various criticisms of these approaches should be noted. Clements queries the proposal that the book of Jonah was aimed at encouraging missionary activity:

> Jonah is clearly in no way to be thought of as a missionary to Nineveh, and his actions are very different from those of the Jews of a later age ... God's mercy which is extended to the people of Nineveh after their repentance and fasting is nowhere related to their embracing of the torah, their rejection of idolatry, their acceptance of circumcision, nor even to so basic a feature as a confession that Yahweh the God of Israel is the only true God. It is true that Nineveh and its inhabitants are shown to be within reach of the divine mercy, but such a broad assumption about Yahweh's dealings with nations is evident very much earlier in the literature of the Old Testament. In itself it does not go as far as the promise that non-Israelite nations will know that Yahweh is God, as asserted by

[1] E. König, 'Jonah', *HDB*, vol. 2, cols. 744–753; Bewer; G. von Rad, *Der Prophet Jona* (Laetare, 1950); B. S. Childs, 'Jonah: A Study in Old Testament Hermeneutics', *SJT* 11 (1958), pp. 53–61; O. Loretz, 'Herkunft und Sinn', pp. 18–29; Wolff (1975).

[2] Burrows, 'Literary Category', pp. 80–107.

[3] S. Goldman, 'Jonah, Introduction and Commentary', in A. Cohen (ed.), *The Twelve Prophets* (Soncino, 1948), pp. 137–150; G. von Rad, *Old Testament Theology*, 2, trans. D. M. G. Stalker (Oliver and Boyd, 1965), pp. 289–292.

[4] M. Delcor, 'Jonas' in *Les petits prophètes*, La sainte Bible 8:1 (Letouzey et Ané, 1961).

Ezekiel and Deutero-Isaiah (Isa. xlix 26; Ezek. xxxvi 36, 38; xxxvii 28).[1]

While the book provides an example of God's dealing with some Gentiles, it can hardly be described as a tract designed to motivate missionary involvement.

Nor can the book be linked with certainty to the time of Ezra and Nehemiah.

> The entire story fails to raise any single example of those issues which we know deeply affected the relationships of Jews with non-Jews in the post-exilic period . . . The so-called separatism of Nehemiah and Ezra was not so much concerned with making a distinction between Jew and Gentile, a distinction which had existed in Israel in national terms for centuries, but with a division between Jews and those who laid claim to being Jews.[2]

On the issue of begrudging divine mercy to Gentiles we may note that this is indeed an important issue in the latter part of the book. However, Jonah's reluctance to go to Nineveh must be contrasted with his willingness to be cast into the sea in order to save the pagan sailors. We must distinguish carefully between Jonah's general view of Gentiles and his particular attitude to the Ninevites; it is the specific deliverance of Nineveh that angers Jonah.

The suggestion that the narrative attacked those who awaited with delight the fulfilment of prophecies against foreign nations is also fraught with difficulties. What part does the episode of Jonah's initial flight and deliverance play in this context? If Jonah is meant to represent those who rejoice in the destruction of Gentiles, why is he portrayed as unwilling to pronounce judgment on Nineveh? Would he not have delighted in the prospect of condemning such a pagan city?

It has been argued by U. Cassuto and S. D. Goitein that the book of Jonah is totally devoid of any antagonism between Jews and Gentiles.[3] Yet the fact that attention is focused on Nineveh is surely significant. As is observed by Allen, 'To deny the foreignness of Nineveh is surely to underestimate the

---

[1] Clements, 'Purpose', p. 18.   [2] *Ibid.*, p. 19.

[3] U. Cassuto, 'Jona', in *Encyclopedia Judaica*, 9, cols. 268–273; Goitein, 'Some Observations', pp. 63–77.

religious and psychological impact of the old Assyrian capital upon a community that had received the book of Nahum as part of its religious heritage'.[1] Nineveh can hardly be viewed in a totally neutral light (*cf.* the book of Nahum, esp. Na. 3:5–6). Yet although Jonah's antagonism towards Nineveh is obviously an important theme in the narrative, it does not, in itself, explain why the narrative was composed.

D. Theodicy

The suggestion that the story examines the relationship between divine justice and mercy has figured prominently in a number of recent discussions on Jonah. This idea, however, is not completely new, and its roots may be traced back to earlier writers. Kaufmann, for example, saw Jonah as the 'champion of divine justice'. 'He is the voice of the ancient idea that sin must be punished.'[2]

Under this general approach various points have been highlighted. According to Trible, Jonah objects vehemently to a divine love which overlooks sin and allows evil to go unpunished.[3] Interestingly, Trible sees this as applying not only to Jonah's attitude towards God's forgiveness of Nineveh, but also to how he himself is treated. Good views Jonah as rebelling against the actions of an unreasonable God: 'What business has a God of justice turning on the mercy act at *Nineveh*?'[4] For T. S. Warshaw the book provides three examples of divine mercy having precedence over retributive justice; apart from forgiving the Ninevites, God rescues Jonah from the sea, and later shelters him from the sun.[5] On the other hand, Fretheim views Jonah as fundamentally concerned with the question of theodicy: 'Are God's *compassionate* actions just?'[6] Can a righteous God possibly forgive the wicked inhabitants of Nineveh? Jonah, according to J. Craghan, emphasizes the absolute freedom of God to act graciously and mercifully towards those

[1] Allen, p. 190; *cf.* T. F. Glasson, 'The Final Question in Nahum and Jonah', *ET* 81 (1969), pp. 54–55.

[2] Kaufmann, *Religion of Israel*, p. 285.

[3] Trible, *Studies in the Book of Jonah*, pp. 273–279.

[4] Good, *Irony in the Old Testament*, pp. 39–55.

[5] T. S. Warshaw, 'The Book of Jonah', in K. R. R. Gros Louis, J. S. Ackerman, T. S. Warshaw (eds.), *Literary Interpretations of Biblical Narratives* (Abingdon, 1974), pp. 191–207.

[6] T. E. Fretheim, *The Message of Jonah*; *idem*, 'Jonah and Theodicy', *ZAW* 90 (1978), pp. 227–237; *cf.* Ackerman, 'Satire and Symbolism', pp. 213–246.

who are deserving of divine retribution.[1] God will not be bound by Jonah's attempt to restrict divine love by playing off righteousness against love. E. Levine suggests that Jonah is a philosophical text, examining the nature of justice.[2] What is the relationship between justice and repentance?

The relationship between justice and mercy is clearly an important theme in Jonah. Yet before leaving this issue, one further observation must be made. From his statement in 4:2, it is quite apparent that Jonah acknowledges the divine prerogative to exercise mercy. Indeed Jonah has already experienced, and gladly accepted, divine deliverance from death at sea (*cf.* 2:2–9). Throughout the story Jonah does not object to divine mercy or forgiveness as such, but rather to its recipient, the Ninevites; how can God possibly pardon this particular people?

Of the various proposals for the purpose of Jonah, it is apparent that there is little to choose between them; it is easy to see why no clear consensus has yet been reached. Having said this, however, the view that Jonah is ultimately concerned with justice and mercy has at least one major advantage over the others. While the other proposals rightly reflect important themes in the story, they can all be satisfactorily subsumed under the heading of theodicy.

In our survey we observed that Jonah's reaction to Nineveh does not reflect his attitude to Gentiles in general. To say that the Ninevites are representative of all Gentiles creates real difficulties in trying to determine the purpose of Jonah. It is the deliverance of Nineveh, and this alone, which is the cause of Jonah's dissatisfaction. This, however, prompts a further series of questions: Why should Jonah object so vehemently to Nineveh? What was there about this particular city that evoked such strong antagonism?

The most obvious response would be that Nineveh, as capital of the Assyrian Empire, was responsible for the destruction of the northern kingdom of Israel (*cf.* 2 Ki. 17:1–23). This explains Jonah's antipathy for Nineveh; he perceives the eventual outcome of his mission and passionately feels that he cannot be party to something which would

[1] Craghan, pp. 164–193.
[2] E. Levine, 'Jonah as a Philosophical Book', *ZAW* 96 (1984), pp. 235–245.

ultimately mean the destruction of his own nation.[1] How can God possibly pardon these pagan Ninevites and then have them destroy Israel? For Jonah God's action is incomprehensible, and so initially he seeks to evade his calling.

There is no escape from God, however. Redirected to the city, Jonah proclaims his message of doom. Without the slightest sign of protest, the entire city, clothed in sackcloth, seeks forgiveness. Jonah's worst fears are realized; God relents from his punishment of the city. Outside the city Jonah sulks angrily. Why did God warn the Ninevites? Could he not just have punished them? What had Nineveh ever done to deserve such mercy? For Jonah, death is now preferable to life.

God responds to Jonah's impudence, however, by graciously providing a plant to shade him from the heat of the day. But Jonah's relief is short-lived, for within a day God sends a worm to kill the plant. Again Jonah reacts in anger. Has God no mercy? Must he act in such an uncaring, thoughtless way?

Having passed judgment on God's handling of these situations, Jonah is now taken to task. God pitied Nineveh, but destroyed the plant. Jonah, on the other hand, pitied the plant, but demanded the destruction of Nineveh. At odds with God, Jonah typifies those who see the divine attributes of justice and mercy as functioning for their own convenience; mercy for themselves, but justice for their enemies. Fortunately, however, these attributes are not directed by human motives or desires. As the book of Jonah makes plainly obvious, God is sovereign, his justice is totally impartial, and his mercy may extend to anyone.

The destruction of Samaria in 721 BC by the Assyrians and the subsequent deportation of the ten northern tribes must have raised many questions and doubts in the minds of God's people. How could God allow the Assyrians to do this? Was this actually part of his sovereign will? Did Israel really deserve such harsh treatment? The book of Jonah offers a very relevant response to these issues. By focusing on the issue of theodicy, it addressed those who, like Jonah, questioned the wisdom of God's sovereign purpose at this time. In the light

[1] Jerome comments, 'He knew, by inspiration of the Holy Spirit, that the repentance of the Gentiles would be the ruin of the Jews, and, as a lover of his country, was actuated not so much by envy of the salvation of Nineveh, as by unwillingness that his own people should perish' (quoted by C. F. Keil, p. 391).

of this, it seems reasonable to date the composition of the book towards the end of the eighth century BC, when the issue of God's dealings with Israel and Assyria would have been of major interest.

In Matthew 12:38 Jesus is approached by some Pharisees and teachers of the law who demand of him a miraculous sign. In response Jesus informs them that the only sign they shall receive will be 'the sign of the prophet Jonah' (12:39). Matthew 16:1–4 records a similar incident, although on this occasion it involves a group of Pharisees and Sadducees. Again Jesus tells them that the only sign they will get is 'the sign of Jonah'. Luke also provides an account which contains the same basic elements as the first of the Matthean episodes, but in a slightly different order (Lk. 11:29–32).

What Jesus meant by 'the sign of Jonah' is not immediately obvious, and detailed study of the issue has generated a number of possible solutions. A helpful summary of the ways in which the sign of Jonah has been interpreted is provided by J. Jeremias.[1] Dismissing several less likely solutions, he focuses on the two most commonly suggested possibilities: the sign of Jonah refers to either (1) the preaching of Jonah or (2) his deliverance from the belly of the great fish.

A. The preaching of Jonah
Beginning with Luke 11:29–32 it is argued that the sign of Jonah refers to his preaching to Nineveh. Confirmation of this is found in verse 32, which focuses on the response of the Ninevites to Jonah's message: 'The men of Nineveh will stand up at the judgment with this generation and condemn it; for they repented at the preaching of Jonah, and now one greater than Jonah is here' (*cf.* Matt. 12:41). Thus, it is suggested, the only sign which Jesus will give to his contemporaries is the summons to repentance which forms the

---

[1] J. Jeremias, 'Iōnas', *TDNT* III, pp. 408–410; for a fuller discussion of the redaction history of these passages, see R. A. Edwards, *The Sign of Jonah in the Theology of the Evangelists and Q*, Studies in Biblical Theology, 2nd series, 18 (SCM Press, 1971).

basis of his preaching.[1]

Although this view has enjoyed considerable support, there are a number of factors which weigh heavily against it. Firstly, it is unlikely that the preaching of repentance would have been considered a sign. As Jeremias comments, 'It is highly unusual to describe the preaching of repentance as a *semeion*, since a sign consists, not in what men do, but in "the intervention of the power of God in the course of events".'[2] Secondly, in Matthew 12:40 and Luke 11:30 Jesus clearly states that the sign will be given in the future. Yet from the very beginning of his public ministry Jesus had already been summoning people to repent; this, therefore, can hardly be the future sign which he envisages. Thirdly, P. Seidelin observes that at this time Jewish interest in the book of Jonah focused principally on the initial two chapters of the book rather than on the account of Jonah's activities in Nineveh which comes in chapter three.[3] Finally, this interpretation of the sign requires the deletion of Matthew 12:40 as a later addition to the text. Although there is some support for this proposal, the evidence is not completely compelling.[4]

B. *Jonah's deliverance from the belly of the fish*
If the sign of Jonah does not refer to the preaching of repentance, then another possibility is that it refers to the miraculous deliverance of Jonah from death by means of the great fish. This is certainly the emphasis of Matthew 12:40: 'For as Jonah was three days and three nights in the belly of a huge fish, so the Son of Man will be three days and three nights in the heart of the earth.' Here Jesus draws a comparison between the experience of Jonah and his own future resurrection from the dead; like Jonah, he too will appear alive after three days.

Some writers see a difficulty here in that Jesus seems to adopt a negative understanding of Jonah's stay within the fish, whereas in the book of Jonah the fish is actually represented as the means of deliverance from death. However, it needs to be

---

[1] *Cf.* A. D. Martin, *The Prophet Jonah: The Book and the Sign* (Longmans, Green and Co., 1926), pp. 69–82; Scott, 'The Sign of Jonah', pp. 17–18.

[2] Jeremias, 'Iōnas', p. 409.

[3] P. Seidelin, 'Das Jonaszeichen', *Studia Theologica* 5 (1951), pp. 119–131, esp. p. 130.

[4] The arguments against the deletion of Mt. 12:40 are ably presented by R. T. France, *Jesus and the Old Testament* (Tyndale Press, 1971), pp. 80–82.

emphasized that the correspondence between Jonah's experience and that of Jesus is not exact. Jonah, unlike Jesus, does not actually die; he merely experiences a very close encounter with death. It is therefore important not to push the parallels too far. Jesus draws attention to the fact that he, like Jonah, will reappear alive after three days.

According to Jeremias, what Jesus has in mind is 'the authorisation of the divine messenger by deliverance from death'.[1] This suggestion, however, presents a problem, because it is nowhere suggested in the book of Jonah that his deliverance from death was a factor in persuading the Ninevites to repent. On the contrary, Jonah was convinced from the very outset that the Ninevites would respond favourably to his message (*cf.* 4:2); indeed it was this very fear which caused him to flee to sea, setting in motion the series of events which led to his being cast overboard. Although Jesus refers here to his being raised from the dead after a period of three days, the significance of this does not lie in the 'authorisation of the divine messenger'.

As the above discussion reveals, Jesus is able to make several comparisons between Jonah and himself: both preach repentance; both reappear alive after three days. There are, however, two other similarities which are worth noting. Firstly, neither of the above interpretations takes into account the context in which Jesus mentions the sign of Jonah. In each of the three instances in which the sign is mentioned in the Synoptic Gospels, Jesus describes those who demand a sign as either 'a wicked and adulterous generation' (Mt. 12:39; 16:4) or 'a wicked generation' (Lk. 11:29). Jesus' response to their request possibly indicates that the only sign they will receive will be one denoting judgment. In this connection it is interesting to observe that Jonah's mission to Nineveh ultimately resulted in disaster for Israel. Is Jesus indicating here that just as Jonah's mission led to the deliverance of Gentiles and the destruction of Israel, so too will his own (*cf.* Lk. 19:42–44; Rom. 11:11–15)?

Secondly, about this time some Jews possibly saw in the book of Jonah an example of a prophet sacrificing his own life in order to save others. This idea obviously underlies the following remark from Mekhilta Exodus, 12:1: 'R. Jonathan

[1] Jeremias, 'Iōnas', p. 409.

[*c.* 140 AD] said: The only purpose of Jonah was to bring judgment on himself in the sea, for it is written: "And he said to them, Take me and cast me into the sea" [Jon. 1:12]. Similarly, you find that many patriarchs and prophets sacrificed themselves for Israel.' In the light of this understanding of Jonah, Jesus could also be alluding to the fact that his own death will take the form of a substitutionary sacrifice.[1]

Clearly it is possible to draw a number of parallels between Jesus' experience and that of Jonah. Maybe it is a mistake to restrict 'the sign of Jonah' to any one of these; perhaps we ought to see in Jesus' reference a combination of some, if not all, of the factors mentioned above.

VI. THE TEXT OF JONAH

The most recently printed edition of the Hebrew text of Jonah is that edited by K. Elliger in *Biblica Hebraica Stuttgartensia* (1970). This reproduces the text of Jonah found in the Leningrad Codex, which, according to its colophon, was copied in AD 1008 from a text prepared by the famous Tiberian textual scholar Aaron ben Moses ben Asher. The Leningrad Codex is but one of a number of surviving medieval codices produced by Jewish biblical scholars, known as Massoretes, who were keen to preserve the original text, and pronunciation, of the Hebrew Bible.[2]

Since 1947 the discovery of various caches of ancient documents along the western shore of the Dead Sea has provided further evidence concerning the text of Jonah. Of particular significance was the recovery in March 1955 of a manuscript of the Twelve (Minor) Prophets from a small cave in Wadi Marubba῾at. This scroll, copied shortly prior to AD 135, confirms that the Hebrew text of Jonah was carefully preserved by the Massoretes. But for a few minor differences in

[1] *Cf.* J. Woodhouse, 'Jesus and Jonah', *Reformed Theological Review* 43 (1984), pp. 33–41, esp. p. 40.

[2] There are three codices containing the text of Jonah which are slightly older than the Leningrad: the Cairo Codex on the Prophets (AD 895); the Petersburg Codex on the Prophets (AD 916); the Aleppo Codex (*c.* AD 925); *cf.* E. Würthwein, *The Text of the Old Testament* (SCM Press, 1980), pp. 34–35. For a discussion of the relative merits of these codices, see M. H. Goshen-Gottstein, 'The Rise of the Tiberian Bible Text', in A. Altmann (ed.), *Biblical and Other Studies* (Harvard, 1963), pp. 79–122; *idem*, 'The Aleppo Codex and the Rise of the Massoretic Bible Text', *BA* 42 (1979), pp. 145–163.

orthography, this text is identical to that of the best medieval manuscripts.[1]

Early translations into Greek, Aramaic, Syraic and Latin also provide evidence regarding the text of Jonah. When allowance is made for some freedom in translation, it is apparent that these ancient versions were based on a Hebrew text identical to that preserved by the Massoretes.[2] Where these versions do diverge from the Hebrew it is generally accepted that they do not provide a superior reading. For example, the important fourth-century AD Greek manuscripts Vaticanus and Sinaiticus omit in 1:8 the phrase, 'Who is responsible for our trouble?' (*cf.* NEB). A. Rahlfs and J. Ziegler, in their critical editions of the LXX, both conclude that the shorter Greek reading is inferior; the phrase was accidentally omitted due to homoeoteleuton (*i.e.* a Greek copyist unfortunately jumped in the verse from the first occurrence of *hēmin* to the next).[3] Similar explanations account for other differences. There is therefore no compelling *textual* evidence to suggest that the Massoretic text of Jonah ought to be emended.

Having said this, however, some scholars argue on other grounds that it is necessary in a few instances to emend the Hebrew text. Thus a number of purely conjectural emendations have been proposed. For example, a number of commentators suggest that the last clause of 1:10, 'because he had already told them', is out of sequence chronologically and ought, therefore, to be deleted as a gloss.[4] Yet there is no textual evidence to suggest that the authenticity of the phrase should be doubted, and it is possible to make sense of the Hebrew as it now stands.[5] Thus although various emendations have been suggested, the present form of the

---

[1] P. Benoit, J. T. Milik and R. de Vaux, *Les Grottes de Murabba'at: Texte*, Discoveries in the Judean Desert II (Clarendon Press, 1961), pp. 50, 69, 181–184, 190–191, 205.

[2] *Cf.* Trible, pp. 1–65, esp. 57–65.

[3] A. Rahlfs, *Septuaginta*, II (Privilegierte Württembergische Bibelanstalt, 1935); J. Ziegler, *Septuaginta: vol. XIII, Duodecim Prophetae* (Vandenhoed & Ruprecht, 1943). In favour of the Greek reading it has been argued that the phrase under consideration was introduced into the Hebrew text by a copyist who erroneously repeated an almost identical phrase in v. 7. For arguments to the contrary, see Allen, p. 209, n. 31.

[4] *Cf.* Bewer, p. 37; Smart, p. 883; Trible, p. 89.

[5] *Cf.* N. Lohfink, 'Jona ging zur Stadt hinaus', pp. 193–195; Keller, p. 275, n. 1; Wolff (1975), p. 42; Allen, p. 210, n. 37.

text presents few real difficulties. Indeed there is widespread agreement that the text of Jonah has been remarkably well preserved.

ANALYSIS

I. JONAH AT SEA (1:1–2:10)
    A. Jonah's initial call (1:1–3)
    B. Jonah and the sailors (1:4–16)
    C. Jonah's gratitude for his own deliverance (1:17–2:10)

II. JONAH AT NINEVEH (3:1–4:11)
    A. Jonah's second call (3:1–3)
    B. Jonah and the Ninevites (3:4–10)
    C. Jonah's anger at Nineveh's deliverance (4:1–11)

COMMENTARY

I. JONAH AT SEA (1:1 – 2:10)

A. Jonah's initial call (1:1–3)

With remarkable simplicity of style and a minimum of words, the author of Jonah quickly captures our attention by skilfully juxtaposing Jonah's divine commission to go to Nineveh with his flight to Tarshish. Specific details are kept to a minimum, yet sufficient information is provided to enable the reader to grasp immediately the opening scene.

1. For the original Hebrew audience, the story starts in a most conventional manner. The expression *The word of the LORD came to* . . . introduces a divine communication to a prophet in over one hundred instances in the Old Testament. What follows is usually the message which the prophet is to deliver (*e.g.* Joel 1:1; Mi. 1:1; Zp. 1:1; Hg. 1:1; Zc. 1:1; Mal. 1:1). Sometimes, however, it introduces specific instructions for the prophet (*e.g.* 2 Sa. 7:4; 1 Ki. 17:2, 8; 21:17). Such is the case here.

The recipient of this divine communication is named as *Jonah son of* [*ben*] *Amittai*. Unfortunately the text is silent about his background. There is, however, good reason to assume that he is the prophet mentioned in 2 Kings 14:25. On the basis of this latter passage various observations may be made. Firstly, he is portrayed as being active during the reign of Jeroboam II, who was king of the northern kingdom of Israel from 782/81 to 753 BC. This enables us to date the events concerning Nineveh to the first half of the eighth century BC. Jonah was thus a contemporary of the prophets Amos and Hosea. That the book of Jonah contains no date formula has been taken by some scholars to indicate that the author did not intend his narrative to be taken literally. It may be, however, that he saw no reason to specify precisely when these events occurred (*cf.* 1 Ki. 17:2). Secondly, Jonah is described as being from Gath-hepher. Joshua 19:13 situates this town on the border of the territory allocated to the tribe of Zebulun. The site of ancient Gath-hepher is now associated with Khirbet ez-Zurra´, a mound situated approximately twelve miles west of the Sea of Galilee (Lake Chinnereth) and three miles north-east of Nazareth.[1] Surface remains indicate that the site was occupied from about 1550 to 600 BC. Just to the north is the village of Meshhed, the traditional site of the tomb of Jonah. Thirdly, Jonah prophesied in favour of the expansion of Israel's borders, and this in spite of the fact that Jeroboam is described as doing 'evil in the eyes of the LORD' (2 Ki. 14:24). The significance of this will be developed later.

2. *Go.* There is an initial imperative 'arise' (*qûm*), which is omitted in the NIV and other more recent English translations (NEB, GNB). Although the Hebrew verb *qûm* frequently indicates the physical action of rising up (*cf.* Gn. 24:54), the imperative is often used in conjunction with other verbs to indicate the need for a prompt response.[2] Jonah is not necessarily being ordered to get up; he is, however, being instructed not to delay his departure for Nineveh.

The great city of Nineveh. Jonah's destination was the Assyrian city of Nineveh, situated on the eastern bank of the river Tigris. Today its ruins lie opposite the city of Mosul in northern Iraq. Since the mid-nineteenth century the site has been subjected to numerous archaeological excavations, providing considerable information on the city up to its destruction by the Medes in August 612 BC.[3] The expression *the great city of Nineveh* denotes not just the walled city but also the surrounding region, including possibly the city of Calah (Tell Nimrud), twenty-five miles to the south (*cf.* Gn. 10:11–12). For a fuller discussion of the problems associated with the size of Nineveh, see the Introduction pp. 56–59.

With the briefest of instructions Jonah is commanded to denounce the city of Nineveh: *preach against it, because its wickedness has come up before me.* Although the Hebrew particle *kî*, 'because', may on occasions be translated by 'that' (Gn. 1:10;

[1] See *NBA*, p. 35.
[2] *Cf.* Gn. 19:15. Gn. 27:19 highlights well the problem of translating *qûm* into English; a literal translation would be 'arise, sit down'.
[3] For further details on the city of Nineveh, see *IBD* 2, pp. 1089–1092.

1 Ki. 21:15), it is never used to introduce direct speech.[1] For this reason the JB translation, 'inform them that their wickedness has become known to me', must be rejected. The actual wording of the proclamation which Jonah is to address to Nineveh is not revealed.

Its wickedness has come up before me. Some scholars see a connection here with Genesis 18:20–21, and suggest that the author of Jonah draws upon the account of the overthrow of Sodom and Gomorrah (Gn. 18 – 19). Allen comments, 'Jonah's role is that of the divine messengers sent to announce the destruction of Sodom (Gn. 19:1, 15). This rather than any previous prophetic experience is the precedent for Jonah's mission.'[2] This link, however, is extremely tenuous. The roles performed by Jonah and the divine messengers are not identical.[3]

3. Jonah's response is immediate: the initial verb *wayyāqom*, 'he arose', which is omitted by NIV (cf. AV), corresponds with the opening imperative of the divine command (see v. 1 above). However, the following words dramatically reveal that Jonah has no intention of obeying God's instructions. Summoned to go eastward, he *ran away* in the opposite direction. His preferred destination is the city of *Tarshish*.

The exact location of *Tarshish* has yet to be established. In the 'Table of Nations' (Gn. 10:1–32) Tarshish is listed, along with Elishah, Kittim and Dodanim (possibly a corruption of Rodanim; *cf.* 1 Ch. 1:7), as one of the sons of Javan. 'From these the maritime peoples spread' (Gn. 10:5). Javan is associated with the Ionian Greeks, Elishah and Kittim with Cyprus, and Rodanim with Rhodes.[4] In line with these identifications we would expect Tarshish to be located in the eastern Mediterranean. However, it ought to be recalled that by about 1000 BC Phoenician merchants had established important trade links as far west as Spain, and it is possible that the name Tarshish designated one of their western settlements. Many

[1] A. Schoors, 'The Particle *kî*, *OTS* 21 (1981), pp. 240–276, esp. pp. 256–259; *cf.* F. Zorell, 'Gibt es im Hebräischen ein "kî recitativum"?' *Bib* 14 (1933), pp. 465–469.

[2] Allen, p. 176.

[3] *Cf.* Alexander, 'Jonah and Genre', pp. 49–50; the correspondence between the Hebrew text of Gn. 18:20–21 and Jon. 1:2 is not as close as some English translations may suggest.

[4] *Cf.* C. Westermann, *Genesis 1–11. A Commentary*, trans. John J. Scullion (SPCK, 1984), pp. 505–508.

scholars favour the identification of Tarshish with Tartessos, a Phoenician colony on the Atlantic coast of southern Spain at the mouth of the river Guadalquivir. Apart from the similarity in names, two factors favour this identification. Firstly, several biblical references associate Tarshish with distant places (Ps. 72:10; Is. 66:19). The same impression is given by a short comment in a cuneiform inscription of the Assyrian king Esarhaddon (680–669 BC): 'All kings who live in the midst of the sea, from Cyprus and Javan as far as Tarshish, submit to my feet.'[1] Secondly, Tarshish was renowned as a source of silver, iron, tin and lead (Je. 10:9; Ezk. 27:12), and, significantly, after 1000 BC one of the most important sources of these metals in the ancient world was the Iberian peninsula. Although alternatives have been suggested, south-west Spain remains the most likely location for Tarshish.[2]

From the LORD. RSV has, more literally, 'from the presence of the LORD.' At first sight this phrase seems to imply that Jonah believed it possible to escape from God's presence; by fleeing to Tarshish, he would place himself beyond the Lord's jurisdiction. This interpretation, however, is at odds with Jonah's later acknowledgment that the Lord is 'the God of heaven, who made the sea and the land' (1:9). Nor does it concur with the general picture which the Old Testament presents regarding the omnipresence of God:

> Where can I go from your Spirit?
> Where can I flee from your presence?
> If I go up to the heavens, you are there;
> if I make my bed in the depths, you are there.
> If I rise on the wings of the dawn,
> if I settle on the far side of the sea,

[1] R. Borger, *Die Inschriften Asarhaddons Königs von Assyrien*, Archiv für Orientforschung 9 (Ernst Weidner, 1956), p. 86; this appears to be the only known cuneiform reference to Tarshish.

[2] For a comprehensive discussion, see M. Koch, *Tarschisch und Hispanien. Historisch-geographische und namenkundliche Untersuchungen zur phönikischen Kolonisation der Iberischen Halbinsel*, Deutsches Archäologisches Institut Abteilung Madrid: Madrider Forschungen 14 (Walter de Gruyter, 1984); *cf.* R. R. Stieglitz, 'Long-distance Seafaring in the Ancient Near East', *BA* 47 (1984), pp. 134–142; *IBD* 3, pp. 1517–1519. Apart from Spain, the name Tarshish has been associated by W. F. Albright, 'New Light on the Early History of Phoenician Colonization', *BASOR* 83 (1941), pp. 14–22, with a site in Sardinia. R. D. Barnett, 'Mopsos', *Journal of Hellenic Studies* 73 (1953), p. 142, n. 3, suggests Tarsus in Cilicia.

even there your hand will guide me,
your right hand will hold me fast. (Ps. 139:7–10)

How, then, should we interpret this expression? The prophet Elijah employs a somewhat similar idiom, 'in whose presence I stand' (1 Ki. 17:1; *cf.* 1 Ki. 18:15; Je. 15:19), to indicate that he is a servant of the Lord (*cf.* NIV, 'whom I serve'). By fleeing from the Lord's presence Jonah announces emphatically his unwillingness to serve God. His action is nothing less than open rebellion against God's sovereignty.[1] Such an occurrence must have shocked those who first heard or read the story. Had not Amos, the contemporary of Jonah, stated, 'The lion has roared – who will not fear? The Sovereign LORD has spoken – who can but prophesy?' (Am. 3:8; *cf.* Je. 20:9)?

He went down to Joppa. Archaeological excavations reveal that the east Mediterranean port of Joppa (modern Jaffa) was settled at least as early as the seventeenth century BC.[2] As the only natural harbour on the coast of Palestine south of the Bay of Acco, it was an important seaport for the surrounding region, especially Jerusalem (*cf.* 2 Ch. 2:16; Ezr. 3:7). Here Jonah embarks on a ship which would take him as far from Nineveh as was then physically possible. On the theme of going down, see the commentary on 2:6.

Significantly, no explanation is given here for Jonah's flight; for this we must await the events of chapter 4. For the present we do not need to know. We must, therefore, restrain our

[1] The repetition of the phrase 'to Tarshish from the Lord's presence' underlines this fact. Lohfink, 'Jona ging zur Stadt hinaus', p. 200, draws attention to the concentric structure of the verse:

Jonah arose to flee to Tarshish from the presence of Yahweh
and he went down to Joppa
and he found a ship
going to Tarshish
and he paid its fare
and he went down into it
to go with them to Tarshish from the presence of Yahweh.

[2] There are a few references to Joppa in Egyptian records of the fifteenth and fourteenth centuries BC. It was probably controlled for most of the early part of the first millennium BC by the Philistines who settled in the coastal region to the south of Joppa. This possibly explains why it is only rarely mentioned in the Old Testament; *cf.* Jos. 19:46; 2 Ch. 2:16; Ezr. 3:7. In the New Testament it is mentioned in connection with the account of Peter's visit to Cornelius (Acts 9 – 11).

curiosity, avoid making conjectures, and patiently allow the author to disclose the motive when the time is right.

B. Jonah and the sailors (1:4–16)

The consequences of Jonah's flight to Tarshish are developed in the remaining verses of chapter 1. After the ship's departure from Joppa the Lord intervenes by unleashing a fierce storm. In the ensuing narrative the behaviour of the pagan sailors is contrasted very favourably with that of Jonah, adding to the prophet's already tarnished image.

Of all the different parts of the book, this section contains the clearest indications of having been carefully composed. Through the repetition of key words and phrases, the narrative has been skilfully bound together in a concentric pattern, revolving around verses 9–10. For a fuller discussion of this structure, see the Additional Note on the structure of 1:4–16, pp. 106–109.

4. Jonah's actions evoke a dramatic response: *the LORD sent a great wind on the sea*. The storm is no coincidence. The author emphasizes its divine origin by placing the subject, *the LORD*, at the very start of the sentence, reversing the more usual Hebrew word order of verb–subject.

Threatened to break up. The expression is literally 'thought to break up'. As this is the only occurrence in the Old Testament of the Hebrew verb *ḥiššaḇ*, 'think', with an inanimate subject, various writers have suggested that the phrase *ḥiššᵉḇāh lᵉhiššāḇēr* be emended.[1] However, the author may have deliberately opted for this pairing of words, because they exhibit close assonance.

5. The differing reactions of the sailors and Jonah to the storm are here closely contrasted. Attention is focused initially on the response of the sailors to their desperate plight.

All the sailors were afraid. The theme of fear is prominent at the beginning, middle and end of the concentric structure underlying verses 4–16. A literal translation of the opening words of verses 5, 10 and 16 highlights not only the close link which exists between them, but more importantly the development which occurs as the sailors progress from fearing the storm to fearing the Lord:

[1] For a brief outline of various suggestions, see Allen, p. 207, n. 21.

the sailors feared (v. 5)
the men feared with great fear (v. 10)
the men feared with great fear the Lord (v. 16).[1]

Each cried out to his own god. The crew members probably came from various nations, and, consequently, worshipped different deities. In the face of the storm their own inadequacy is all too apparent, and so they turn to their gods for help. By the end of the episode, however, an important transformation occurs: they cry out to the Lord (v. 14).

They threw the cargo into the sea to lighten the ship. What the sailors actually jettisoned is not clear; the Hebrew *kēlîm* could refer to the cargo, or it could designate the ship's equipment (*cf.* Acts 27:19). Their policy may have been designed to lighten the ship, and so help it ride the storm, or the cargo may have been intended as a sacrifice in order to appease either the sea (*cf.* 1:15, 'its raging') or an offended god. In either case their efforts prove completely futile. Interestingly, the sailors' action parallels closely the picture, in the previous verse, of God hurling a storm at the sea; their ability to hurl, however, cannot match that of the Lord (*cf.* v. 15).

But what of Jonah? The author returns to him in a flashback:[2] *But Jonah had gone below deck, where he lay down and fell into a deep sleep.* His downward descent continues (*cf.* 1:3, 2:6). Below deck he lies down and falls soundly asleep, the Hebrew term *yērāḏam* signifying a particularly deep sleep (*cf.* Gn. 15:12; 1 Sa. 26:12). Consequently, when the storm breaks, Jonah remains oblivious to all that is going on around him, especially the frantic activities of the sailors above deck.

6. Jonah's slumber is suddenly disturbed by the captain. The translation *How can you sleep?* (*cf.* 'What are you doing asleep?', GNB) is preferable to 'What do you mean, you sleeper?' (RSV; *cf.* AV, RV). The irony of the ensuing request can hardly have escaped Jonah: *Get up and call on your god!* After all, Jonah's sole reason for being on board the vessel was to flee from the presence of his God. Moreover, by repeating the imperatives *qûm*, 'arise', and *qᵉrā'*, 'call', the captain parodies closely Jonah's initial summons from God (v. 2). Each word mocks him.

---

[1] See the Additional Note on the structure of 1:4–16, pp. 106–109; the theme of fear also appears in v. 9.

[2] *Cf.* 1:10; 4:2. Landes, 'The Kerygma', pp. 13–15, draws attention to this stylistic device.

The sea-captain's petition is carefully couched: *Maybe he will take notice of us, and we will not perish.* He knows only too well that the gods are not genies, to be summoned up at the rubbing of a lamp to do our bidding. Interestingly, his remark is later paralleled by the king of Nineveh (3:9), and the theme of divine freedom to act irrespective of human desires is particularly significant in chapter 4.

7. The thought of apportioning blame for a 'natural' occurrence may appear like pure superstition to the twentieth-century Westerner. Yet the author of Jonah has already revealed that divine responsibility for the storm rests with the Lord (v. 4), and human responsibility with Jonah. The sailors, however, have still to discover what the reader already knows. Thus they resort to casting lots in order to identify the guilty party.[1] It comes as no surprise when Jonah is singled out; this is just a further demonstration of God's sovereign control of events. *This calamity* is literally 'this evil' (RSV, AV, RV). The same word, *rāʿāh*, is used in verse 2 to designate the wickedness of Nineveh.

8. Jonah is immediately placed on trial; but this is no ordinary courtroom interrogation. The questions are formulated, not by a ruminating barrister absorbed in the finer details of the case, but rather by terrified sailors clinging on for their lives in the midst of a howling gale. A salvo of questions are fired at Jonah, their brevity in keeping with the circumstances.

For many, the initial question, *Who is responsible for making all this trouble for us?* seems superfluous; surely the culprit has already been identified.[2] The sailors, however, may have wished confirmation of what the lots indicated. Alternatively, they may have viewed the entire procedure as merely isolating the one capable of identifying the guilty party.[3] The remaining questions are clearly intended to elucidate information about their unknown passenger. 'What is your business?' (NEB, JB) may be understood in one of two ways. (1) What is your usual

---

[1] Jos. 7:16–21; 1 Sa. 14:38–43; Pr. 16:33; *cf.* J. Lindblom, 'Lot casting in the Old Testament', *VT* 12 (1962), pp. 164–178; S. Abramsky, 'About Casting Lots in Order to Catch a Sinner', *Beth Mikra* 86 (1981), pp. 231–266.

[2] *Cf.* NEB, JB. The omission of the question in various manuscripts also supports its deletion. However, see the discussion in the Introduction, pp. 94–96.

[3] Fretheim, p. 91, n. 10; Walton, pp. 19–25.

occupation? (*cf.* NIV, AV, RSV). (2) What is your business on this ship? (*cf.* GNB). In the context this latter meaning seems more likely (*cf.* Ps. 107:23, RSV).

9. Only part of Jonah's reply to the sailors is reported in detail (*cf.* v. 10). Firstly, he identifies himself as *a Hebrew*, a term commonly used in foreign contexts to refer to an Israelite.[1] Secondly, he identifies his god, *the LORD, the God of heaven*. Although the epithet, 'God of heaven' has been judged by many scholars to indicate a date of composition in the Persian period,[2] B. Porten argues that it would have been most appropriate in addressing Phoenician sailors who probably worshipped Baal Shamem 'lord of heaven'.[3] By describing the Lord as the maker of sea and land (cf. Ps. 95:5), Jonah leaves the sailors in no doubt that his God is responsible for the present crisis. *I worship* (see also GNB, JB, NEB) is literally 'I fear' (*cf.* RSV, RV, AV). In the light of his wilful disobedience, Jonah's words have an extremely hollow ring to them.

10. Jonah's confession that he fears the Lord is almost immediately followed by a further reference to fear: *This terrified them* (lit. 'the men feared a great fear'). The author uses here a form known as a cognate accusative (*i.e.* the verb and direct object derive from an identical root in Hebrew).[4] This construction, which strengthens the meaning of the verb, is found also in 1:16; 3:2; 4:1 and 4:6. There is no need to delete, as some suggest, the final clause, *because he had already told them so*. As we have observed in verse 5, our author is not tied to a strict chronological order of presentation.[5]

11–12. Having identified the source of their trouble, the sailors still require a solution to the ever-worsening situation. They turn to Jonah for advice. His words are reminiscent of verses 4 and 5: *throw me into the sea*. For the sailors to survive his life must be sacrificed. The final part of verse 12, *I know that it is my fault that this great storm has come upon you*, answers the almost identical question in verse 7, and in so doing forms an inclusion, binding together the material in

[1] Gn. 40:15; Ex. 1:19. In Gn. 10:21 Eber is one of the sons of Shem; *cf. IBD* 2, pp. 626–627.

[2] The epithet occurs mostly in the books of 2 Ch., Ezr., Ne. and Dn.; but see also Gn. 24:3, 7.

[3] Porten, 'Baalshamem and the Date of Jonah', pp. 240–241.

[4] *Cf.* G–K, p. 117, *p-r*.   [5] *Cf.* Allen, p. 210, n. 37.

verses 7–12 (see the Additional Note on the structure of 1:4–16, below).

13–14. To avoid casting Jonah overboard the sailors make a valiant effort to bring the ship to shore. They struggle, however, in vain. Whereas they had previously cried to their gods (v. 5), now they call to the Lord. Their reference to *an innocent man* does not imply that Jonah is guiltless; rather, the sailors are worried lest in casting Jonah into the sea, they themselves will be held accountable for his death. Like their captain (v. 6), they too recognize the absolute sovereignty of God: *you, O LORD, have done as you pleased*. Ultimately, Jonah also will have to take cognizance of this very fact (*cf.* ch. 4).

15–16. When Jonah's instructions are eventually obeyed, the predicted results follow immediately. With the calming of the sea the sailors are filled with awe; the narrative stresses yet again their fear. However, an important development has occurred; they now worship (lit. 'fear') the Lord (*cf.* v. 9). Consequently, they offer him sacrifices and make vows (*cf.* Ps. 116:17–18). The double occurrence of God's name in verse 16 emphasizes that the sailors are now familiar with his identity. Thus, in spite of Jonah's disobedience, they acknowledge his God as their own.

Additional Note on the structure of 1:4–16

The earliest writer to draw attention to the possibility of a structural pattern underlying most of chapter 1 was Lohfink. In 1961 he suggested that the account of Jonah's sea voyage (1:4–16) formed a concentric structure:[1]

A	1:4–6
B	1:7f.
Centre	1:9–10aα
B^1	1:10aβ, 11
A^1	1:12–16

Although this proposal was criticized by Trible,[2] it became the basis of Pesch's more detailed analysis.[3]

---

[1] Lohfink, 'Jona ging zur Stadt hinaus (Jon 4,5)', p. 201.

[2] Trible, pp. 207–209.

[3] R. Pesch, 'Zur konzentrischen Struktur von Jona 1', *Bib* 47 (1966), pp. 577–581; *cf.* Cohn, pp. 51–52; Magonet, p. 57; Allen, p. 197–198.

1	Narrative and 'fear' motif: vv. 4–5aα
2	Sailors' prayer: v. 5aβ
3	Narrative: vv. 5b,c–6aα
4	Captain's speech: v. 6aβ,b
5	Sailors' speech (1): v. 7a
6	Narrative: v. 7b
7	Sailors' speech (2): v. 8
Centre	Jonah's confession and 'fear' motif: vv. 9–10aα
VII	Sailors' speech (II): v. 10aβ,b
VI	Narrative: v. 10c
V	Sailors' speech (I): v. 11
IV	Jonah's speech: v. 12
III	Narrative: v. 13
II	Sailors' prayer: v. 14
I	Narrative and 'fear' motif: vv. 15–16a

Like Lohfink, Pesch envisaged the narrative as forming a mirror image centred around vv. 9–10a.

More recently an alternative analysis of the same passage has been proposed by Fretheim.[1] Whereas Lohfink separates the pericope into five sections, forming an ABCBA pattern, Fretheim uncovers six elements comprising an ABCCBA structure. He offers the following detailed analysis:

A. NARRATIVE FRAMEWORK (4–5a)
1. God hurls a wind and the storm starts (4).
2. Sailors fear, cry to their gods and sacrifice to them (5a).

B. NARRATIVE/REQUEST (5b–6)
1. Jonah sleeps deeply in the face of the storm (5b).
2. Captain requests Jonah to pray to his God so that they do not perish (6a).

A1. NARRATIVE FRAMEWORK (15–16)
1. Sailors hurl Jonah and the storm stops (15).
2. Sailors fear Yahweh, speak their vows and sacrifice to him (16).

B1. NARRATIVE/REQUEST (13–14)
1. Sailors strive to bring ship to land (13).
2. Sailors pray to Jonah's God so that they do not perish (14a).

[1] Fretheim, pp. 73–74.

3. Captain professes sovereign freedom of God (6b).

3. Sailors profess sovereign freedom of God (14b).

C. DIALOG (7–9)
1. Sailors speak to one another to determine who has done wrong (7a).
2. Report – Jonah is revealed by lot (7b).
3. Sailors request information from Jonah (8).
4. Jonah responds – I fear (9).

C1. DIALOG (10–12)
1. Sailors speak to Jonah to determine what he has done wrong (10a).
2. Report – Jonah's wrong is revealed (10b).
3. Sailors request information from Jonah (11).
4. Jonah responds – I know (12).

The analyses of Pesch and Fretheim both take as their starting point the clear parallels which exist between the opening and closing verses of the passage: God hurls a great wind upon the sea and the storm begins (v. 4); the sailors hurl Jonah into the sea and the storm ceases (v. 15); the sailors are filled with fear and pray to their gods (v. 5a); the sailors fear Yahweh and offer sacrifices to him (v. 16). Fretheim's suggestion, however, that the captain's speech in verse 6 finds a counterpart in the sailor's prayer in verse 14 seems preferable to the view of Pesch that the captain's speech parallels Jonah's speech in verse 12; verses 6 and 14 have in common the themes of 'perishing' and 'divine sovereignty'. Consequently, the two analyses diverge considerably as regards the structure of the inner part of the pericope.

Although Fretheim improves upon the structure suggested by Pesch, his analysis of the central section (vv. 7–12) is not as convincing as that of the surrounding verses. The parallels which he observes between verses 7–9 and 10–12 do not exhibit the same type of thematic links as those which bind together the outer parts of the concentric structure. An alternative analysis of the central part of the narrative is possible, however.

The middle part of the narrative (vv. 7–12) is concerned with the identification of the one responsible for bringing disaster upon the voyage. Verses 7 and 12 correspond closely and form a fitting inclusion for this section of the narrative: verse 7 states the sailors desire to identify the one responsible for their misfortune; verse 12 contains Jonah's admission of responsibility.[1] The turning-point of the story comes in verses 9–10 with Jonah's confession that he fears Yahweh (v. 9) and the resulting fear of the sailors (v. 10).[2] Significantly, the motif of fear comes also at the very beginning and end of the structure (vv. 5a, 16).[3] Finally, verses 8 and 11 correspond to each other; in both verses the sailors question Jonah.[4] On the basis of these observations the following outline of the structure is suggested:[5]

A   Yahweh hurls a wind on the sea; the storm begins; sailors fear and cry to their gods (vv. 4–5a)

B   Jonah sleeps; cry to your god; we shall not perish; divine sovereignty (vv. 5b–6)

C   that we may know on whose account (v. 7)

D   the sailors question Jonah (v. 8)

E   I fear (v. 9)

E[1]   the sailors fear (v. 10)

D[1]   the sailors question Jonah (v. 11)

C[1]   I know that it is on my account (v. 12)

B[1]   sailors strive for land; sailors cry to Yahweh; let us not perish; divine sovereignty (vv. 13–14)

A[1]   sailors hurl Jonah into sea; the storm ceases; sailors fear Yahweh and sacrifice (vv. 15–16)

---

[1] 'That we may know on whose account this evil has come upon us' (v. 7); 'for I know it is because of [on account of] me that this great tempest has come upon you' (v. 12).

[2] Allen, p. 209, comments, 'Verses 9, 10a represent the focal point of the section.' In their analyses of 1:4–16 Lohfink and Pesch both place these verses as the centre.

[3] On the development of the theme of fear, see the commentary on 1:5.

[4] Each verse begins with the statement, 'they said to him'.

[5] For a somewhat similar, although not identical, analysis of the structure of these verses, see P. Weimar, 'Literarische Kritik und Literarkritik: Unzeitgemässe Beobachtungen zu Jon 1,4–16', in L. Ruppert, P. Weimar and E. Zenger (eds.), *Künder des Wortes. Beiträge zur Theologie der Propheten* (Echter, 1982), pp. 217–235, esp. pp. 219–223; D. L. Christensen, 'Andrzej Panuknik and the Structure of the Book of Jonah: Icons, Music and Literary Art', *JETS* 28 (1985), p. 136.

C. Jonah's gratitude for his own deliverance
(1:17 – 2:10).[1]

By focusing on the sailors in verse 16, we lose sight of Jonah. As far as they are concerned there can be no hope of his surviving the turbulent waters (*cf.* v. 14). The Lord, however, has not yet finished with Jonah, and by means of a great fish he snatches him from a watery grave. In gratitude Jonah celebrates his timely rescue by composing a psalm of thanksgiving.

17. *The LORD provided a great fish.* Just as Jonah's flight to Tarshish was halted by divine intervention, so again God exercises his sovereign power. The author leaves us in no doubt that God was responsible for Jonah's rescue. The verb *wayman*, 'he appointed', translated *provided* in NIV, comes also in 4:6, 7, 8, and refers in each instance to God's ability to control nature as he desires.

Much speculation has centred on the great fish which serves as Jonah's lifeboat. Any attempt to classify the type of fish involved is pointless. The Hebrew original is no more specific than the English translation 'great fish', and although the Greek translation employs the term *kētos*, which is rendered 'whale' in some translations of Matthew 12:40 (AV, RV, RSV), the word can also designate a large fish (*cf.* GNB, NIV) or sea-monster (RV mg., NEB, JB).

Not surprisingly the idea of Jonah being swallowed by a fish and surviving inside it for three days is viewed with considerable scepticism by many modern readers. Such an event, it is reasoned, is too incredible to have actually happened. This naturally raises questions concerning the historicity of the account.

To make the account more acceptable to present-day readers, various approaches have been adopted. A few conservative writers have sought to justify the accuracy of the account by drawing attention to modern examples of men being swallowed by fish and surviving. These, however, have proved to be less than convincing.[2] A more popular approach

---

[1] In the MT this section is numbered 2:1–11; 1:17 in the English translations is the first verse of chapter 2 in the Hebrew text.

[2] A. J. Wilson, 'The Sign of the Prophet Jonah and its Modern Confirmations', *PTR* 25 (1927), pp. 630–642, esp. pp. 635–638, cites, along with two other examples, the case of a whaler, James Bartley, who in February

has been to suggest that the whole book is a literary fiction, and ought not to be viewed as historical. Although this position enjoys widespread support, it is questionable whether the author of Jonah envisaged his account as anything other than factual.[1] Other more ingenious, but even less satisfactory, solutions have been offered. It has been suggested, for example, that Jonah recovered from his ordeal at sea by spending three days and nights in an inn called 'The Fish'. This proposal, however, requires that the text be manipulated in a quite unacceptable manner. As the book stands it is extremely difficult to avoid the conclusion that the narrative presents the survival of Jonah within the fish as a miracle. The question therefore arises, Did Jonah actually survive for three days within a fish?

If one starts with the view that miracles never occur, then it follows automatically that Jonah could not have been returned to land inside a great fish. Such an assumption, however, prejudges the issue. It is the author's belief that this miraculous event did occur, and he asks the reader to accept his testimony to that effect. Consequently we are left with the choice of accepting either the modern dictum, 'If miraculous, unhistorical', or the witness not only of the author of Jonah but of other biblical writers that in certain circumstances miracles did occur. It remains for each reader to decide which position to adopt.[2]

Before leaving this issue, we ought also to observe the manner in which this miracle is presented. The account of Jonah's unique rescue is not embellished with vivid descriptions of either the fish or Jonah's stay therein. Indeed, the fish is mentioned in only two verses (1:17; 2:10), and even then very briefly. The author's portrayal of this most peculiar event

---

1891 during an attempt to harpoon a large sperm whale in the south Atlantic was swallowed by the animal. When the whale was eventually killed and dissected, Bartley was found alive, although unconscious, within its stomach. While Wilson argues that the incident was carefully investigated and its veracity confirmed by Sir Francis Fox and two French scientists, Allen, p. 176, n. 5, observes that the widow of the ship's captain later denied that it occurred.

[1] On the question of authorial intention, see the Introduction, pp. 69–77.

[2] The idea of God acting in history has been debated at length by historians, philosophers and theologians, and continues to be. For a helpful introduction to this debate, see C. Brown, 'History and the Believer', in C. Brown (ed.), *History, Criticism and Faith* (IVP, 1976), pp. 147–224.

is very low key; it has certainly not been included in order to heighten the dramatic quality of the narrative. This being so, why should the author have invented it, if it did not really happen?

Jonah remained within the fish *three days and three nights*. Landes observes that a journey of three days and three nights represented in ancient Near Eastern mythology the time required to journey to the underworld.[1] This is noteworthy, especially as Jonah's psalm contains various references to the world of the dead. However, there is insufficient evidence within the Old Testament itself to demonstrate that this is how a Hebrew reader would have interpreted the phrase. It must remain, therefore, an interesting speculation.

2:1. *Jonah prayed to the LORD his God*. Only here and in 4:2 does the text contain the usual Hebrew verb *hitpallēl*, 'to pray'. Elsewhere the verb *qārā'*, 'to call', is used (*e.g.* 1:5; 3:8).

From inside the fish. It is objected by some that Jonah's psalm of praise could not have been composed while he remained inside the fish. This arises, however, from a failure to appreciate the fish's function; it is the means by which Jonah is delivered from death by drowning. On the relationship of the psalm to the rest of the book, see the Introduction, pp. 63–69.

Verses 2–9. In contrast to the surrounding material, verses 2–9 are poetic in form. Some uncertainty still exists regarding the precise nature of Hebrew poetry. It is marked primarily by 'parallelism'; that is, the second line corresponds to the first through the repetition of related words and phrases. Thus, for example, expressions concerning Jonah's cry for help and God's answer are found in both halves of verse 2. Attempts to uncover some form of poetic metre have focused on counts involving (1) syllables, (2) stress groupings, or (3) morae.[2] To date, however, no consensus has been reached regarding which approach ought to be followed. In view of the uncer-

---

[1] G. M. Landes, 'The "Three Days and Three Nights" Motif in Jonah 2,1', *JBL* 86 (1967), pp. 446–450; *cf. idem*, 'The Kerygma', pp. 11–12.

[2] For a brief outline of these different approaches, see Christensen, 'The Song of Jonah', pp. 217–231, esp. pp. 220–222. Other recent studies on the poetic nature of Jonah 2:2–9 are Walsh, 'Jonah 2,3–10', pp. 219–229, and F. M. Cross, 'Studies in the Structure of Hebrew Verse: The Prosody of the Psalm of Jonah', in H. B. Huffmon, F. A. Spina, A. R. W. Green (eds.), *The Quest for the Kingdom of God: Studies in Honor of George E. Mendenhall* (Eisenbrauns, 1983), pp. 159–167.

tainties which pertain to metrical analysis, it is perhaps surprising that some scholars argue on the basis of metre for the deletion of particular words and phrases in the psalm.[1]

A further feature of the psalm which is often commented upon is the use made of expressions found in the Psalter.[2] Jonah, however, cannot be accused of plagiarism. His composition clearly relates to the situation in which he found himself, and although he uses a variety of phrases similar to some found in the Psalter they are not, with one exception (2:3; *cf* Ps. 42:7), exactly identical. In all likelihood Jonah has been influenced in his choice of words and phrases by expressions which were familiar to him through the recital of psalms in worship.

Jonah's psalm falls into two parts: (1) verses 2–7 record his experience when first cast into the waters. In particular he stresses the danger of his situation and God's willingness to answer his cry for help. This part of the psalm is bound together by the inclusion formed in verses 2 and 7 by the reference to God hearing Jonah's plea. (2) Verses 8–9 contain Jonah's positive appraisal of the Lord, and his personal response to God's saving actions.

2. At the very start of his song of thanksgiving Jonah refers to an earlier prayer which he uttered soon after being hurled into the water. As is typical in Hebrew poetry the same set of actions are expressed in two slightly differing ways: Jonah cried for help and God answered. This initial verse summarizes the reason for Jonah's gratitude. In verses 3–7 the details of what took place are outlined more fully.

From the depths of Sheol (see NIV mg.). The term translated *depths* is *beṭen*, 'womb', 'belly'. Some commentators have taken this to refer to the stomach of the great fish. However, in verse 1 (Heb., v. 2) a different term *mēʿê*, 'inner parts', denotes the inside of the fish. The precise connotation of the term *Sheol* is disputed. However, it probably designates the place where the wicked remain until their final judgment.[3] It is not annihilation in death that Jonah fears here, but rather the prospect

---

[1] *E.g.* Allen, p. 214, n. 1, suggests the deletion of *mᵉṣûlāh*, 'the deep' (2:3), on 'both grammatical and metrical grounds'.

[2] *Cf.* Magonet, pp. 44–49.

[3] The AV translates *šᵉʾôl* as 'grave' thirty-one times, and as 'hell' thirty times; *cf.* D. Alexander, 'The Old Testament view of life after death', *Themelios* 11 (1986), pp. 41–46.

of being abandoned in Sheol, and consequently separated thereafter from God. However, although Jonah is on the verge of entering into Sheol, the Lord hears his cry and delivers him. The theme of God answering a cry for help is a common element in the Psalter (*cf.* Pss. 18:6; 118:5; 120:1). The switch from third person (*he answered*) to second person (*you listened*) need not be viewed as reflecting an inconsistency in composition. The same kind of change even occurs in some modern prayers.

3. Although Jonah was physically cast into the sea by the sailors (1:15), he readily acknowledges that ultimate responsibility rests with God. Here again the absolute sovereignty of God is emphasized. Jonah's words portray vividly his descent beneath the waves.

Into the deep, into the very heart of the seas. Some scholars argue that the word *mᵉṣûlāh*, 'depths', is a later addition to the text and ought to be deleted. This contribution is based on two considerations. Firstly, the line is considered to be too long. This objection, however, arises from the way in which the metre is reckoned. If an alternative approach is adopted, no problem exists.[1] Secondly, from a grammatical point of view, one would have expected the noun to have a preposition indicating motion towards. This presents something of a difficulty. However, the proposal that the term was subsequently introduced as a gloss is no less problematic, and it is difficult to see why the word should have been inserted afterwards into its present context.

The currents swirled about me. The word *nāhār*, normally translated 'river' or 'stream', is used here to denote the current.[2] Similar descriptions occur in other psalms without denoting the physical action of drowning (*e.g.* Ps. 69:1–2, 14–15; 88:6–7, 17). This is, however, no reason to deny, as some do, that these words were not composed by Jonah in the light of his own dramatic experience. *All your waves and breakers swept over me.* An exactly identical statement comes in Psalm 42:7 (Heb., v. 8).

4. Floundering in the sea, Jonah's initial thought is that he has now been completely rejected by God: *I have been banished from your sight* (*cf.* Ps. 31:22; Heb., v. 23). Having attempted

---

[1] *Cf.* Christensen, 'The Song of Jonah', p. 223.
[2] *Cf.* Landes, 'The Kerygma', p. 6, n. 14.

earlier to flee to Tarshish from God's presence, he now finds himself destined for Sheol, where he will be permanently isolated from God.

It is often suggested that the first word in the second half of this verse ought to be emended to read *'êk*, 'how'. Thus Jonah asks the question, 'How will I look again to your holy temple?' (*cf.* RSV, JB). As it stands the MT has the word *'ak*, 'yet', 'nevertheless'. By retaining this reading, the second part of the verse contrasts with the first: *Yet I will look again towards your holy temple* (*cf.* AV, RV). Although the NIV takes these words to be a direct continuation of Jonah's speech in the first half of the verse, it is possible that they arise from Jonah's confidence that having been rescued by the fish he will again worship in the Temple in Jerusalem. Thus the latter part of the verse probably originates not from the time when Jonah was in the water, but rather following his rescue. Interestingly, both parts of the verse have as a common element the idea of 'seeing'.

5. Surrounded on every side, Jonah is a prisoner of the sea: *The engulfing waters threatened me* (or *waters were at my throat,*[1] NIV mg.), *the deep surrounded me.* Even the seaweed binds itself around him. Try as he may, Jonah cannot free himself from his watery prison. Death by drowning seems inevitable.

6. *To the roots of the mountains.* Although the MT connects this phrase to what follows, a number of English versions take it to be the conclusion of the previous verse (RSV, JB, NEB). Instead of rendering the Hebrew preposition *lᵉ* as 'to', they translate it by 'at' or 'in'. This division of the text, it is suggested, best suits the poetic metre. However, although the present punctuation was first introduced in the Middle Ages, those responsible, the Massoretes, endeavoured to preserve the form of the text as previously transmitted. Thus the GNB and NIV retain the MT verse division.

There is some uncertainty as to the precise meaning of the expression *qiṣbê hârîm, the roots of the mountains*, which occurs only here in the whole of the Old Testament. From the context it probably refers to the mountain bases which extend down to the very bottom of the sea. Support for this comes in Ecclesiasticus 16:19, where the same expression is used in

---

[1] The AV and RV translates *nepeš* as 'soul'. It can, however, refer to the neck or throat (*cf.* JB, NEB, NIV mg.). *Cf.* H. F. Peacock, 'Translating the Word for "Soul" in the Old Testament', *The Bible Translator* 27 (1976), pp. 216–219.

conjunction with the phrase 'the foundations of the contin-ents'.¹ Thus Jonah descends to the lowest depths of the sea.

Jonah, however, also envisages his descent to the bottom of the sea as a descent towards the world of the dead: *the earth beneath barred me in for ever.* The Hebrew noun *'ereṣ*, 'land', 'earth', has here the special sense of 'underworld'.² Like a Palestinian city, Jonah views the underworld as having a gate which was locked secure by bolts and bars: there could be no escaping from it. Once in Sheol, Jonah would be imprisoned there for ever.

Having charted his descent towards the land of the dead, Jonah now introduces an all-important contrast: *But you brought my life up from the pit.* Since the noun *šaḥat*, 'pit' or 'grave', often parallels in Hebrew poetry the term Sheol, there is good reason to understanding it as referring here to the abode of the dead.³ At length the downward journey ceases and Jonah's descent is dramatically reversed. This change in the direction of Jonah's movement brings to an end a series of descending steps which may be traced back to the beginning of chapter 1. From his initial flight in 1:3 Jonah's progress has always been downwards (*cf.* 1:3, 5, 15; 2:2) and each stage symbolizes a further movement away from God.⁴ Now, when Jonah can sink no lower, the Lord intervenes and raises him upward.

7. *When my life was ebbing away.* The initial words of this verse have been translated in a variety of ways: 'When my soul fainted within me' (RSV; *cf.* JB); 'As my senses failed me' (NEB); 'When I felt my life slipping away' (GNB). The Hebrew verb *hiṭʿaṭṭēp̄* conveys the idea of growing faint or losing consciousness (*cf.* Pss. 142:3; 143:4). On the brink of passing out for lack of oxygen, Jonah's thoughts suddenly turn to God.

I remembered you, LORD. By inserting 'you' after 'remembered' the NIV appears to follow M. Dahood's suggested emendation

---

¹ The RSV and JB both avoid the problem of translating the term *qiṣbê* in Ecclus. 16:19 by omitting it completely.

² *Cf.* N. Tromp, *Primitive Conceptions of Death and the Nether World in the Old Testament,* Biblica et Orientalia 21 (Pontifical Biblical Institute, 1969), pp. 23–46; M. Ottosson, ''erets' in *TDOT,* 1, pp. 399–400.

³ Tromp, *Primitive Conceptions,* pp. 69–71; V. P. Hamilton, 'shahat', in *TWOT,* 2, p. 918.

⁴ Walsh, 'Jonah 2,3–10', pp. 226–227; Christensen, 'The Song of Jonah', pp. 226–227.

of the Hebrew particle '*et* to '*attā*, 'you'.[1] This however, is quite unnecessary.[2] So, 'I remembered the LORD' (RSV) is to be preferred. Jonah, however, not only remembers the Lord, but he also prays (*cf.* Pss. 88:2; 102:1). In the light of verse 6 it is clear that Jonah's request was favourably received (*cf.* v. 2). The expression *your holy temple* comes also at the end of verse 4 (*cf.* Ps. 18:6).

8. Although it only consists of five words in Hebrew, this verse presents various difficulties. The initial three words refer to those who practise idolatry; an almost identical phrase comes in Psalm 31:6. The word translated 'idols' (GNB, NIV, RSV) means literally a 'snare'. The final two words are generally understood in one of several ways: (1) 'they have abandoned their loyalty to you' (GNB; *cf.* RSV, NEB); (2) 'they forfeit the grace that was theirs' (JB; *cf.* AV, NIV). The reason for these alternatives is to be found in the term *ḥasdām*, from the noun *ḥesed*, which here means either 'their loyalty' or 'their loving-kindness'. In the first instance the noun is taken as referring to the loyalty of human worshippers, and in the second to the 'loving-kindness' which God extends to those who trust him. Although there is little to choose between these possibilities, the former interpretation seems preferable. If, as seems likely, this verse forms a contrast with what follows in verse 9, then Jonah expresses here the opinion that those who worship idols will discover in times of trouble how impotent they really are, and as a result will no longer show loyalty, or love, to their supposed gods. Those who worship the Lord, however, will always find him trustworthy and reliable. Thus it seems best to translate the verse as follows: 'Those who cling to worthless idols will abandon their loyalty to them.'

9. Having experienced in his own life God's power to rescue him from the very jaws of death itself, Jonah, as an expression of his gratitude, promises to offer sacrifices and fulfil his vows to the Lord. His words echo the response of the sailors in 1:16. Finally, Jonah brings his psalm of personal thanksgiving to a climax in the wonderful statement, *Salvation comes from the LORD.* No other words could summarize better

---

[1] M. Dahood, 'Ugaritic and the Old Testament', *Ephemerides Theologicae Lovanienses* 44 (1968), p. 37. Dahood argues that this emendation removes the third person reference to God and brings this line into harmony with the next. *Cf.* GNB.

[2] *Cf.* Allen, p. 214, n. 5. RSV, JB and NEB all follow MT.

Jonah's appreciation of all that God has done for him. The Lord saves! Ironically, however, it is this very same fact which fills Jonah with intense anger in the final chapter of the book.

10. The text reverts again to prose to record Jonah's somewhat unconventional, and very unceremonious, return to land: *And the LORD commanded the fish, and it vomited Jonah onto dry land.*

II. JONAH AT NINEVEH (3:1 – 4:11)

A. Jonah's second call (3:1–3)

After Jonah's remarkable rescue and restoration to terra firma, he is again instructed to go to Nineveh. This time he makes no attempt to escape from the Lord's presence, but willingly complies. By paralleling here the book's opening remarks, almost word for word, the author skilfully conveys the idea that Jonah is being offered a new beginning. In spite of his earlier refusal, he has a fresh opportunity to fulfil the divine commission.

1–2. Apart from the replacement of 'son of Amittai' (1:1) by the Hebrew term *šēnît*, 'second' (3:1), the initial words of chapters 1 and 3 are identical. The first significant divergence occurs after the verb *proclaim*. Whereas Jonah is commanded in 1:2 to cry *ʿal*, 'against', Nineveh, here in 3:2 he is instructed to cry *ʾel*, 'to', it (*cf.* RSV, NIV). Opinions are divided on the importance of this change of wording. Many writers see no significant difference in meaning between the prepositions *ʾel* and *ʿal* when used with the verb *qārāʾ*, 'call'.[1] However, as J. M. Sasson has forcefully argued, *qārāʾ ʿal* (*cf.* 1:2) probably carries the connotation 'to denounce' (*cf.* NEB), whereas *qārāʾ ʾel* means merely 'to proclaim to'.[2] This subtle change in the wording of Jonah's call is perhaps intended to prepare the reader for the unexpected consequences of his mission.

The message I give you. These words emphasize the divine origin of Jonah's proclamation; the message he communicates

---

[1] An important reason for this is the fact that no distinction is drawn between these expressions in the LXX translation.

[2] J. M. Sasson, 'On Jonah's Two Missions', *Henoch* 6 (1984), pp. 23–29; *cf.* Keil, p. 389.

is not his own, it comes from God.[1] The JB and GNB follow the LXX translation of this expression by using the past tense: 'as I told you to' and 'the message I have given you' respectively. The Hebrew original, however, can also be understood as referring either to the present, 'the message I am giving you' (*cf.* Vulg.), or to the future, 'the message I shall give you' (*cf.* Syr.). Of these three possibilities the first appears the least likely; had the past tense been definitely intended another form of the verb 'tell' would have indicated this better.[2]

3. Jonah's ready compliance is emphasized not only by the repetition of the verbs 'arose' and 'went' (see RSV, AV), both found in the preceding divine command (v. 2; see the commentary on 1:2–3), but also by the inclusion of the expression, 'according to the word of the LORD' (RSV, AV).

The phrase *Nineveh was a very important city* ought not to be interpreted as indicating that the book was composed after the destruction of the city in 612 BC. The author is merely stating that at the time of Jonah's mission the city was large (see the Introduction, pp. 56–58). *A very important city* is literally 'a great city to God'. Many scholars understand the term *'ĕlōhîm*, 'God', as denoting here a superlative (*cf.* Gn. 23:6; 30:8; Ex. 9:28; 1 Sa. 14:15; Pss. 36:7; 80:11). However, in the light of the book's plot, it is perhaps best to understand this phrase as meaning 'a city important to God'.[3] 'Of three days' journey' (AV) is a precise statement of

---

[1] The Old Testament prophets constantly draw attention to the fact that their message comes directly from God. For an impressive list of phrases, all drawn from the book of Isaiah, which illustrates this, see E. J. Young, *My Servants the Prophets* (Eerdmans, 1952), pp. 171–175. Similar lists could be constructed for other prophetic books.

[2] Price, pp. 51–52.

[3] D. W. Thomas, 'A Consideration of Some Unusual Ways of Expressing the Superlative in Hebrew', *VT* 3 (1953), pp. 209–224, discusses at some length the use of the divine name to form a superlative. He concludes, 'In the O.T. it is, I believe, difficult, if not impossible, to point to any unambiguous example of the use of the divine name as an intensifying epithet and nothing more' (p. 218). Furthermore, the actual form of the expression used here is not found elsewhere in the Old Testament. Of all the instances of *'ĕlōhîm* being understood as a superlative, this is the sole example of it being preceded by the preposition *l*, 'to'.

the time required to traverse the city.[1]

These remarks about Nineveh provide a suitable interlude in the narrative between the departure of Jonah (v. 3) and his arrival at Nineveh (v. 4). As Nineveh was approximately five hundred miles, or a month's journey, from Israel, this brief description of the city enables a smooth transition to be effected between verses 3 and 4.[2] It also sets the scene for the following episode.

B. Jonah and the Ninevites (3:4–10)

It is perhaps surprising that having focused so much attention on the efforts to get Jonah to Nineveh, his activity there is recorded with remarkable brevity (v. 4). Prominence is given to the repentance of the Ninevites, which forms the core of this section (v. 5–9), and the resulting divine turnabout (v. 10).

4. The account of Jonah's prophetic ministry in Nineveh is exceptionally concise. The words *On the first day, Jonah started into the city. He proclaimed* . . . can be interpreted in several ways; the Hebrew is literally 'he began to enter the city a journey of one day and he proclaimed'. Most commentators take this to imply that Jonah started to preach only after he had gone a day's journey into the city. Alternatively, it could mean that he proclaimed his message when he initially entered the city, which required in all three days to traverse (v. 3). With either interpretation it is evident that Jonah did not delay his proclamation until he had reached the very heart of the great metropolis; on his first day within the boundaries of the city he set about informing the population of their divine condemnation.

The gist of Jonah's message is summarized in the short statement: *Forty more days and Nineveh will be overturned.* In all likelihood Jonah probably addressed those he encountered at greater length than this. The author, however, playing down Jonah's ability as an orator, condenses his message into five

[1] On the size of Nineveh, see the Introduction, pp. 56–59. The translation in the 1978 edition of the NIV, 'it took three days to go all through it', conveys the idea that this was the time required to walk through all the streets of the city. This impression is not supported by the wording of the Hebrew text. The 1984 edition of the NIV reads, 'a very important city – a visit required three days', following the view of Wiseman, 'Jonah's Nineveh', p. 38, that this refers to the day of arrival, the day of visiting, and the day of departure.

[2] There is no need to rearrange the order of the text, as in the NEB.

words in Hebrew. Although a few scholars have preferred the LXX reading of 'three' days, rather than 'forty', the former was probably introduced by a copyist who mistakenly observed 'three days' in the previous verse. The number 'forty' is no arbitrary figure; in the Old Testament it is often associated with periods of special religious significance.[1]

Will be overturned. The verb *hāpak*, 'overturn', is used elsewhere to describe the destruction of Sodom and Gomorrah (Gn. 19:25; La. 4:6; Am. 4:11). The basic idea underlying the verb is 'to turn'. On occasions it means 'to overturn' (2 Ki. 21:13, 'to overturn a plate'). However, it can also mean 'to turn around', 'transform' (1 Ki. 22:34, 'to turn around a chariot'; Jer. 13:23, 'to transform one's appearance'). With these different connotations the use of the word here is hardly accidental. Although Nineveh was not overturned, it did experience a turn around.[2]

5. The reality of imminent divine judgment strikes home to the hearts of the Ninevites. The text clearly implies that the response to Jonah's preaching was immediate. His proclamation is followed directly by a description of the people's reaction; nothing intervenes between the prophetic pronouncement and the penitence of the Ninevites. Furthermore, there is no indication that Jonah continued to preach beyond his first day within the city (*cf.* v. 4).

The expression *the Ninevites believed God* (lit. 'the men of Nineveh believed in God') has been understood in two ways: (1) the Ninevites believed God's word (NEB; *cf.* AV, RSV, GNB, NIV); (2) the Ninevites believed in God (JB). The Hebrew idiom *he'emîn b*ᵉ, 'believe in', denotes more, however, than just believing what someone has said; it expresses the idea of trusting a person.[3] Significantly, the response of the Ninevites is presented here in terms of what God expected from his own people (*cf.* Ex. 14:31; 2 Ch. 20:20), but frequently did not

---

[1] *E.g.* Ex. 24:18; 34:28; Nu. 13:25; 1 Ki. 19:8; *cf.* J. B. Segal, 'Numerals in the Old Testament', *JSS* 10 (1965), pp. 2–20, esp. pp. 10–11. He rejects the suggestion, often made, that the number forty merely represents a round figure.

[2] *Cf.* Good, *Irony in the Old Testament*, p. 48; Wiseman, 'Jonah's Nineveh', pp. 48–49.

[3] *E.g.* 1 Sa. 27:12, 'Achish trusted David'; Gn. 15:6, 'he [Abram] believed the LORD'. D. Kidner, *Genesis* (IVP, 1967), p. 124, comments, 'Abram's trust was both personal (*in the Lord*, AV, RV) and propositional (the context is the specific *word of the Lord* in verses 4, 5)'.

receive (*cf.* Nu. 14:11; 20:12; Dt. 1:32; 2 Ki. 17:14; Ps. 78:22).

As a consequence of trusting God, *they declared a fast, and . . . put on sackcloth*. This was a common means in the ancient world of expressing grief, humility and penitence – the hallmarks of true repentance. When denounced by the prophet Elijah, the Israelite king Ahab responded in a similar fashion: 'He tore his clothes, put on sackcloth and fasted. He lay in sackcloth and went around meekly' (1 Ki. 21:27; *cf.* Ne. 9:1–2; Is. 15:3; Dn. 9:3–4). The prophet Joel, possibly a contemporary of Jonah, demanded that his hearers should fast and don sackcloth as a sign of their repentance (Joel 1:13–14). The sackcloth used was a thick coarse cloth, normally made from goat's hair; to wear it symbolized the rejection of earthly comforts and pleasures. The response of the Ninevites was unanimous: *from the greatest to the least*. No class or section of Ninevite society felt exempt from the need to humble itself before God.

6. By focusing in on the king, the author adds detail to the general picture of verse 5.[1] Through the repetition of particular details he reinforces his initial observation that the inhabitants of Nineveh, from the greatest to the least, truly repented of their evil.

The title *king of Nineveh* is peculiar to the book of Jonah. For this reason it is viewed by some scholars as indicating that the book was composed in the Persian period (*c.* 539–331 BC), when Assyria was a vague memory; the usual designation is 'king of Assyria' (*cf.* 2 Ki. 19:36). However, if Jonah's mission is dated to the middle of the eighth century BC, a time of Assyrian weakness and vulnerability, the title 'king of Nineveh' may not be altogether inappropriate (see the Introduction, pp. 59–60).

The Hebrew original is ambiguous as to what the king actually heard; the term *dābār* can mean 'word', 'affair', 'thing'. It denotes here either the actual content of Jonah's proclamation or the reaction of the city's population. The description of the king's behaviour forms a neat chiastic pattern: he arose, put off, put on, sat down. Rising from his throne and replacing his royal robes with sackcloth, the king sits on the ground amid dust or ashes. In so doing he symbolizes his human frailty and worthlessness (*cf.*

---

[1] The AV and RV mg. have 'For word came unto the king', taking v. 5 as a general summary, followed by an explanation of how this occurred.

Jb. 2:8,12–13).

7–8. The issuing of a joint *decree* by *the king and his nobles* to both men and animals is viewed by many scholars as indicative of a late date of composition. It is suggested on two grounds that this action reflects not Assyrian practice, but rather Persian. 1. There is no documentary evidence from Assyria of (a) a king issuing a decree in conjunction with his nobles, or (b) of animals being clothed in sackcloth. 2. Both of these practices, however, are known to have occurred in the later Persian period. Although this line of argument seems to point conclusively towards a post-exilic date of composition, we have already observed that on purely linguistic grounds such a date is unlikely. We can only suppose that the lack of reference to these practices in the Assyrian records is either an unfortunate coincidence or an indication that such actions were extremely rare, in which case they emphasize further the unusual nature of the Ninevite response; the inclusion of the animals clearly underlines the severity of the threat which the king and his nobles perceived. Furthermore, the first half of the eighth century BC is one of the most poorly documented periods of Assyrian history. (For a fuller discussion, see the Introduction, pp. 60–61.)

The official edict to fast contains two different verbs concerned with eating. The first, which can apply equally well to both men and animals, is the verb *ṭāʿam*, 'to taste'. The other verb comes from the root *rāʿāh*, 'to pasture' or 'to graze', and applies only to cattle and sheep. Interestingly, both verbs may be linked with other terms found in this passage, providing yet further examples of our author's love for word-play. Thus the verb 'to taste' has the same root consonants as the noun *ṭaʿam*, 'decree' or 'edict'. Similarly, the verb 'to graze' may be linked with the adjective *rāʿāh*, 'evil', which comes in verses 8 and 9.[1]

The royal summons to *call urgently on God* is reminiscent of earlier statements concerning prayer (1:6, 14; 2:2). Fervent prayer was to accompany the fasting and wearing of sackcloth. Finally, the king demands of his subjects genuine repentance: *let them give up their evil ways and their violence*. No outward show

---

[1] *Cf.* B. Halpern and R. E. Friedman, 'Composition and Paranomasia in the Book of Jonah', *HAR* 4 (1980), pp. 79–92, esp. p. 85; D. L. Christensen, 'Anticipatory Paranomasia in Jonah 3:7–8 and Genesis 37:2', *RB* 90 (1983), pp. 261–263.

of piety will deliver Nineveh from her approaching destruction; only a radical transformation of heart and behaviour offers any hope of a reprieve. Even Israel had to be warned of the dangers of religious pretence when it came to prayer and fasting (*e.g.* Is. 58:3–9).

9. Like the pagan sea-captain (1:6) and his crew (1:14), the king and his nobles acknowledge the absolute freedom of God to do as he pleases. They realize only too well that pious actions and prayers can never merit or guarantee divine forgiveness (*cf.* Joel 2:13–14); God is under no obligation to pardon. There remains, however, the hope that he may look upon them with mercy and turn away his fierce anger. A complete turnabout by the Ninevites (v. 8) may possibly encourage God to do likewise. *We will not perish* echoes the earlier hope of the pagan sailors (1:6, 14).

10. The theme of repentance which dominates verse 9 continues here with the repetition of the verbs *šûḇ*, 'repent', and *niḥam*, 'relent'.[1] As a result of the penitent actions of the people of Nineveh, God relents from punishing them as he had threatened. Unfortunately, various English versions translate the verb *niḥam* as 'repent' (*cf.* AV, RV, RSV), and this, quite naturally, creates difficulties for many readers. Is it possible for God to repent? However, whereas the English term 'repent' conveys the idea of a change of behaviour from worse to better, the Hebrew verb *niḥam* refers rather to a decision to act otherwise, and does not necessarily imply that the first action is inferior to the second. The English verb 'relent' (JB, *cf.* NIV) conveys better the meaning of the Hebrew. Furthermore, as Jeremiah 18:7–8 makes clear, prophetic pronouncements of judgment were not absolute, but conditional: 'If at any time I announce that a nation or kingdom is to be uprooted, torn down and destroyed, and if that nation I warned repents of its evil, then I will relent and not inflict on it the disaster I had planned.' The fact that God changes his mind here does not represent a divine failing, but rather reveals his earnest desire to be true to his own immutable nature.[2]

[1] In vv. 8–10 the verb *šûḇ* occurs four times, twice with God as the subject and twice with the Ninevites as subject. The verb *niḥam* comes twice, and, as is almost always the case regarding its use in the Old Testament, God is here the subject in both instances.

[2] *Cf.* W. C. Kaiser, *Towards Old Testament Ethics* (Zondervan, 1983), pp. 249–251; 'He [God] is patient with you, not wanting anyone to perish, but everyone to come to repentance' (2 Pet. 3:9, NIV.)

For many writers the promptness, extent and sincerity of the Ninevite repentance seems totally unrealistic. Is it likely that the entire population of Nineveh would have responded so readily to the preaching of a foreign prophet? Furthermore, it is noted that the Assyrian annals of the eighth century BC contain no mention of these happenings. Yet surely one would have expected some reference to such remarkable events? For these reasons doubts are raised about the historical accuracy of the account.

Certain observations may be made in response to these objections. Firstly, it must be stressed again (see the Introduction, pp. 79–80) that there is a sparsity of Assyrian source material from the first half of the eighth century BC. This is a period of Assyrian history about which we are unfortunately very poorly informed. Secondly, the repentance of the Ninevites need not be thought unusual or unexpected, especially if Jonah's mission coincided, as Wiseman suggests,[1] with the period of national tension and turmoil which existed during the reigns of Ashur-dan III (772–755 BC) and Ashur-nirari V (754–745 BC). Thirdly, the text does not imply that as a result of their repentance the Ninevites became worshippers of the Lord, the God of Israel. Significantly, whereas the divine name Yahweh (the LORD) is used in connection with the pagan sailors in chapter 1, it is absent in chapter 3. Although the Ninevites repented there is no indication that they were converted to Yahwism. Furthermore, while their repentance is portrayed as being sincere and genuine this need not imply that Jonah's mission had lasting effects upon the population. Even in Israel, repentance did not always bring a prolonged transformation. This is true, for example, in the case of Ahab, who repented regarding the death of Naboth, and was forgiven (1 Ki. 21:27–29). Yet even so he still acquired the reputation of being one of the most evil kings of Israel (1 Ki. 21:25–26).

C. Jonah's anger at Nineveh's deliverance (4:1–11)

In considering the unity of the book of Jonah we observed that this present section corresponds closely to 1:17 – 2:10. This makes the contrast between Jonah's joy over his own rescue and his anger at the deliverance of the Ninevites all

[1] Wiseman, 'Jonah's Nineveh', pp. 44–51.

the more striking. Indeed, Jonah's harsh attitude towards God and the Ninevites becomes all the more resprehensible when viewed against the events of chapters 1 and 2.

1. Jonah, who drops out of view in the second half of chapter 3, suddenly reappears here. His reaction to the repentance and forgiveness of the Ninevites is stated in no uncertain terms: *Jonah was greatly displeased.*[1] This stands in stark contrast to the remarks of the previous verse, and sets the tone for the final section of the book: in their attitudes to the repentant Ninevites, God and Jonah are diametrically opposed. Whereas God turns away from his anger (3:9), Jonah becomes *angry*. This entire section is marked by the deep gulf which separates the Lord and Jonah.

2-3. The short prayer which Jonah utters provides at last the reason for his earlier attempt to evade his divine commission (1:3). From the very outset Jonah was fully persuaded that his summons to preach to the inhabitants of Nineveh would result in their being divinely pardoned: *is this not what I said when I was still at home?*[2] His personal conviction that this would be the case rests on his knowledge of God:[3] *you are a gracious and compassionate God, slow to anger and abounding in love, a God who relents from sending calamity.* Undoubtedly this detailed description of God derives ultimately from Exodus 34:6-7: And he [the LORD] passed in front of Moses, proclaiming, 'The LORD, the LORD, the compassionate and gracious God, slow to anger, abounding in love and faithfulness, maintaining love to thousands, and forgiving wickedness, rebellion and sin.' The existence of similar statements elsewhere in the Old Testament (*e.g.* Ne. 9:17; Pss. 86:15; 145:8; Joel 2:13) indicates that Jonah's description is in complete

[1] A literal translation of the Hebrew is, 'It was evil to Jonah a great evil/calamity.' The same type of construction, a cognate accusative, comes in 1:10, 16; 4:6. G. I. Davies, 'The Uses of R" Qal and the Meaning of Jonah IV 1', *VT* 27 (1977), pp. 105–111, rejects the view of Wolff (1975), pp. 38–39, that this verse refers to the 'wickedness' of Jonah. While this is probably correct, the implication that Jonah is acting wickedly is nevertheless present. The use of the noun *rāʿāh* 'evil' and the related verb *rāʿaʿ* 'to be evil' links this section to the preceding verses, as does the reference to anger (*cf.* 3:9).

[2] Jonah contrasts here his word, 'What I said' (lit. 'my word') with that of the Lord (1:1). His prayer focuses to a very large extent on himself. As Wolff (1975), p. 118, observes, the terms 'I' and 'my' occur nine times in vv. 2–3.

[3] Whereas the king and his nobles are uncertain as to how God would act, 'who knows . . .?' (3:9), Jonah asserts with confidence, 'I knew'.

harmony with the orthodox Hebrew perception of God. Moreover, God's loving-kindness and his willingness to forgive were major themes in the preaching of the prophet Hosea, a contemporary of Jonah (*cf.* Ho. 3:1–5; 11:1–11; 14:1–4).

Jonah is here, however, highly critical of these divine attributes, and views them as regrettable weaknesses in the divine make-up. The strength of his feeling is all too apparent; he is adamant that there is no point in continuing to live: *Take away my life, for it is better for me to die than to live.* Later, in verse 8, he repeats this death wish. Like Elijah in 1 Kings 19:4, he now prefers death to life.[1]

In the light of his earlier experience it is ironic that Jonah now desires to die on account of God's gracious and compassionate nature. Had he himself not benefited from these very attributes when confronted by death (2:7–8)? And had he not rejoiced that *Salvation comes from the* LORD (2:9)? Clearly, he fails to see the incongruity of his own prayers.

Although his words give us an important clue as to why Jonah is enraged, they do not of themselves provide the final answer. We have yet to discover why the deliverance of the Ninevites should anger Jonah so. For this we must examine the remainder of the chapter.

4. Jonah's death wish is greeted with almost complete silence. With the briefest of questions (three words in Hebrew) God responds: *Have you any right to be angry?*[2] Ironically, having condemned God for not being angry, Jonah is now challenged concerning his own anger. In the verses which follow, God responds to Jonah's rage by subjecting him to the intense heat of the Eastern climate. This treatment takes on a special significance when one observes that the Hebrew verb *ḥārāh* means not only 'to be angry' but also 'to be hot'.

5. Jonah has nothing further to say. Having voiced his objection, he departs from the city eastwards and finds a suitable place to observe what will become of Nineveh.[3] He is

---

[1] Fretheim, p. 121, observes that whereas Elijah is distraught because of failure, it is Jonah's success that makes him desire death.

[2] Chr. H. W. Brekelmans, 'Some Translation Problems', *OTS* 15 (1969), pp. 175–176, suggests that this sentence should be translated, 'It seems, you are really angry' (*cf.* NEB). The context, however, suggests that God is questioning Jonah's right to be angry.

[3] If the author, as we have suggested, views Jonah as having preached to 'Greater Nineveh', then we may assume that 'the city' refers here to this same area.

determined to persevere in the hope that God, given time, will reconsider his position and exact retribution upon the Ninevites. In the meantime, to shade himself from the scorching heat of the sun, he constructs a makeshift shelter of branches and leaves, similar to the type used during the Feast of Tents (Lv. 23:40–42). That this was necessary indicates that there must have been a significant lack of natural shade in the spot where Jonah commenced his unusual vigil. The scene is thus set for verses 6–11.

6. *The LORD God provided a vine* ('gourd' AV). Like the great fish (1:17), the gourd is divinely commissioned to shelter Jonah, providing for him a welcome relief from the raging heat of the sun. The phrase *to ease his discomfort* (lit. 'to deliver him from his evil/calamity') may well contain a double meaning. The verb *lᵉhaṣṣîl*, 'to deliver', can also be read as *lᵉhāṣēl*, 'to shade', and this is apparently how the translators of the Greek Septuagint understood the word. Furthermore, the phrase also contains the noun *rāʿāh*, which is used elsewhere in Jonah to mean 'distress' (*e.g.* 1:8) or 'wickedness' (*e.g.* 1:2). Consequently, it is possible to interpret the phrase as meaning either, 'to shade him from his distress', referring to the sun (*cf.* RSV, GNB, NIV), or, 'to deliver him from his wickedness', referring to Jonah's unjustified anger (*cf.* JB). Jonah's response to the gourd is summarized in a phrase which, translated literally, reads, 'Jonah rejoiced concerning the gourd a great rejoicing';[1] his mood is entirely transformed by the unexpected divine provision of shade.

The plant cannot be identified as a gourd with absolute certainty. In the whole of the Old Testament the Hebrew noun *qîqāyôn* occurs only in this passage. B. P. Robinson, in a recent study on the interpretation of this term,[2] observes that the earliest translators of the book of Jonah adopted one of three approaches. The noun *qîqāyôn* was either translated by the Greek or Latin words for (1) a gourd or (2) an ivy, or alternatively, (3) it was merely transliterated, with no attempt being made to specify the nature of the plant. In the sixteenth century two further solutions were suggested: (1) a castor-oil plant (or ricinus) and (2) a vine. Finally, because of the difficulties surrounding the translation of *qîqāyôn*, a number of

---

[1] This is a further example of the author using a cognate accusative; *cf.* 1:10, 16; 4:1.

[2] B. P. Robinson, 'Jonah's Qiqayon Plant', *ZAW* 97 (1985), pp. 390–403.

modern translations use the general designation 'plant' (RSV, GNB). Of these various alternatives, the weight of evidence seems to favour a climbing plant, probably a type of gourd. When the leaves on Jonah's shelter withered in the hot sun, a climbing gourd would have provided a fresh covering of leaves, giving him renewed protection.[1] The fact that the *qîqāyôn* was destroyed by a worm suggests that the stem of the plant must have been supple, like that of a gourd.

7. Jonah, however, does not have long to enjoy the relief brought by his leafy companion. At dawn the next day God appoints a *worm* which attacks the gourd, causing it to wither up. Although verses 6 and 7 have almost identical beginnings, they introduce two opposite aspects of God's nature: his ability to deliver and to destroy. The contrast between these is further emphasized by the use in verse 6, but not in verse 7, of the divine name, the LORD, which is particularly associated with mercy and deliverance.[2] In a work which stresses divine compassion and mercy, the destruction of the gourd appears strangely out of place. It dramatically reveals, however, that God's sovereignty is not restricted to acts of compassion. As the one who gives life, he also has the right to bring it to an end. Furthermore, the destruction of the gourd by the worm, both divinely appointed, symbolizes the future destruction of Israel by the Assyrians. Through this incident God highlights the root cause of Jonah's antagonism.

8. When the sun rises, God sends *a scorching east wind*. The same form of the verb *wayman*, 'he appointed' (NIV, 'provided'), is used here as in 1:17 (Heb., 2:1), 4:6 and 4:7. To add to Jonah's discomfort *the sun* beats down on his head. The action of the sun is described in the same way as that of the worm destroying the gourd; the verb *wattak*, 'it attacked', is used in both instances. As a result Jonah becomes faint, probably suffering from sunstroke. All this is too much for him, and like Elijah under the broom tree, he expresses his desire to die.[3] Though the final words of the verse are identical in the Hebrew original to those at the end of verse 3, NIV has *It would*

---

[1] This also explains why Jonah requires the shade provided by the plant; see Robinson, 'Jonah's Qiqayon Plant', pp. 397–398.

[2] A comparable distribution of the divine names 'God' and 'LORD' comes in Gn. 22. *Cf.* Kidner, 'Distribution', pp. 77–87; Magonet, pp. 33–38.

[3] 1 Ki. 19:4. The same expression, *wayyiš'al 'et-nap̄šô lāmût̠*, 'he desired to die', comes in both passages.

be better for me to die than to live. Significantly, although Jonah's mood in verses 3 and 8 is similar, quite different factors are responsible for this. Whereas in verse 3 he questions God's right to deliver, here he challenges God's right to destroy.

9. As in the earlier part of the chapter God greeted Jonah's death wish with a question, so also here. Indeed, but for several minor variations,[1] the Hebrew wording is identical to that of verse 4: *God said to Jonah, 'Do you have a right to be angry about the vine?'* Once again the narrative highlights the issue of anger.

However, whereas Jonah remained silent the first time God questioned him concerning his anger (*cf.* v. 5), this time he responds in a very forthright manner: 'I have every right to be angry – angry enough to die!' (GNB). Jonah can take no more. Although he had offered God the opportunity to reverse his decision regarding the future of the Ninevites, God has merely demonstrated how absurd and incomprehensible he really is. His behaviour is totally inconsistent. One minute he brings comfort, the next he brings destruction. Jonah can see no rationale to all this; God's ways are beyond him. If God must act so perversely, then Jonah sees no point in continuing to live; he would be better off dead.

10–11. The last word, however, rests with the Lord. By contrasting Jonah's attitude to the gourd with his attitude towards the Ninevites, God highlights where the real absurdity lies. Jonah is filled with compassion regarding a mere plant, yet remains hard-hearted towards the entire population of a city. He shows concern for one small item of God's creation, yet fails to care for a large mass of people, who, like Jonah himself, were made in the divine image. The inconsistency rests not with God but with Jonah.

Furthermore, God emphasizes that the Ninevites cannot be held as fully accountable for their wicked deeds as Jonah imagines. They lack moral perception. The phrase *who cannot tell their right hand from their left* does not designate children, as many commentators suggest. Rather, as Wiseman observes, it concerns the ability of individuals to make moral judgments.[2] Finally, lest Jonah should still lack compassion towards the 120,000 inhabitants of Nineveh, God reminds him of the *cattle*

---

[1] The divine name 'LORD' is replaced by 'God', and specific reference is made to the gourd.
[2] Wiseman, 'Jonah's Nineveh', pp. 39–40; see the Introduction, pp. 58–59.

which live within the city. Even if Jonah does not care about the people, perhaps, God suggests, he may have some compassion for their cattle.

The final verses of the book clearly focus on God's right to destroy or to deliver. For Jonah the problem of God's forgiving Nineveh, lies not so much in their wickedness, although this is obviously a related factor, but rather in the fact that they will be responsible for the destruction of Israel. How can God allow this to happen? Here was the real dilemma confronting Jonah.

His reaction is all the easier to appreciate when we recall that, according to 2 Kings 14:25, Jonah prophesied that Israel's borders would be expanded during the reign of Jeroboam II. Having acted for the benefit of Israel, he now finds himself being an unwilling accomplice in its future destruction.

In the light of these observations, the destruction of the gourd takes on a special significance. In this action, which symbolizes the fate of Israel, God demonstrates that as the source of life, he also has the right to take it away. Like the captain (1:6) and his sailors (1:14), and the king and his nobles (3:9), Jonah is forced to acknowledge the absolute sovereignty of God. The Lord is ultimately free to act as he pleases (*cf.* Mt. 20:1–16). *Salvation comes from the* LORD.

MICAH

AN INTRODUCTION AND COMMENTARY

by

BRUCE K. WALTKE, B.A., TH.D., PH.D.

*Professor of Old Testament, Westminster Theological Seminary,
Philadelphia*

AUTHOR'S PREFACE

When Professor D. J. Wiseman honoured me with an invitation to contribute the commentary on Micah for the Tyndale Old Testament Commentaries, I did not anticipate the rich spiritual banquet that awaited me. Through God's grace I hope this commentary will enable readers to share in the feast.

Many helped me to prepare the food. The NIV served as a good basic translation, and when I disagreed with it, I could almost always find what I wanted in another version. The commentary identifies some from whom I learnt. Surprisingly, I often learnt most when I disagreed. I commenced the work in an Old Testament seminar led by myself and Professor Carl Armerding at Regent College in the spring of 1984. We stretched and encouraged each other in a way neither one of us will forget.

Others helped me set the table. Here I should mention the editors of Inter-Varsity Press and my superb teaching assistant Mr John Marcott. Elaine, my wife, patiently listened to the commentary, giving me assurance that the layman could eat and enjoy the fare without suffering from indigestion. She found one of the introductory dishes, 'date and authorship', difficult to digest, but appreciated my difficulty in trying to summarize over a century of assiduous research in order to condense a critical appraisal of it into several pages.

BRUCE WALTKE

INTRODUCTION

Two prophets bear the common Hebrew name Micah: Micaiah son of Imlah, a prophet in the northern kingdom at the time of Ahab, *c.* 874–52 BC (1 Ki. 22:8–28; 2 Ch. 18:3–27), and Micah of Moresheth, *c.* 740–690 BC (Mi. 1:1), the author of the canonical book. His name is shorter than that of the first mentioned prophet because the received Hebrew text faithfully represents the development of the shorter form in Judah by the second half of the eighth century BC.[1]

Micah, by artfully inserting his name in the forgiven people's hymn of praise at the end of his book (7:18), applies the meaning of his name, 'Who is like Yahweh?', to the Lord's incomparable quality to forgive his guilty people and to be true to his promises to the patriarchs. God's memorial name, Yahweh, became famous in the early days of Israel's history when he hurled the Egyptian army into the depths of the sea. Its lustre is added to when he promises to hurl the iniquities of his people Jacob into the depths of the sea (7:19).

To judge from the names of other prophets (*e.g.* Micaiah son of Imlah and Isaiah son of Amoz), Micah's identification by his hometown of Moresheth (1:1, 14; see the commentary) implies that he was an outsider to Jerusalem, where he functioned as one of the professional prophets who helped shape the character and policies of Israel (Micah's term for both kingdoms). By contrast, Amos, who preached a generation earlier in Samaria, was not regarded as a professional prophet but as a shepherd (*cf.* Am. 1:1; 7:14–15). Micah's powerful voice changed Hezekiah's heart, reshaped Judah's policies and

---

[1] Ziony Zevi, 'A Chapter in the History of Israelite Personal Names', *BASOR* 250 (1983), pp. 14–15.

so saved the nation from immediate catastrophe (*cf.* Je. 26:17–19).

He distinguished himself from his false peers by speaking the truth (*cf.* 2:6–11) and by upholding the values of the Mosaic covenant (*cf.* 3:5–8). Because false prophets differed from the true ones in character, they also differed in their messages. In order to ingratiate themselves with the rich and ruling classes the false prophets preached the Lord's gracious attributes at the expense of his righteousness and justice. Their ungodly ways and wrong doctrine led the nation into a false sense of security and to eventual ruin. Micah, filled with the spirit of justice, preached judgment upon sin and grace for the repentant, and so saved Jerusalem for the time being. Whereas his rivals were self-seeking, Micah was filled with zeal for the oppressed, his own tell-tale sign of being filled with the Spirit (3:8). He has often been called 'the prophet of the poor'; more accurately, he is a 'prophet of the middle class', who were being reduced to poverty by the rich (see commentary at 2:1–5, 6–11). Above all, he was the plenipotentiary of the Lord, who champions their cause (*cf.* Lk. 6:20). He was God's holy property, and whoever touched him in the past or abuses his book today incurs God's wrath.

In contrast to the so-called major prophets, Isaiah, Jeremiah and Ezekiel, he gives us no autobiographical information about his call to prophesy. Nevertheless, Micah 1:1 assures us that the word of the Lord came to him.

II. HISTORICAL BACKGROUND

Micah delivered his messages to Samaria and Jerusalem during the reigns of Jotham (742–735 BC), Ahaz (735–715 BC) and Hezekiah (715–686 BC). From Amos a generation earlier we have first-hand knowledge of the moral rot at work inside Samaria (*cf.* Am. 2:6–7; 4:6–9; 5:10–12; 8:4–6). According to Hosea a generation later the same sorry situation obtained, and from inside information given us later by Isaiah and Micah we learn that it came to prevail in Samaria's prostitute sister Jerusalem as well. A shocking contrast between extreme wealth and poverty was exacerbated by egregious injustices on the part of the élite rich and ruling class against the stalwart landowners, who were driven off their land and into a dependent economic status (2:1–3, 8–9; 3:1–3, 9–10). Dishonest practices prevailed everywhere, since the judges were venal and the poor had no redress (6:10–11; 7:1–4a). Moral corruption was so rife that it even debauched the nation's religious leaders. Gifted prophets (2:6, 11; 3:5–7) and educated priests (3:11) prostituted themselves for their élite pimps. To be sure the nation looked religious as it thronged the Temple and offered lavish gifts, but the moral covenant, which mandated a loving spirit towards God and one's neighbour, had been replaced by a covenant between the powerful to spoil the poor (chs. 2–3). Ahab's false religion leavened the whole nation within a little over a century (6:16).

Just as the Lord waited for the iniquity of the Amorites to become full before handing them over to Joshua's sword and driving them off the land, so also the Lord waited for Israel's sin to ripen and rot before handing the nation over to the Assyrian army that stomped through the pleasant land during the second half of the eighth century, casting one city after another into exile. Blinded by their own cupidity, the false prophets saw no connection between Israel's sin and the rampaging army, but the true prophet saw the Lord marching above it (*cf.* 1:3–7) fulfilling the curses he had threatened when he gave Israel her moral covenant at the beginning (6:1–5, 13–16; see the commentary). The church today needs men like Micah who can see the connection between the Western world's spurning of its Christian heritage and the international crises that surround it.

The arrogant and ruthless Tiglath-pileser III (744–727 BC) (= Pul, his Babylonian throne name, 1 Ch. 5:26) set out to regain and extend Assyria's rule in the west. He received tribute from Menahem among other western rulers in 743 or 738 BC. A certain 'Azriyau of Yaudi', which some maintain is Azariah (*i.e.* Uzziah) of Judah,[1] instigated a short-lived revolt (*cf.* 2 Ki. 15:7) at about the same time. Shortly after this Tiglath-pileser III organized North Syria into an Assyrian province. He put down another uprising in the west during the reign of Pekah (736–732 BC), and may have cut off part of Israel at this time.[2] From now on it is not merely a matter of

---

[1] *Cf.* H. Tadmor, 'Azriau of Yaudi', *Scripta Hiersolymitana* 8 (1961), pp. 232–242 versus S. Hermann, *A History of Israel in Old Testament Times*, trans. J. Bowden (SCM Press, 1975), p. 244.

[2] D. J. Wiseman, 'A Fragmentary Inscription of Tiglath-pileser III from Nimrud', *Iraq* 18/2 (1956), pp. 117–129.

paying tribute – that had happened before in Israel's history. Rather, something new and of the gravest theological concern was happening: the Assyrian was beginning to appropriate to himself the land where one should enjoy life with the Lord (*cf.* Dt. 6:1–3; Mi. 2:4). This new event signalled that the covenant had been so broken that its intended curses, including exile, were now being fulfilled. The Assyrians were content merely to accept tribute until a state withheld it and cherished ideas of rebellion. Then they would reduce the rebel, deport its leadership, appropriate the land and govern it.

Pekah, having assassinated Pekaiah because of his policy of submission to Assyria, allied himself to Rezin king of Damascus. Together they brought pressure on Jotham to join them in order to increase their strength and to protect their southern flank. Isaiah, however, advised him and his successor, Ahaz, to remain neutral. Pekah marched up to Jerusalem to depose Ahaz in order to put a puppet king, one Tabeel, on Judah's throne (Is. 7:6). Although he inflicted heavy losses on Ahaz (2 Ch. 28:5–8), he failed to depose him (2 Ki. 16:5). The Edomites (NIV, not Syrians, *cf.* AV) on Ahaz' south at this time regained Elath (2 Ki. 16:6), and the Philistines on his west raided the Shephelah, Judah's western foothills, and the Negev, Judah's southern dry region (2 Ch. 28:16–18).

Faced with this anti-Assyrian coalition, and spiritually unable to embrace Isaiah's faith in the Lord (Is. 7:1–8:18), the apostate Ahaz (*cf.* 2 Ki. 16:2; 2 Ch. 28:22–26; Mi. 5:12–14) sought to preserve his throne by submitting himself as a vassal to Tiglath-pileser and by offering him a huge sum of money in exchange for his help. Tiglath-pileser devastated Damascus in 732 BC and invaded Israel as far south as Galilee (2 Ki. 15:25–29). He boasted that he placed Hoshea on the throne of Israel after the latter had assassinated Pekah (2 Ki. 15:29–30).

When Tiglath–pileser was succeeded by his son Shalmaneser V in 726 BC, the time seemed opportune for Hoshea to rebel. He formed an alliance with the king of Egypt and withheld his annual tribute. The Bible matter of factly describes what happened in 2 Kings 17:5–6. It correctly attributes the siege to Shalmaneser V, though his successor Sargon II claimed credit for the capture of Samaria. Exacting an extreme measure of subjugation, he deported the upper classes – the large property holders, rulers and religious leaders – from Ahab's splendid capital, which had been adorned by Phoenician craftsmen brought south by his wife Jezebel. The Lord dropped the curtain on the final act of the northern kingdom's tragedy (*cf.* Mi. 1:3–7). In the debris excavators have found richly decorated ivory fragments, which illustrate the ostentatious luxury denounced by the prophets.

Sargon's armies conducted four campaigns to whip the rebellious western states into line in 720, 716, 713 and 712 BC. When Ashdod rebelled in 714, depending on Egypt for help and looking to Judah for additional support, Isaiah took an extreme measure to influence official policy in Judah against joining their folly. He went around Jerusalem barefoot and stripped to depict the plight of an exile and as a warning against all those who thought of making a pact with Egypt (*cf.* Is. 20). In this case Hezekiah obeyed the prophet and waited. Just as Isaiah had pictured it, in 712 BC Sargon came, whipped the Egyptians and Nubians, stripped the captives, exposed their buttocks, and deported them.

Hezekiah was of a different mind to his father Ahaz. For him, might was not necessarily right, and a line had to be drawn between prudent submission and moral rectitude. He was willing to pay the tribute but not to sell his soul. He initiated a sweeping reform, partly in response to Micah's preaching against the turpitude, venality and injustices that characterized Judah (2 Ki. 13:3–6; 2 Ch. 29–31; Je. 26:18). Perhaps Micah drew a veil over the king in his denunciations against the nation because of these reforms (*cf.* 3:1; 5:1; 7:3). Hezekiah tried but failed to reconstruct a true Israel consisting of both north and south (2 Ch. 30:1–12). Instructively, Micah refers to Judah by the term Israel (1:5, *etc.*), which heretofore had been used as a theological term for the whole nation, but never as a political term that included Judah.

When Sennacherib (705–681 BC) succeeded his father Sargon II to the Assyrian throne, Hezekiah thought the time propitious to withhold the tribute. From a political viewpoint his judgment seemed sound. Merodach-Baladan had successfully re-established himself as king of Babylon. He encouraged the western states to rebel and probably at this time sent envoys to Hezekiah (2 Ki. 20:1–21; Is. 39). Hezekiah received them gladly and showed them his armoury and treasury, two essentials to support a revolt. Moreover, Shabako (*c.* 710/9 –696/5 BC), an energetic king, ruled Egypt. But spiritually Hezekiah was wrong, for Isaiah had denounced the rebellion (Is. 30:1–2) and forewarned that as a result of his folly in exposing his military might and wealth Babylon would one day carry Judah off into captivity (Is. 30:6–8). Micah confirmed Isaiah's dire predictions and went about stripped and wailing (1:8–9) as he pictured the Assyrian plundering his homeland (1:10–16) and reaching right up to the gate of Jerusalem (1:9, 12). To Isaiah's prophecy that Judah would ultimately fall to Babylon, Micah added that the Lord would redeem Israel from there (4:9–10).

In 701 BC Sennacherib appeared on the scene (2 Ki. 18:17 – 19:37; 2 Ch. 32:1–12; Is. 30 – 31; 36 – 37.[1] He marched down the plain of Sharon, subduing all resistance. Once Joppa, at the southern end of the Sharon, had been captured, he moved through the Philistine coastal plain at will. Padi, king of Ekron, wanted to submit, but his officials handed him over as a prisoner to Hezekiah. At the same time Sennacherib took the major defensive cities in the Shephelah (Judah's western foothills) that protected Jerusalem. He boasted:

> As for Hezekiah, the Jew, he did not submit to my yoke. I laid siege to 46 of his strong cities, walled forts and to the countless small villages in their vicinity, and conquered [them] by means of well-stamped [earth-]ramps, and battering-rams brought [thus] near [to the walls] [combined with] the attack by foot soldiers, [using] mines, breeches as well as sapper work. I drove out [of them] 200,150 people, young and old, male and female, horses, mules, donkeys, camels, big and small beyond counting, and considered [them] booty.[2]

These 'strong cities' included the town mentioned by Micah (1:10–15).[3] The most important city he captured was Lachish (*cf.* 1:13), as evidenced by its size and the prominence given to it in the reliefs in Sennacherib's palace.[4] Excavations there

---

[1] *ANET*, pp. 287–288.   [2] *Ibid.*, p. 288.
[3] A. F. Rainey, 'The Biblical Shephelah of Judah', *BASOR* 251 (1983), p. 2.
[4] Archaeologists are divided over the dating of the destruction of Lachish

have revealed a huge pit into which the Assyrians, presumably, dumped some 1,500 bodies, covering them with pig bones and other rubbish.

At the same time as his army was besieging Lachish, Sennacherib also marched up to Jerusalem. At this point, it seems, Tarhaqa, brother of Shabako, led the combined forces of Nubia and Egypt to intervene. When Sennacherib decisively defeated them in the plain of Eltekeh, a part of the coastal plain level with Jerusalem, Hezekiah repented. Isaiah joined him in prayer and with Micah (Mi. 2:12–13; 7:8–10) boldly predicted the city's miraculous deliverance (2 Ki. 18:17 – 19:34; 2 Ch. 32:1–23). Sennacherib boasted that he shut up Hezekiah as a prisoner in Jerusalem 'like a bird in a cage', but implicitly admits his failure to take the city. The angel of the Lord (2 Ki. 19:35; 2 Ch. 32:22–23) apparently struck his mighty army with a bubonic plague, at least to judge from Herodotus' account that the Assyrian army had been overrun by a plague of mice (rats?).

The Assyrians, the rod in the Lord's hand, enjoyed military superiority because their troops were well disciplined (*cf.* Is. 5:26–29)[1] and, above all, because they used a standing army, unlike the conscripted levies that the western states relied upon. The Assyrians not only had professional soldiers who came from their own people but also used mercenaries of various nationalities. In fact, the Assyrian kings took over the mercenary armies of the conquered states and supported this international army by the huge tributes they exacted from their subjects (*cf.* 4:11).[2] The kings of Israel foolishly tried to match strength with strength and false religion with false religion (*cf.* 5:10–15). According to Micah, however, salvation belonged to the Lord, and he demanded repentance and renunciation of sin.

III. Recent excavations there under D. Ussishkin seem to have shifted the balance in favour of the Assyrian date: see D. Ussishkin, 'Answers at Lachish', *BAR* 5/6 (1979), pp. 16–39; W. H. Shea, 'Nebuchadnezzar's Chronicle and the Date of the Destruction of Lachish III', *PEQ* 111 (1979), pp. 113–116.

[1] Hermann, *History of Israel*, p. 244, said of the text: 'Every detail in this saying of Isaiah's is based on exact observation of Assyrian techniques and practices in war.'

[2] J. Lindblom, *Micha literarisch untersucht*, Acta Academiae Aboensis, Humaniora VI:2 (Abo: Abo Akademi, 1929). He compares Is. 22:6; 29:7f.; *cf.* Ho. 10:10, cited by Allen, p. 247, n. 28.

III. FORM AND STRUCTURE

Luther complained about the prophets: 'They have a queer way of talking, like people who, instead of proceeding in an orderly manner, ramble off from one thing to the next, so that you cannot make head or tail of them or see what they are getting at.'[1] This abrupt transition from one form and theme to another reflects the manner in which the prophet or his disciples edited the book. Micah's prophecy contains once-independent announcements of judgment, oracles of salvation, controversy sayings, lawsuit speeches, instructions, laments, prayer, hymn, and a proclamation of the Lord's epiphany. One could think of it almost as a preacher's file of sermons delivered on different occasions in the life of the capital. But unlike a drawer of sermon-files, the careful student will discern that the messages have been skilfully fitted together like pieces of a mosaic by means of catchwords and logical particles. In the commentary we will point out some of these unifying links.

Micah's distribution of oracles, however, presents a unique phenomenon in comparison to the composition of other prophetic books. It deviates from the usual scheme – oracles against Israel, oracles against the nations, oracles giving Israel hope – by repeating the oracles threatening Israel (consisting of many different forms such as lament and judgment) and oracles giving Israel hope (also consisting of many types such as the composite song of victory that concludes the book). Some want to analyse the repetition as chapters 1–3 (threat), 4–5 (hope), 6–7 (threat). Others, with more sophistication, follow the same scheme, but divide chapters 6–7 into 6:1–7:6 (or 7) (threat) and 7:7 (or 8)–20 (hope). Yet others divide the material into chapters 1–5 (oracles addressed to the nations, *cf.* 1:2) and 6–7 (oracles addressed to Israel, *cf.* 6:1). An intractable oracle of hope, however, in 2:12–13, calls these analyses into question. An old analysis, recently well developed and defended by J. T. Willis in his doctoral dissertation, seems best. He divides the book thus: 1:2 – 2:13; 3:1 – 5:15 and 6:1 – 7:20. The first section moves from oracles of doom against Israel (beginning with the Lord's punitive epiphany, 1:2–7, followed by a lament song, 1:8–16, a funeral lament, 2:1–6, and a controversial saying, 2:7–11), to the short

---

[1] Cited by Allen, p. 257, n. 56.

144

oracle of hope, 2:12–13. The second division, marked off by the editorial suture, 'Then I said', moves from three oracles of doom (more specifically oracles of reproach or judgment) sharing the same form (3:1–12), to a number of diverse oracles promising the nation hope (4:1 – 5:15). Willis has demonstrated beyond reasonable doubt the unity of 3:9 – 4:3 (see the commentary). Some have mistakenly interpreted 5:10–15 as an oracle of doom, but in fact it is a promise that God will rid Israel of her besetting sins. The third section, marked off by an editorial anacrusis (see the commentary at 6:1a), also moves from diverse kinds of doom oracles threatening the nation, concluding with a lament song (6:1b – 7:7), to a victory song, a composite of hymns of confidence and praise. The motif of confidence (7:7), present in most lament songs, forms a transition into the final song of victory.

This striking threefold repetition points to the book's unity, as Willis has cogently argued, reinforced by striking affinities on a horizontal axis between the oracles of doom and of hope and, as stated, by a vertical coherence linking the oracles to one another by catchwords and logical particles. Regarding the affinities on the horizontal axis, suffice it here to note that the three sections commence with the imperative 'hear' or 'listen' (1:2; 3:1; 6:1) and that their hope sections contain the motif of shepherding (2:12; 4:8; 5:4; 7:14).

IV. DATE AND AUTHORSHIP

Many literary and historical critics commence their labours with a profound scepticism towards the Bible's own statements regarding its date and authorship and, also, so restrict the prophetic gift that predictions are dated to the time of their fulfilment. By observing abrupt transitions of themes, jerkiness of style, and thinking it improbable that a prophet would have weakened the effect of his messages of doom by introducing oracles of hope, they analyse the text into diverse literary sources. The isolated sources in turn are dated by means of the historical conditions presupposed in them and by theological and literary typologies; that is, their religious ideas and language are correlated with the evolution of the Hebrew religion as drawn up by Wellhausen[1] and dated accordingly.

[1] J. Wellhausen, *Geschichte Israels*, 1 (G. Heimer, 1878).

Ewald[1] in 1867 initiated this approach to Micah even before Wellhausen's classic *Geschichte Israels* (1878) appeared. In an epoch-making article which appeared in 1881, Stade,[2] systematically employing this kind of literary-historical approach, laid the foundation for all future research. There is now a widely held consensus that Micah is not the author of 2:12–13; 4:1 – 5:9; 7:8–20.

In the decade 1915–24, the form-critical approach began to supplement the literary-historical approach in deciding the date of the oracles in Micah. Form critics identify the literary genre of the isolated units and attempt to reconstruct the setting-in-life in which they originated and were at home. Finally, they trace both the development of the oracle from its brief (usually thought to be) oral form to its final form and its incorporation into larger bodies of material, right on to its present position in a book. Hans Schmidt[3] initiated this approach to Micah in 1915, and Johannes Lindblom[4] wrote the most influential work from this viewpoint in 1929. According to him, among other things, 1:2–7, 8–16; 6:9–16; 7:1–4 and 7:13 were originally written, perhaps as pamphlets, and disseminated among the people at appropriate places. Lindblom dealt extensively with the delimitation and type of each oracle in Micah. Recent form critics, such as Weiser,[5] assign the life-setting of as many oracles as they can to Israel's cultus. This approach led Kapelrud[6] to defend the traditional authorship of many more oracles. For example, he assigns the hope oracles in chapters 4 – 5 to the autumnal new year festival before the destruction of the Temple.

Redaction criticism builds on both of these approaches and seeks to understand the reamplification, rearrangement and reapplication both of individual oracles and of the final form

---

[1] G. H. A. von Ewald, *Jesaja mit den Uebrigen aelteren Propheten erklaert. Die Propheten des Alten Bundes erklaert*, 2 Aufl., 1 (Vandenhoeck & Ruprecht's Verlag, 1867), p. 523. Ewald later retracted this position.

[2] B. Stade, 'Bemerkungen ueber das Buch Micha', *ZAW* 1 (1881), pp. 161–172.

[3] H. Schmidt, 'Micha', *Die Schriften des Alten Testaments*, 2 (1915), pp. 130–153.

[4] Lindblom, *Micha literarisch untersucht*.

[5] A. Weiser, *Das Buch der zwoelf Kleinen Propheten*, 4 Aufl. (Vandenhoeck & Ruprecht, 1963), pp. 228–290.

[6] A. S. Kapelrud, 'Eschatology in the Book of Micah', *VT* 11 (1961), pp. 392–405.

of the book in the life of the community that held it sacrosanct. Critics today mostly date the final form of the book to the exilic[1] or the post-exilic period[2] before the dynamic activity of Ezra and Nehemiah. For example, Renaud (1977; pp. 246f.), who mostly uses the techniques of literary criticism, thinks that 5:3 is a redactional gloss to justify to restored Israel the delay in the fulfilment of the eschatological-Messianic promises found in 4:9 – 5:6 and to renew their hope in them.

Here we aim critically to appraise in a general way the techniques that are basic to all the approaches *vis-à-vis* the linguistic and theological typologies, and the psychological problem of mixing hope oracles with doom oracles; to examine briefly the oracles scholars have been prone to deny to Micah; and to challenge the conclusion that the book reached its final form in the exilic or the post-exilic communities.

The grammar of Micah is pre-exilic, displaying none of the characteristic features of post-exilic Hebrew.[3] Moreover, vocabulary tests are extremely difficult to control because texts can be archaized or modernized, and words can disappear from the limited texts reflecting a dead language and then later reappear.[4]

Furthermore, most of the allegedly later religious ideas in Micah are found in Jeremiah. Willis (pp. 306–310) in fact collected some thirty-one parallels between the two. Critics are prone to assume that this means Micah borrowed from Jeremiah. For example, Renaud (1977; p. 112) thinks that he can establish the exilic date of 2:12 by the following argument: 'Jer. 23:1–6 is the only passage to make God say (in the first person as in Micah): "And I, I will gather the remnant of my ewes" (Jer. 23:3), and to link therefore the three concepts of reassembling, of herd and of remnant.' But how can he be so sure that Micah depended on Jeremiah, especially since Micah is explicitly quoted in Jeremiah 26:18? Besides, Willis (p. 200) reached the opposite conclusion. According to him the verse

[1] R. Ungerstern-Sternberg, *Der Rechtsstreit Gottes mit seiner Gemeinde, Der Prophet Micha* (Calwer Verglag, 1958); W. Harrelson, *Interpreting the Old Testament* (Holt, Rinehart & Winston Inc., 1964), p. 362; Willis, p. 303.

[2] Renaud; Allen, p. 252.

[3] D. A. Robertson, *Linguistic Evidence in Dating Early Hebrew Poetry* (Society of Biblical Literature, 1972), p. 154.

[4] R. Polzin, *Late Biblical Hebrew: Toward an Historical Typology of Biblical Hebrew Prose* (Scholars Press, 1976), p. 7; K. A. Kitchen, 'Egypt', *NBD*, p. 350.

looks back to the Davidic tradition because the verbs 'gather' and 'bring together' occur in passages in which David gathers Israel to fight. Another problem arises because themes sometimes contradict one another, as observed in our Additional Note on the date of the complex oracle in 4:1–5 (see pp. 170–175).

Allen (p. 251) has cogently rebutted the psychological argument about mixing oracles of hope and doom as follows: 'Certainly a message of comfort would weaken one of condemnation if both were uttered in the same situation to the same audience, but literary juxtaposition is no proof of contemporaneity. Oracles collected from years of prophetic ministry and different spiritual climates can reasonably range over a host of prophetic moods from stormy to fair.' Besides, the double focus of the prophet on destruction and renewal is succinctly summarized in Jeremiah 1:10, and both moods find expression in Lamentations 3, a poem unified by a strict acrostic structure. Finally, the announcement of hope in 5:9–15 is so closely connected with Isaiah 2:6–8, dated by all to late eighth century BC, that most critics do not deny it to Micah.

Let us now look more particularly at the disputed oracles of hope. In the commentary we will argue, as does Allen, that the setting of 2:12–13 is the time of Sennacherib's invasion in 701 BC.

Micah 4:1–5 is so complex and important that we argue its date at some length in the Additional Note (pp. 170–175) in which we reach the conclusion that it probably predates Isaiah 2:2–4.

Allen (p. 244) notes that 4:6–8 shares in common with 2:12–13 the motifs of the remnant, sheep and divine kingship, but, none the less, denies the oracle to Micah because 'remnant' appears as a technical term full of hope for the elect that survive God's judgment. He awards the first use of the term in this sense to Jeremiah, without noting that Amos 5:15 represents the first appearance of this technical meaning. It is hard to see why Micah could not have been among the earliest prophets to use the term in this way, since he was one of the elect who survived the Assyrian onslaught that took thousands of Judaeans into captivity and left only a remnant in Jerusalem. In fact, Isaiah (Is. 37:32 = 2 Ki. 19:31; Is. 37:4 = 2 Ki. 19:4) uses the term in precisely this connection. (Many critics, however, doubt the authenticity of this piece.) Surprisingly Allen (p. 248) says about 5:7–9, where 'remnant' occurs with the same sense as in 4:6–8, that 'there is nothing in the oracle to rule out an eighth-century provenance'.

The 'now' of distress in 4:9 – 5:1 fits well into the Assyrian crisis. The reference to nations in 4:11 is not apocalyptic (a literary genre that arose in Israel after Micah), as some have assumed, but refers to the nations comprising the Assyrian imperial army. Note that restoration from Babylon in 4:10 is seen as something remote in time and place. In sum, the provenance of these oracles is implicitly Jerusalem in the pre-exilic epoch.

The date of 5:1–6 can be determined by the mention of Assyria and the land of Nimrod in 5:5–6. Even Renaud (p. 253), who denies the integrity of the oracle, is forced to concede that 5:5b–6 'comes from a time when Asshur reigned over Babylonia, which would really correspond to the epoch of Isaiah and of Micah'.

There is nothing in 5:7–9 and 7:8–20 to rule out an eighth-century provenance. Allen (p. 251) bows to the scholars who assign 7:8–20 to an exilic or post-exilic date, but offers no evidence to validate his scepticism.

If one rejects the posture of scepticism towards 1:1, there is no compelling reason to urge against the authenticity of any oracle in Micah.

We have already argued that the book is a unity and suggested that its provenance is consistently Palestinian at the time of the Assyrian invasions. The editorial notice in 1:1 (note the singular, 'the word of the Lord', *contra* Je. 1:1, Am. 1:1) and the editorial suture 'Then I said' in the first person in 3:1 together suggest that Micah had a hand in editing the book traditionally assigned to him.

ANALYSIS

The heading (1:1)

COMMENTARY

The heading (1:1)

The heading puts the accent on the divine origin of Micah's book by making the topic *the word of the Lord*, instead of the words of the prophet (*cf.* Is. 1:1; Je. 1:1; Am. 1:1), and by stating it without a predicate. Our shoes should be off our feet as we hear this word. The two modifying clauses (*cf.* NEB) present the historical situation into which it came (see the Introduction, pp. 138–143). *Came* means 'happened' as a dynamic and powerful event. Filled with the Spirit (3:8), Micah addresses his audience with messages from the same voice that created the cosmos and directed Israel's history heretofore. He dates his message only by the southern kings, because in the north kings had been made without prophetic sanction (Ho. 8:4). Micah would not dignify these pretenders by naming them. *Saw* (AV, RSV; Heb., *ḥāzâ*) refers to an audition, though it could be accompanied by visions as well.[1] Micah's book is God's word.

I. JUDGMENT AND DELIVERANCE (1:2 – 2:13)

A. Samaria to be levelled (1:2–7)

Micah's oracle, announcing the fall of Samaria, has four parts, each with two sub-divisions: (1) The prophet *summons* the nations to a trial (v. 2a) as defendants (v. 2b). (2) The Lord is going to descend in a punitive *epiphany* (v. 3) to convulse the earth (v. 4). (3) Samaria (v. 5a) and Jerusalem (v. 5b) are *accused* of breaking covenant. (4) The King hands down the *sentence* that Samaria will be levelled (v. 6) and its idols destroyed (v. 7).

2. God's condemnation of Israel serves as a typical example

[1] *TDOT* 4, p. 283; *THAT* 1, p. 536.

of the judgment he will exact upon all peoples that forsake the living God for idols. Ironically, Israel, called to be a priestly nation, now functions as a warning to them (*cf.* Lv. 18:28). The Lord's universal rule is underscored explicitly by *all* (twice) and more subtly by the title 'Sovereign' (NIV). He manifests that rule by giving prophecies that are unrivalled for their morality, specificity and comprehensiveness (*cf.* Is. 41:21–29).[1] *Temple* more properly means 'palace' (Heb., *hêkal*), where the throne of judgment sat. For another judgment scene, see 6:1–2.

3–4. Behind the scenes described in verses 6–7, Micah saw the march of God. *High places* and *valleys*, better 'plains', signify the whole – every high and stable thing crumbles beneath him. Men feel secure so long as God remains in heaven, but when he comes to earth in judgment they are gripped by the terrifying realization that they must meet the holy God in person. If men would tremble before God, instead of before each other, they would have nothing to fear.

5. Micah accuses *Jacob* (= the northern kingdom) and *Israel* (= all Israel) of *transgression* (= breaking covenant) and of *sin* (= not keeping its stipulations). The Lord's relationship with Israel was not contractual but covenantal, calling for heartfelt allegiance to him. The unethical conduct entailed in breaking covenant with God will be specified in chapters 2 – 3 and 6:9–12. The judgment against Judah is to be depicted in 1:8–16. *Samaria* and *Jerusalem* by metonymy stand for the corrupt leadership of the northern and southern kingdoms respectively.

6–7. *Therefore* shows that the sentence fits the crime. The punitive epiphany and the sentence are linked by 'pour down' (RSV, AV, NEB). *Idols* were the tangible symbols of Samaria's pagan world-view, from which sprung her twisted value system and unethical conduct (*cf.* Rom. 1:18–31). These enticing idols, so attractive to the flesh and demanding no moral rectitude, seduced Samaria's leaders into breaking covenant and to committing crimes even as sex and drugs do today. Golden images, of such monetary value yet so spiritually and politically worthless, were constructed from the wages of cult prostitutes (cf. NIV). The conquerors will break

---

[1] *Cf.* P. van Imschoot, *Theology of the Old Testament*, 1, trans. K. Sullivan, R. S. C. J. and F. Buck, SJ (Desclee Company, 1965), pp. 167–171.

them up and use the money to repeat the same cycle. Only the heart of depraved man could worship gods like that!

B. Lament over the towns of Judah (1:8–16)

Micah's lament over the fall of Judah has three parts: (1) an *introduction*, stating his intention to mourn (vv. 8–9), (2) a *lament song*, commemorating the fall of the Judaean strongholds by a play on words (vv. 10–15), and (3) a *conclusion*, calling the house of David to join in mourning rites because it will go into exile. The song, like Isaiah 10:24–32, features word plays between the name of the town and its predicted doom. The regularly occurring alliteration, the rapid shift from one locality to another, images juxtaposed in opposition to one another (apart from v. 13), along with imperatives and parallels, give the song a dynamic and dramatic effect. One feels the excitement before the dreaded march of the enemy.

Here is a chart of the towns and their identification:

City	Identification
Gath	Tell eṣ-Ṣafi
Beth Ophrah	uncertain
Shaphir	uncertain
Zaanan	uncertain
Beth Ezel	Deir el-Aṣal?
Maroth	uncertain
Jerusalem	Jerusalem
Lachish	Tell ed-Duweir
Moresheth Gath	Tell ej-Judeideh
Aczib	Tell el-Beida
Mareshah	Tell Sandahanna
Adullam	Tell-esh-Sheikh-Madkur

The arrangement is not according to the order of Sennacherib's march – it makes no sense topographically[1] but literarily. The known towns form a circle with a radius of fourteen kilometres around Micah's hometown, Moresheth-Gath. Micah's description of the invasion complements Sennacherib's account of it, even to the point of stating that it reached the gate of Jerusalem, without mentioning its fall

---

[1] A. F. Rainey, 'The Biblical Shephelah of Judah', *BASOR* 251 (1983), pp. 2ff.

(vv. 9, 12). The concluding pronouncement that the house of David will go into exile did not come to pass at that time, because Hezekiah repented (*cf.* Je. 26:7–8, 18–19).

8–9. Unlike some tub-thumping modern preachers of fire and damnation, Micah preaches judgment out of such love that he weeps for his audience. For mourning customs in Israel, see Genesis 50:10; Jeremiah 6:26; Ezekiel 24:17.

Possibly the word rendered *her wound* (Heb., *makkôteyhā*) conceals an original abbreviation (*makkat yah* = 'the blow from the Lord'), because the masculine form of the verb rendered *reached* (Heb., *nāga‘*) is unexpected. If that be so, verse 9b, c should read 'it [= the blow] has come to Judah, *he* [= the Lord] has reached the gate of my people' (*cf.* AV and NIV mg.). The prophet again interprets the international crisis as God's punishment (*cf.* vv. 12, 15).

10. The Daughter of Zion should ventilate her grief not in Philistine Gath but in its own Beth Ophrah. Verse 10 begins *bᵉgaṯ ’al-taggîdû/bāḵô’al-tiḇkû: Tell it not in Gath;/weep not at all.* Note that the initial consonants on both sides of the caesura are *b*, *’*, *t*, and that the vowel pattern with the verbs at the ends is *a*, *i*, *u*. Unlike the cities that follow, with the exception of Adullam (v. 15), the assonance with *Gath* does not entail the doom of Gath; rather it links Micah's lament with David's lament over the death of Saul and Jonathan, Israel's first king and heir apparent, under similar circumstances (2 Sa. 1:20). The borrowed command ominously hints at the death and defeat of David's descendants, a threat made clear in verses 15b–16. Gloating at Israel's defeat misinterprets history, derogates God while exalting the tyrant, and rejoices in human misery. *Beth Ophrah* ('House of Dust') puns the feminine singular command to the Daughter of Zion (= Jerusalem's rulers) to *roll in the dust*, a vivid way of expressing grief over a humiliating defeat (Jos. 7:6; 1 Sa. 4:12; Jb. 16:15; Je. 6:26).

11. Whereas *Shaphir*, meaning 'Beauty-Town', which once prided itself on its splendour, will now go forth as a captive, stripped and put to shame, *Zaanan*, meaning 'Going Forth Town', will cower behind its walls instead of boldly going forth to battle. *Beth Ezel*, meaning 'House of Taking Away', will 'take [away] its place' (= its protection to Judah) because it has been annexed by the conqueror. *You* (a masculine plural form) refers to either Shaphir and Zaanan and/or all Judah.

12. *Maroth* means 'bitter'. As all that are bitter hope for something better, so also the inhabitants of 'Bitter Town' waited 'anxiously' (RSV) for 'good' (= *relief*, NIV) from the one quarter they might have expected aid. But no (*cf.* AV), the Assyrian marched right up to the great *gate of Jerusalem*.

13. *Lachish* sounds like *lārekeš*, 'to the steeds' (RSV, NEB). In pungent irony, Lachish is commanded to harness its war chariots to racing horses (*cf.* AV and RSV). The town is the beginning of sin to Israel because idolatry got a foothold at Lachish and quickly leavened all Israel. Lachish's spiritual role in Israel reminds one of Hollywood, which promoted adultery.

14. With the loss of Lachish, Judah's key defensive point, the king must be prepared to pay tribute (*cf.* 2 Ki. 18:14–16). *You*, feminine singular, refers to the Daughter of Zion. *Moresheth* may be related to either *yāraš*, meaning 'possess/dispossess', or to *mᵉʼōrāśâ*, 'betrothed'. If the latter, then, instead of *parting gifts*, the more explicit meaning 'dowry' is to be preferred (*cf.* 1 Ki. 9:16). The combination yields an intense *mot de jeux* involving biting sarcasm. Judah's rulers must give as a dowry (= the hated tribute) the town once betrothed to them, but now pledged to the enemy. When we fail to win the world for God, we find instead that the world conquers us. *Aczib* means 'deception'. Instead of *town* (NIV) read 'houses' (AV, RSV), more specifically, 'workshops' (*cf.* 1 Ch. 4:21–23 and Je. 18:2).[1] The king lost revenue both by having to pay the hated tribute and because Aczib, now in enemy hands, would no longer yield him taxes. The rulers who had once fleeced their flock (3:2), are now fleeced by the Assyrian. A man reaps what he sows (Gal. 6:7).

15. *Conqueror* (Heb., *hayyōrēš*) literally means 'the one who dispossesses another from his property' (= 'heir', 'new owner'; *cf.* Je. 8:10) and designates Sennacherib. 'Inhabitants of Mareshah' (RSV; Heb., *yôšebet mārēšâ*) sounds like *yôrēš* ('conqueror'). Possibly by popular etymologizing, *Mareshah* was associated with the verb 'dispossess'. A new heir will dispossess the old heritage of Judah. The prophet no more intends a lament over *Adullam* than over Gath. Both cities evoke a literary and historical allusion against the house of David. As David fled to Adullam as a fugitive from Saul at the beginning of his dynasty (1 Sa. 22:1; 2 Sa. 23:13), so the nobility of Israel will

---

[1] A. Demsky, 'The Houses of Aksib. A critical note on Micah 1:14*b* (*cf.* 1 Chron. 4:21–23)', *IEJ* 16 (1966), pp. 211–215.

also be driven out of the land into exile by a hostile king at the end of the monarchy. *Glory of Israel* (NIV, RSV, NEB; *cf.* 2 Sa. 1:19–20) refers to 'men of rank' (*cf.* Is. 5:13; NIV).

16. The imperatives, which are feminine singular in form, again address the Daughter of Zion. Her *children* going into exile are the nobles. A (griffon-)*vulture*'s neck and head are destitute of feathers. The wages paid out by the Lord to Israel as poetic justice for her sin were disaster, defeat and death – high wages indeed.

C. Venal land barons sentenced to exile (2:1–5)

Augustine divided mankind into two cities 'formed by two loves: the earthly by the love of self, even to the contempt of God; the heavenly by the love of God, even to the contempt of self'.[1] In this oracle of judgment Micah announces that those who had 'succeeded' in the earthly city, are about to lose forever their share in the heavenly. The oracles against Samaria and Judah in the first chapter speak in general terms of their rebellion and sin and put the accent on immediate political destruction. This oracle indicts them for specific crimes and puts the accent on the eternal and theological punishment.

The oracle of doom falls into three parts: (1) Micah *addresses* the deceased by *accusing* activities (vv. 1–2). (2) The Lord *sentences* them to a galling and humiliating exile (v. 3), entailing spiritual death (v. 4). (3) Micah's conclusion consigns the landgrabbers to an eternal spiritual death and evokes hope for others (v. 5). The motifs of accusation and sentence are linked together by two expressions: *those who plot evil* (*ra'*) contrasts with *I am planning disaster* (*ra'*), and *they covet fields* contrasts with 'he hath divided our fields' (AV). Once again the word plays reflect the principle of *lex talionis*.

1–2. *Woe to* in the mouths of prophets may express grief over those sentenced to death by the Lord (*cf.* 1 Ki. 13:30; Je. 22:18; 34:5; Am. 5:16–17);[2] but here, as in Isaiah

---

[1] St. Augustine, *The City of God*, 14.28.

[2] R. J. Clifford, 'The Use of HOY in the Prophets', *CBQ* 28 (1966), pp. 458–464; J. G. Williams, 'The Alas-oracles of the Eighth century Prophets', *HUCA* 38 (1967), pp. 45–91; W. Janzen, 'Mourning Cry and Woe Oracle', *BZAW* 125 (1972), *passim*. *Hôy* means 'alas' in contexts of funerary rites and 'woe' in contexts of accusation and threat.

29:15; 33:1, it means 'woe', not 'alas'. With criticism and scorn the prophet accuses the land barons of cupidity and recounts the Lord's sentence handing them over to exile and eternal death. During the night the venal landowners plan to get rich by violence. *Iniquity* entails negative power and deception.

At morning's light is ironic. Thieves usually cover their black deeds with the darkness of night. Court was held in the ancient Near East when the sun rose because it symbolized the dispelling of the darkness that covered the crime (*cf.* Jb. 38:12–13). The 'legal sharks' against whom Micah inveighed, however, performed their perfidious acts at daybreak by perverting the legal system. Today, in more than one country, lawyers teach criminals how to circumvent the law and make mockery of it. Perpetrators go free and witnesses languish in jail.

Covet strikes right at the heart of man's spiritual malady and unethical behaviour (*cf.* Ex. 20:17; Dt. 5:21; Rom. 7:8). Verse 2a would be better rendered, 'whenever they covet fields, they seize them', suggesting that this perfidy went on regularly.

Defraud represents a situation where the stronger takes away, either directly or indirectly, the produce and labour of the weaker, giving nothing in exchange. It may be done by using dishonest scales (Ho. 12:7–8) or by extortion, either by employing naked force (Is. 52:4; Je. 50:33) or by manipulating the legal system (*contra* Lv. 6:2 [Heb., 5:21]; 6:4 [Heb., 5:23]; 19:13; Dt. 1:17; 17:8–13). The parallel in Amos 5:7, 10–17 suggests the latter is in view here. The objects of their rapacity were the fields and houses of Israel's stalwart citizens (see also vv. 8–9).

Man (Heb., *geber*, v. 2c) depicts him at his most competent and capable level. *Fields* (v. 2a) were a sacred trust. In that agrarian economy a man's life and freedom depended on owning them. Deprived of them, he might at best become a day-labourer; at worst, a slave.

3. *Therefore* once again (*cf.* 1:8) matches the sentence with the crime. Once again the Lord himself hands it down. *Disaster* came in the form of the crack troops of the invading Assyrian armies. 'Family' (rsv) denotes Israel as a corporate solidarity bound together by blood, covenant and history. The whole 'family' suffered for the sins of individuals within it, especially of its leaders, because of this solidarity (*cf.* Jos. 7; 2 Sa. 24:17). The NIV's *from which you cannot save yourselves* paraphrases 'from which [yoke] (*cf.* Je. 28:14) you cannot remove your necks' (RSV) to make it plain that disaster is certain, but it conceals the notion that it will be galling. *You will no longer walk proudly* adds humiliation to the punishment.

4. In Isaiah the expression *in that day* is found either at the beginning or the end of an oracle to make clear the results of an event.[1] Here it introduces a new starting-point to explain the consequences of the divine sentence. The second part of the judicial sentence is stiffer than the first: they will lose their sacred land! *We are utterly ruined* (Heb., *šādôd neʾšaddûnû*) sounds like *our fields* (Heb. *šādênû*), another instance of word play reflecting *lex talionis*. As the strong and mighty in Israel ruined others by taking their fields, so now others stronger than they will take theirs – 'All who draw the sword will die by the sword' (Mt. 26:52). *Possession* (Heb., *ḥeleq*) is a quasi-technical term relating the fertile land essential for life to both the giver and the receiver, who have an equal interest in it. As owner of the land, the Lord had distributed it to the tribes and families through the casting of the sacred lot (Jos. 12 – 22). Without these sacred portions the priestly nation could not exist. The Owner gave it as a usufruct (*cf.* Lv. 25:23). Israel could enjoy the land freely and fully as long as she served the interest of the covenant, but should she abuse her gift by using it apart from the covenant's designs the Lord retained the right to take it away from his faithless people and give it to her enemies (Lv. 26:33; Dt. 28:49–68). The pronoun *he* is used instead of 'the Lord' so as not to allow the mockers to blaspheme the divine Name. *Šôbēb*, misunderstood as a participle meaning 'turning away' in the AV, means 'the rebellious' (RSV mg.; *cf.* Je. 49:4), and is a reference to the obstinate, arrogant, and wilful Assyrian (*cf.* Is. 10). The same Lord still divides up the nations according to his own good pleasure and justice (Acts 17:26), and directs the building of his church by taking away spiritual advantage from those who apostatize, giving it to others (in this case to the faithful; *cf.* Rom. 11:17–21; Rev. 2:16; 3:16), and by giving spiritual gifts to his people (Rom. 12:3–8; 1 Cor. 12; Eph. 4:7–13).

---

[1] A. Lefèvre, 'L'expression "en ce jour-là" dans le livre d'Isaie', in *Mélanges bibliques rediges en l'honneur d'Andre Robert* (Bloud et Gay, 1957), pp. 174–179.

5. The landgrabbers will not participate in the future redistribution of the land in the eschatological assembly. The sentence, looking to a future beyond the Exile (see v. 4), evokes eternal spiritual death for them and the hope of life for others (*cf.* Gn. 17:8; Dt. 30:1–10).

D. Polemic against false prophets (2:6–11)

Micah accuses those who glory in their own power of refusing to repent when confronted by true prophecy. (1) In an *introduction* Micah rebuffs their command to stop prophesying (v. 6); (2) in *the body* of the indictment the Lord corrects false prophets (v. 7), accuses the powerful of exploiting the defenceless (vv. 8–9), and sentences them to exile (v. 10); and (3) in a *conclusion* Micah sarcastically describes the kind of prophet the people want to hear (v. 11).

6. *Do not prophesy* is plural, probably lumping Micah together with his peers Hosea and Isaiah, and with the disciples of true prophets (*cf.* Is. 8:16). As in the days of Elijah, the Lord has always preserved a spiritual remnant (Rom. 11:1–6). The *vox populi* finds expression through *their prophets*, the official theologians of those times. *These things* links this polemic with the preceding reproach. True prophets continue to preach against the lies by which men seek to justify their life-styles, for through its double-edged sword the kingdom in men's hearts will come (*cf.* 1 Ki. 22:8–27; Je. 11:21; Am. 2:12; 7:12–13; Acts 4:1–21). The last clause should read: 'The shame will not withdraw' (NAB). Whereas Israel's glory departs, its *disgrace* (the loss of land and eternal death) will not depart.

7. Once again the false theologians are quoted and then rebuked. In Micah *house of Jacob* refers to all Israel (*cf.* 3:1). *Spirit* with *angry* means 'impatient' (*cf.* NEB; Jdg. 16:16; Jb. 21:4). The popular theologians, probably building their theology on Exodus 34:6, focused exclusively on God's love. Their theology founders on two rocks. First, it is a half-truth (*cf.* Ex. 34:7). The whole truth is that God will both keep his covenantal promises to Israel as a nation and that he does *good* only *to him whose ways are upright*. Second, they misapplied texts (*cf.* Pr. 26:9; Lk. 4:10–11). False teachers today apply the doctrine of the believer's security to those who disown their Lord and do not bring forth the fruit of repentance from sin (*cf.* Mt. 7:24–27; 12:50; 1 Cor. 6:9–11; Gal. 5:21; 2 Tim. 2:12).

8–9. In a rising crescendo the Lord accuses Israel's ruler's of stripping off the men's rich robes, seizing the women's luxurious houses, and taking away for ever the children's splendour. A *rich robe* displayed a man's dignity. Israel's stalwart men felt as secure within their own borders as a soldier feels when returning home from battle. But Israel's leaders, regarding their offices as prizes they had won instead of as opportunities to serve, pillaged them. *Blessing*, better 'splendour', refers to the riches the Lord conferred on Israel (*cf.* Ezk. 16:9–14). The accusation indirectly gives an insight into the nation's wealth at the time it fell.

10. In another *lex talionis* the Lord sentences the criminals by using the same words they had used to oust their victims from the land. *Resting place* carries the spiritual notion of well-being with it. *Defiled* refers to something that is ritually unclean and therefore abhorrent to God, which needs to be removed from the Lord's presence.

11. Micah rakes both the false prophets and his audience. Isaiah also used *people* derogatorily for his stubborn audience (Is. 6:10, *etc.*). The profiteers do not bother to verify the authenticity of so-called prophets, for they are not the least surprised or offended by preachers who share their cupidity and venality.

E. A remnant survives in Zion (2:12–13)

The first section of the book ends with a promise that Israel's Shepherd-King will gather his sheep into a protected area (v. 12) and then deliver them (v. 13). The speaker changes from the Lord (v. 12) to Micah (v. 13) and Israel is seen first as a corporate singular (*remnant, flock*) and then as a plurality of individuals. The scene changes from the gathering of Israel into a fold to her being led out of it by the Lord himself.

Most scholars interpret the oracle with reference to Israel's salvation from the Babylonian captivity, and accordingly place it into the mouth of an exilic or post-exilic prophet. Allen (pp. 242, 244 and 301), however, more plausibly interprets it as a metaphorical reference to Jerusalem's deliverance from Sennacherib's blockade. This interpretation is confirmed by verbal links between it and 2 Kings 19:31 (*i.e.* 'remnant' and 'going out'), and this setting admirably fits the text's imagery and Micah's situation. The *gate* is that of Jerusalem (*cf.* 1:9, 12) and *pen*, according to Willis (p. 207), refers to Zion. Mays (pp. 74f.) observes: 'V. 13 thinks of some walled place, apparently a city, out of which YHWH will lead his people.' Amazingly Mays thinks only of Nebuchadnezzar's siege of Jerusalem. The small glimmer of hope in the preceding oracles of judgment that there would be a remnant (see 1:9, 12 and 2:5) is now exploited.

12. The verb rendered *throng* means in Psalm 55:2 (Heb. 55:3) 'to be distraught' and *with* would be better rendered as 'by reason of' (the Heb. reads literally 'from'). Accordingly the commotion is caused not by the crowd of men within Jerusalem but comes from the *people* (*i.e.* the besieging Assyrian army) without who threaten them.

13. The release from Jerusalem occurs in three stages: Israel's Shepherd-King goes up and breaks open the blockaded gate; the masses break out and pass through the opened bay; and their King takes his rightful position at their head. Israel's earthly kings failed; her heavenly King will triumph.

II. FALSE LEADERS DENOUNCED, A RIGHTEOUS KING PROMISED (3:1 – 5:15)

A. Shepherds turned cannibals (3:1–4)

The following three oracles of judgment are of equal length (four verses) and share a common form: an *address*, on to which is grafted the *accusation* introduced by 'who' (vv. 2, 5, 9) and a concluding *sentence* introduced by 'then' (v. 4) or 'therefore' (vv. 6, 12). The first two oracles move to the climactic third. Among the accused it gathers together the rulers (v. 1) and the prophets (v. 5), and adds to them the priests (*cf.* v. 11a). It accuses all three groups of justifying their guilty behaviour theologically, thus making them feel secure and immune from divine retribution (v. 11b). The judicial sentences move from God's silence (v. 4), to his silence plus darkness (vv. 6–7), and to his absence when the Temple is destroyed (v. 12).

1. For *then I said*, see the Introduction (p. 145). Micah brings first into the dock the rulers themselves, who in ancient Israel were also her judges. Ultimately the responsibility for justice resided in the king (2 Sa. 15:3; 2 Ch. 19:4–11). We have already noted that *Jacob* and *Israel* include Judah (*cf.* 3:12). *Justice* refers to the decisions collected in the sacred law (*cf.* Ex. 21:1 – 23:19) and to other verdicts of the court (*cf.* Dt. 17:8–11), as well as to deciding cases fairly (*cf.* 1 Ki. 3:28; 7:7). *Know* designates not merely intellectual appreciation of the law or of legal exigencies, but also personal knowledge of it so that out of sympathy for the afflicted one punishes the wrongdoer and re-establishes the outcast of fortune in his right.

2–3. Whereas righteous leaders delighted in God's law (*cf.* Ps. 1:2; 19:7–11), the leaders of Micah's day despised it (*cf.* Is. 1:17, 21–23, 26; 5:7–8). Micah looks straight into their evil hearts and sees the source of the wrong which is wrecking the climate of justice and fraternity that should mark the covenant community. Nothing short of new appetites, resulting from the new birth (Jn. 3:3–8) can remedy moral corruption. The Lord Jesus Christ will not judge by superficial appearances but by his spiritual perception of the heart and by truth (*cf.* Is. 11:1–5; Jn. 5:19–30; Rom. 2:5–8). Instead of using their privileged offices to defend the defenceless, the magistrates abused the law so as to circumvent it, enabling themselves to live luxuriously off the labours of their abused and defenceless subjects. Since the grinding poverty of the poor was leading them to an early grave, the prophet, in a sustained metaphor, depicts the magistrates responsible for creating these conditions as acting like cannibals. This grotesque figure aims to awaken the conscience of the reprobates.

4. Presuming the judgment of utter ruin already threatened (1:9–16; 2:3–5), this sentence adds that God will not relent even though they cry out for deliverance. As the judges turn a deaf ear to the poor, so too God will not listen to their pleas when they are helpless. It is a fearful thing to fall into the hands of an angry God (*cf.* Pr. 1:26; Mt. 25:11–13; Lk. 16:26; 2 Cor. 6:2; Heb. 10:31; 12:17).

B. Prophets who preach for profit (3:5–8)

Micah again censures the gluttonous prophets after the greedy rulers (*cf.* 2:1–5, 6–11). The religious and judicial systems were in cahoots to protect the criminal and leave the victim at his mercy. It was an open secret, as they say.

5. The messenger formula *this is what the Lord says* and Micah's autobiography (v. 8) stress that the source of Micah's authority against the false prophets lies not in himself but in God. It is better to render *as for* by 'concerning' (AV, RSV, NEB) and to refer *my* to Micah instead of to the Lord (*cf.* 1:9). Accordingly, the initial quotation marks should be placed not in verse 5 but in verse 6 (*contra* NIV). As in other pronouncements of judgment, the Lord himself hands down the sentence. These *prophets* are false because they lead the people astray contrary to sound doctrine (*cf.* Dt. 13:1–5), use divination (Dt. 18:14; vv. 6–7a), and give false prophecies through a lying spirit from the Lord (*cf.* Dt. 18:21–22; 1 Ki 22:19–28; v. 7b). False prophets prostitute their gift to curry the favour of kings and to receive handsome rewards (Nu. 22:7, 17; 24:11; Ne. 6:12; Ezk. 13:19). They are not lacking in gift; they are lacking in moral conviction and strength. To judge from Balaam's experience (*cf.* Nu. 22:15–34), God sends prophets lying visions in conformity to their depraved appetites. The verb rendered *feeds* (Heb., *nāšak*; 'bite', AV) in ten of its other eleven uses has to do with snakes. Like malevolent and dangerous serpents they kill their victims to feed themselves. As verse 11 makes plain, for these evil prophets 'money talked louder than God' (Mays, p. 83).

6. *Therefore*. The Lord's sentence hits them on their own ground. By taking away their gift (*cf.* Jdg. 16:20; 2 Sa. 17:14), he removes the source of their illicit gain. *Darkness* is literal in verse 6a – dreams and visions often came at night (*cf.* Nu. 12:6; Dn. 2:9; 7:1; Joel 2:28; Zc. 1:8) – and figurative in verse 6b. As other poets liken the loss of knowledge to darkness (*cf.* Pss. 82:5; 69:23), Micah compares their loss of clairvoyance to the setting of the sun. Their 'crystal balls' will become black.

7. As a consequence of the Lord's sentence, Micah adds that they will be publicly disgraced by their uncleanness. When a prophet was exposed as a fraud, he was regarded as unclean (*cf.* La. 4:13–15). Like unclean lepers they will go about with covered moustaches (*faces*, NIV; Heb., *śāpām*) the very area of their abused gift (*cf.* Lv. 13:45). At the time of judgment 'their profession will become as empty of reality as the oracles they gave' (Mays, p. 84).

8. *But*, a strong adversative, contrasts the true prophet with the false: his ministry is based on the Spirit, not sensuality; he proclaims sin and judgment, not peace; he establishes justice and does not foster injustice. Filled with *power* (*i.e.* spirit-directed energy and dynamism; *cf.* Ezk. 2:2; 3:12, 14, 24; *etc.*) and *might* (*i.e.* valour, making him equal to redoutable adversaries), Micah, with other inspired men, puts aside his chaste veil of modesty in controversy (*cf.* Am. 7:14–15; 2 Cor. 11:16–32). The sign of his being filled with the Spirit is speaking of *justice*. 'Micah', Mays observes (p. 86), 'focuses on the sin in Israel, not its gross national product, because it is only in seeing themselves under the judgment of God that the guilty can grasp the reality of what is happening to them in history.'

C. Jerusalem to be levelled (3:9–12)

This third, and climactic (see vv. 1–4, 5–8), oracle of judgment in chapter 3 follows the classic form: invitation to listen (v. 9a), accusation (vv. 9b–11), and judicial sentence (v. 12). The oracle is delivered directly to the transgressors, with the exception that after the accusation is first stated generally in verse 9b (they distort justice), then concretized in verse 10 (they build Jerusalem through crime), it is explicated in the third person (v. 11). In the first explication the three groups of leaders (rulers, priests, prophets) are accused of prostituting their offices (v. 11a); in the second they are indicted for giving a faulty theological justification for their practices (*i.e.* claiming the Lord is among them, v. 11). The sentence that Jerusalem's fate will be the same as that of apostate Samaria brought Hezekiah to his knees (2 Ki. 18 – 20; 2 Ch. 29 – 31; Je. 26:19). Hezekiah's repentance, in accordance with the principle laid down in Jeremiah 18:8, turned the punishment aside. Because of this principle, judicial sentences are in effect threats. Although God is not credited with this oracle, Israel a century later said of it: 'This is what the Lord Almighty says' (Je. 26:18).

9a. The *leaders of the house of Jacob* (= all Israel) are broken down by Isaiah into: 'the hero and warrior, the judge and prophet, the soothsayer and elder, the captain of fifty and man of rank, the counsellor, skilled craftsman and clever enchanter' (Is. 3:2). Micah probably did not name the king in order to tailor his oracle to take into account Hezekiah's reforms. What amazing grace that prompts God to appeal to these vile sinners to listen.

9b–10. Once again Micah traces the source of the problem back to man's immoral appetite (*cf.* v. 2; Pr. 2:22; Mt. 15:8–9). Instead of delighting in justice, they are repulsed by it (*cf.* Is. 5:20). From their darkened hearts come distorted actions: they twist everything that is upright. Instead of being a theocracy under God's law, Israel has become an oligarchy under tyrants. Under the protective umbrella of the Temple, Jerusalem's 'skyline' reached upwards and its building projects flourished.[1] Micah, however, was not caught up in the *élan* of the capital, praising its businessmen for their bravery in adventuring capital and its architects for their brilliant engineering and sophisticated tastes; rather he saw beneath it to its economic basis *vis-à-vis* the exploitation of the 'poor' (*cf.* v. 10 with 2:2, 9 and 3:2–3). The ten commandments guaranteed all men four rights: the right to life ('you shall not murder'), the right to a home ('you shall not commit adultery'), the right to property ('you shall not steal') and the right to reputation ('you shall not give false testimony'). Israel's leaders, although required to bestow these rights, in fact violated them. *Bloodshed* refers to the violation of the first right and would have reminded Micah's audience that God requires payment in kind (*cf.* Gn. 4:10; 9:6; Nu. 35:33; Dt. 19:11–13; 21:9; 2 Sa. 1:16; 4:11; 1 Ki. 2:31–33; 2 Ki. 9:7; Hab. 2:12). *Wickedness* includes a violation of the other three rights.

11. God mediated his word to the theocracy of Israel through three instruments: the sages (usually members of the ruling class), with their counsel; the priests, with the law (*cf.* Dt. 17:10; 33:10; 2 Ki. 12:2; Ho. 4:6; Mal. 2:7); and the prophets, with messages from God. All three offices had been corrupted by love of money, the root of all kinds of evil (1 Tim. 6:10). For the right price these official hacks did not prize truth but compromised it; moreover, *they lean upon the Lord*, that is, they justified their lives of lies with the half-truth that the Lord's presence guaranteed the nation's security (*cf.* Ex. 17:7; 33:14–16; 34:9; Nu. 14:42; Dt. 7:21; Jos. 3:10; Pss. 46 – 48; 84; 87; Joel 2:27; Zp. 3:5, 15), forgetting that God made his presence contingent on ethical behaviour (Ex. 33:3, 5;

---

[1] 'Build' (Heb., *bānâ*) most frequently has a physical structure as its object. It may take restored 'Israel' as its object (*cf.* Je. 24:6; 31:4, *etc.*).

Nu. 14:14; Lv. 26:1–39, esp. v. 11; Dt. 28; 1 Ki. 9:1–9). Their
half-baked and partisan theology later seemed to be reinforced
by history, for God did indeed spare the Temple (*cf.*
Je. 7:1–15). Some today seek to validate Zionism by pointing
out the apparently successful restoration of the state of Israel.
But ethics, not an incomplete historical record, must validate
truth.

12. The sentence against Jerusalem resembles that against
Samaria: both reduced to a *heap of rubble* and a place for the
cultivation of vines, with all signs of worship gone (the Temple
in v. 12; the idols in 1:7). When the Holy One of Israel forsook
his most holy Temple, it became a profane and unholy place.
Micah speaks of *temple* (lit. 'house') instead of 'house of the
Lord' in order to desacralize it and strip it of its glorious aura.
(*Hill* and 'mountain', 4:1, render the same Hebrew noun, *har*.)
Jesus likewise announced the fall of the Temple (Mt. 24) after
denouncing the religious leaders for misusing the service of
God for their own glory and profit (Mt. 23). These warnings
need to be taken to heart by each generation of religious
leaders.

D. Zion to be exalted (4:1–5)

In a breathtaking shift, Micah moves from the dismantling of
the old Jerusalem to the rebuilding of the new. Five links unite
the two oracles and radically juxtapose the contrasts between
the two Jerusalems. Both are concerned with the role of 'Zion'
(3:10, 12; 4:2). 3:12 announces the diminution of the 'temple
hill' (Heb., *hār*), and 4:1 declares the exaltation of the 'mountain (Heb., *hār*) of the Lord's temple'. The wicked 'leaders'
(Heb. root *rō'š*) of the house of Jacob (3:9, 11) stand in contrast
with Zion as the 'chief' (better 'top', AV; Heb., *rō'š*) of the
mountains (4:1). 3:10 speaks of building Zion with bloodshed
and wickedness; 4:1–2 speaks of establishing it as the centre
from which the Lord's teaching will emanate. 3:11 condemns
the religious leaders of old Jerusalem for judging and teaching
for selfish purposes; 4:2–3 proclaims that in the new Jerusalem
the Lord will 'teach' the nations his ways and 'judge' between
them.[1]

After an anacrusis projecting the vision of the new Jeru-

[1] J. T. Willis, 'The Structure of Micah 3–5', *ZAW* 81 (1969), p. 196, n. 4.

salem into a future beyond Jerusalem's fall (v. 1a), Renaud (1977; pp. 153f.) analyses the body of the oracle into three strophes. In the first strophe (v. 1b) the prophet *sees* Zion raised above the mountains and drawing to itself numerous peoples. In the second (v. 2) the prophet *hears* the nations exhorting one another to go up to the mountain and the Lord's Temple to receive the law and the divine word. In the third strophe (vv. 3–4b) the prophet *reflects upon* and relates in detail the life of this pacified world, the fruit of the conversion of men's hearts, which issues in three unfolding benefits: (1) God arbitrates among the peoples; (2) therefore disputes are no longer settled by recourse to war, so peace prevails among the nations; and (3) as a result, every individual enjoys the fruit of his own labour in security. It ends with a twofold *conclusion* (vv. 4c–5): (1) a concluding saying-formula – the Lord promises to fulfil his prediction (v. 4c), and (2) a liturgical response by the congregation that they will walk in the name of the Lord (v. 5). Alonso-Schoekel shows the movement of the piece by an aesthetic analysis:

> It is the mountain (*har*) where the peoples flow (*nahar*, v. 1). It is solidly founded (*nakon*, v. 2) and serves as a point of attraction for the movements of crowds (*nelka*). It is the center of ways (*derākāw*) and of paths (*orhotaw*). But it is also the starting point of a centrifugal movement, that of the *torah*, which is compared to a path (*orah*), and that of the Word (*dabar*), which is compared to a way (*derek*). From it also issues sovereignty and justice, an efficacious power that creates peace . . . [The streaming towards the mountain] is described in particularly flowing lines which are astonishingly rich in NHRL sounds, and, by contrast, without sibilants, and impoverished in explosive sounds. The opposed movement toward the exterior is introduced by a half-line: *kî miṣṣiyyon tēṣē tôrāh* [= 'for the law will go forth from Zion'], clearly marked by two *s* and by two *t* sounds. It extends itself later to a line in which the number of its explosive sounds increases and issues finally into a third line where seven *t* and two *h* sounds create an onomatopia.[1]

[1] L. Alonso-Schoekel, *Estudios de poetica hebrae* (Barcelona, 1963), p. 209, reprinted in *Das Alte Testament als literarisches Kunstwerk* (Cologne, 1970), pp. 350–352.

1a. 'In days to come' (NEB, JB) is better than *in the last days* (AV, NIV, *cf.* RSV), because, although either one is possible, the oracles of salvation that follow in chapters 4 and 5 envisage the re-establishment of Zion as beginning with Israel's return from the exile rather than exclusively in the last stretch of history, which the New Testament presents as having begun after Christ ascended his heavenly throne and sent his Spirit (*cf.* Acts 2:17; Heb. 1:2). This generic promise, that is one that has a series of successive fulfilments,[1] found a partial fulfilment when the second Temple was rebuilt, is finding a much more intense fulfilment in the heavenly Mount Zion (Heb. 12:22–24), and will find its consummation when the new Jerusalem comes down from heaven (Rev. 21:1, 10, 22–27). The untroubled peace for which sane men hope does not lie exclusively in an unattainable Utopia but is available now to all who will come to heavenly Mount Zion.

1b. *Mountains*, which often raise themselves above the clouds, provide the psychic and spiritual entrance into the heavens. Throughout the ancient Near East temples were located on mountains for this reason. In Egypt the formula 'The gates of heaven are opened' was recited at the daily opening of the sanctuary.[2] In God's revelation to Israel, his heavenly sanctuary and its earthly replica on Mount Zion are inseparable (*cf.* Ex. 25:9; Pss. 11:4; 76:4, 8; Heb. 9:23; *etc.*). As the counterpart of the heavenly throne, Zion was always viewed as towering above all other mountains, though in terms of physical geography it was actually lower (*cf.* Ps. 68:16–17). The great and powerful nations began to discern its true heavenly quality when the Lord raised Zion out of its ashes, and peoples of all nations came to their full senses about it when God raised his Son from the dead and set him at his right hand in heaven.

While Jerusalem was ploughed as a field, tyrannical and bacchanalian Babylon, which boasted itself as the gateway to heaven, towered over the nations and peoples 'streamed' (Je. 51:44) to it. The prophet's eagle eye of faith saw beyond Jerusalem's rubble to its phoenix-like resurrection in days to come and the elect 'streaming' to it (*cf.* Ps. 87; Is. 56:6–8; Zc. 8:21–23; Jn. 12:32; Heb. 12:22; Rev. 21).

---

[1] W. Beecher, *The Prophets and the Promise* (1905; Baker Book House, 1975), p. 13.
[2] O. Keel, *The Symbolism of the Biblical World* (Seabury Press, 1978), p. 172.

Babylon, the creation of man's titanic efforts, resulted in confusion (*cf.* Gn. 11:1–9), but the new Jerusalem offers peace.

2. Micah imaginatively portrays this reversal of history, a reversal beyond human engineering and manipulation, by allowing his audience to overhear the conversation of the elect nations in their dramatic, liturgical procession to the new Jerusalem. Among other things (*cf.* Is. 56:8; 60; 66:18–21), they will come to hear God's *word*. Moses arranged for Israel to make three annual pilgrimages to the central sanctuary, and David with his psalms provided a libretto to accompany their worship. Micah enlarged it to include the nations. In coming to the heavenly Zion to hear the new administration, the peoples will turn their weapons of war into instruments of husbandry because their hearts have been changed. There will be a universal and lasting peace among men of goodwill. He who does not accept peace under this new administration will be broken in a future and final judgment. Commenting on the new order, Mays (p. 98) says: 'people will use the scarce and valuable materials of earth to cultivate life instead of crafting death'.

4a, b. The dream of disarmament is backed up by the dream of agrarian well-being. The two dreams are inseparable: those who have the swollen appetites of consumerism covet the vines and figs of others, and therefore wage war to obtain them. Accordingly they must live in fear of dying by the sword. But those who live according to the law are content with a modest life-style and with living by their own produce, having the happy prospect of peace and domestic felicity.[1] If the nations could trust each other not to exploit one another, they could dismantle their military machines. The ideal of not coveting is fulfilled only in the kingdom of God.

4c. Micah uses the military title for God, *YHWH Ṣᵉbā'ôt* (JB), to underscore the certainty of the promise and to focus our attention not so much on the prediction as on the one who made it.

5. As Micah represented the glorious future by quoting the converted nations (v. 2), so he represents the faith of the hopeful congregation by quoting them. They pledge themselves to walk according to the Lord's way and so serve as

---

[1] W. Brueggemann, ' "Vine and Fig Tree": A Case Study in Imagination and Criticism', *CBQ* (1981), pp. 188–204.

the harbingers of the universal peace to come in the eschaton. In the mean time the promise comforts then in sorrow, restrains them from temptation, and nerves them to fidelity in testings.

Additional Note on the date of Micah 4:1–5

Earlier literary-historical critics denied oracles of promise to the pre-exilic prophets and put this oracle in the mouth of a late exilic or post-exilic prophet. The majority of critics date the oracle in the late exilic or early post-exilic periods.

To help the reader follow the argument that follows, here is a chart of the three epochs in view, with dates and their relevant literatures according to 'normative' biblical criticism.

EPOCH	LITERATURE
Pre-exilic (760–586 BC)	
Early	Amos
	Hosea
	First Isaiah (chs. 1 – 35)
	Micah
	Pss. of Zion (46, 48, 87)
Late	Jeremiah
Exilic (586–539 BC)	
Early	Jeremiah
	Deuteronomist (Dt. – 2 Ki.)
	Ezekiel
Late	Second Isaiah (chs. 40 – 55)
Post-exilic (516–?350 BC)	
Early	Zechariah
	Haggai
	Third Isaiah (chs. 56 – 66)
	Ezra, Nehemiah
Late	Malachi
	Joel

The issue of the date of Micah 4:1–5 has two aspects: its relation to the parallel passage in Isaiah 2:2–4, and the internal evidence of its composition.

Micah 4:1–3 finds a remarkable parallel in Isaiah 2:2–4, aside from a few textual differences. (Mi. 4:4 has no parallel in Isaiah, and Mi. 4:5, while appearing similar to Is. 2:5, has a different theological intention and literary formulation.) Every possible explanation for this relationship has been proposed. The traditional view is that Micah was the author and that Isaiah or his disciples quoted him (so Calvin, C. N. E. Naegelsbach, E. B. Pusey and, most recently, E. Nielsen[1] and J. T. Willis.[2] Two arguments support this view: in the few textual differences Micah's text is generally regarded as superior, and, as we have observed, Micah 4:1–3 is closely linked with 3:9–12. Textual superiority, however, does not prove originality. The same cannot be said about literary dovetailing. The links are not coincidental and therefore owe their origin to creative activity, either that of the prophet or of a later redactor. The latter option is to be ruled out because of the oracle's occurrence in Isaiah.

Some critics regard Isaiah as original because of the affinity between the form (style, vocabulary) and content of Micah's oracle and the Isaianic prediction, which thus makes them think that Micah or his disciples quoted Isaiah. Von Rad[3] has removed the main objection to accepting Isaiah 2:2–4 as authentic by demonstrating that the ideas contained in it are at home in the psalms of Zion (Pss. 46, 48, 87, *etc.*), which most critics today accept as pre-exilic. Moreover, according to him, 'it fits perfectly into the overall pattern of Isaianic thought, but one cannot say the same of the occurrence in Micah'.[4] Wildberger[5] strenuously defends this view. According to him Isaiah 2:2–4 (like Is. 17:12–14; 29:5–8; 14:25) offers close points of contact with the earlier psalms of Zion, which he claims inspired Isaiah, and to which Micah conformed his vocabulary and phraseology. This thesis is not convincing, however, because it cannot be demonstrated that the psalms of Zion are earlier than Isaiah; it ignores the dovetailing of Micah 4:1–3 with 3:9–12; and others think Isaiah 2:2–4 does not fit well into its own context.

F. Hitzig and H. Ewald earlier argued that both Isaiah and

[1] E. Nielsen, *Oral Tradition* (Alec R. Allenson, Inc., 1954), p. 92.

[2] Willis, *loc. cit.*

[3] G. von Rad, 'The City on the Hill', in *The Problem of the Hexateuch and Other Essays* (Edinburgh and London: Oliver & Boyd, 1966), trans. from *EvTh* 8 (1948–49), pp. 442–445.

[4] *Ibid.*, p. 234.

[5] H. Wildberger, 'Die Voelkerwallfahrt zum Sion', *VT* 7 (1957), pp. 62–81.

Micah took up an earlier prophecy, and R. Vuilleumeir[1] and many others have recently defended this position on the grounds of its liturgical character. But this view neither explains satisfactorily the verbal links uniting Micah 3:9 – 4:3 nor is its appeal to liturgical character convincing, because liturgical literature belongs on a time-line extending from the period of the united kingdom to the post-exilic era. As Renaud (1977; pp. 161f.) says: 'It is on this large vector [early and late] that one must put the texts of Isaiah and of Micah 4:1–3, and it is not necessary to place them on the same point.'

Renaud champions the majority view that locates the oracle at the time of the return from exile, and makes the unlikely suggestion that a later redactor slipped it into both books. He bases his arguments on the typologies of theology and of language, giving us opportunity to examine the internal evidence of the composition itself. He begins his argument (pp. 165–169) by noting that the theme of the pilgrimage of the peoples to Zion fits several putative exilic and post-exilic texts (Is. 51:4; 56:3, 6–8; 60; 66:18–21; Hg. 2:7–9; Zc. 8:21, 23). Moreover, he argues effectively that the links with Zechariah are particularly strong. He rightly objects to Wildberger's attempt to link this theme with the so-called first Isaiah (Is. 17:12–14; 29:5–8). Junker[2] seeks to establish a thematic link with 1 Kings 8:41–43. But this link is questionable to most critics because they date Kings to the early exile. Besides, Renaud justly contrasts its individualistic tone with the nationalistic tone of our oracle. More compelling, however, is Psalm 87, which is probably pre-exilic and which affirms that both Babylon and Egypt will be enrolled in the book of life in Zion. Jeremiah 31 also speaks of peoples going up to Zion and contains literary contacts with our oracle; *e.g.* both (*cf.* Je. 31:12) speak of 'flowing' ['streaming'/'come', NIV] to Zion. Instead of flowing to Babylon they will flow to Jerusalem. Renaud insists that Jeremiah must be earlier. But why? Micah is clearly quoted in Jeremiah 26:18. Besides, Renaud fails to note that Alonso-Schoekel has effectively argued that *nāhār* was chosen to match *hār*, 'mountain', an assonance

[1] R. Vuilleumier, C. A. Keller, *Michée, Nahoum* . . . (Delachaux et Niestlé, 1971), pp. 47–48.
[2] H. Junker, 'Sancta civitas Jerusalem nova, eine formkritische und ueberlieferungsgeschichtliche Studie zu Is 2', in *EKKLESIA, Festschrift fuer Bischof WEHR M., TrThS* 15 (1962), pp. 28–29.

missing in Jeremiah. If one wishes to argue that Micah's theology has a more advanced universalistic tone than Jeremiah's more nationalistic one, then let him note that it is also more advanced than the nationalism of Haggai 2:7–9 and Isaiah 60, which, according to Renaud, are later than this oracle.

Renaud (1977; pp. 170–173) now takes up the theme of the heightening of Zion as the centre of the world. If we grant, however, with most critics, that the psalms of Zion (Ps. 46, 48, 87, *etc.*) are pre-exilic, this theme is perfectly consistent with eighth-century prophecy. To circumvent this patent argument, Renaud minimizes the evidence and prejudicially follows Wanke, who defends a post-exilic date for the psalms of Zion. But even Wanke admits that their motifs, which is the issue at stake, may be very old.[1] To hold his view he even has to deny Isaiah 19:24 to first Isaiah and make it a post-exilic addition.

Renaud (pp. 173–174) now turns to the theme of the universal eschatological peace, with its complementary motifs of the arbitration of disputes and the destruction of the weapons of war. He has to grant that these latter are relatively ancient motifs. As noted in the commentary, Isaiah associates them with his picture of the Messianic future (*cf.* Is. 9:5; 11:1–5). Renaud uses nitpicking arguments against this evidence. He argues that in contrast to both Isaiah 9, which is addressed only to the elect people, and to Isaiah 11, which is addressed to the 'poor of the land', Micah 4 extends peace universally. Isaiah, however, also has a universal peace in mind (see Is. 9:7 and the reference to the striking the earth in 11:4). Rowley, innocent of this debate, noted: 'it is to be observed that the pictures of the Golden Age are always of a universal character'.[2] Renaud also objects to the link between our oracle and first Isaiah because it attributes the establishment of justice to the Lord whereas Isaiah links it with the Messiah. Of course, the two are inseparable in prophetic thinking (*cf.* Ps. 2:2–3). But let me advance a counter-argument at this point. This theme is not found in *any* exilic or post-exilic prophet. Just the opposite. Joel, post-exilic according to the scholarly consensus, actually presents an opposite picture:

[1] G. Wanke, *Die Zionstheologie der Korachiten* (Topelmann, 1966).
[2] H. H. Rowley, *The Faith of Israel* (SCM Press, 1956), p. 180.

he calls upon the nations to beat their ploughshares into swords and their pruning hooks into spears in order to rally in war against the Lord who is about to trample them (Joel 3:9–11). In sum, the post-exilic prophet reverses the earlier vision of Micah and Isaiah, who are best dated in the pre-exilic period.

It transpires that the three themes that Renaud thinks support his argument for a later date actually provide better grounds for an earlier date. This external evidence is confirmed by Willis' five links uniting 3:9–12 and 4:1–5. The pre-exilic prophets had dual motifs: destruction and renewal (see the Introduction, p. 148). Should we not expect the post-exilic prophets to exploit the renewal theme? Is it not wrong-headed to isolate the renewal theme from the earlier single unit with its dual focus, and comparing it with post-exilic prophets, who naturally would have used it, redate it by them?

What about vocabulary? As in archaeology, where one does not date strata by older ceramic evidence but by the latest, so also critics date texts by traces of new vocabulary. Renaud finds five late traces: (1) 'In days to come'. He begs the issue here by attributing the expression in Genesis 49:1; Numbers 24:14; and throughout Jeremiah to later redactors. (2) 'In the mountain of the house of the Lord'. Here Renaud arbitrarily discounts the references in the psalms of Zion and points away from Isaiah 30:29 and 'my mountain' in Isaiah 11:9; 14:25 in favour of the one parallel in 2 Chronicles 33:15. (3) 'Flow'. The term is found elsewhere only in Jeremiah 31:12; 51:44. On the basis of Alonso-Schoekel's study we have already established the priority of Micah. (4) 'Powerful nations', without other determinatives, is unique. According to Renaud the singular ($g\hat{o}y$) is never used in the pre-exilic prophetical texts and does not appear before Deuteronomy 9:14; 26:5, which he dates to the early exile, and is found in Isaiah 60:22, a piece close to Micah 4:1–3. It is used, however, in Micah 4:7. The data are, however, too shaky to draw a firm conclusion. The expressions in Zechariah 8:22 probably depend on Micah 4:2. (5) 'They will learn to make war.' The reader can make his own judgment about the strength of the argument from Renaud's own comment: 'uniquely postexilic: Pss. 18:35; 144:1; Song 3:8 and a gloss of Ju. 3:2'. Let us dismiss this whole argument with Renaud's own confession (p. 178): 'None of these observations taken in isolation remains decisive by itself, for the absence of such formula in the Bible before a given date does not mean that it was not used at an earlier period.'

In sum, literary critics, on whom the burden of proof rests, have not disproved the tradition (*cf.* Mi. 1:1). We may suppose that in somewhat the same way that the sage makes the thirty 'sayings of the wise' his own in Proverbs 22:17, Isaiah made Micah's oracle his (*cf.* Is. 2:1).

E. The lame become strong (4:6–7)

Verses 6–7 develop, by using three motifs, the theme that the Lord will restore and rule over afflicted Israel in the open-ended future (v. 6a): (1) the Lord will regather them (v. 6b), (2) he will transform them into a strong nation (v. 7a), and (3) he will reign over them forever (v. 7b).

This oracle shares many links with 2:12–13: similar themes (the Lord *gathering* the *remnant* of Israel like *sheep* into the *security* of Jerusalem), the same mood of hope, similar vocabulary ('gather', 'assemble', 'remnant'), and syntax (a shift from referring to the Lord in first person to third person). But there are differences: (1) 'in that day' points to a more remote future, instead of the immediate future (see 4:1a); (2) 'remnant' here is created by God's salvation, not his judgment; (3) the rule of the Lord becomes eternal; and (4) Israel triumphs by remaining secure within Jerusalem, not by leaving it.

6a. DeVries defined *that day*, the particular time in which God is seen to be active in crucial confrontation with his people, as follows: 'It lies just over the horizon of time. But, when that horizon gets extended, deferred beyond immediate expectation, it becomes . . . "that day", a day out there, beyond man's immediate reach and in the hand of God.'[1]

6b. The word *lame* is very rare in the Old Testament (Gn. 32:31 [Heb., 32:32]; Zp. 3:19), suggesting to Renaud (1977; pp. 187f.) that Micah intends an allusion to the laming of Jacob and his renaming as Israel. Martin-Achard, commenting on Genesis 32:23–32, laid the foundation for Renaud's cross-reference: '[the writer] pre-recognizes that this [adventure of Jacob at Penuel] is exemplary for the children

---

[1] S. J. DeVries, *Yesterday, Today and Tomorrow* (Wm B. Eerdmans, 1975), pp. 283–284.

of Israel. The episode at the ford of the Jabbok prefigures that which will be the fate of the sons of the patriarchs.'[1] *And* is ascensive so that one should read: 'the exiles, *even* those I have brought to grief'.

7a. The *remnant*, that which remains after most of Israel is destroyed in judgment (v. 6),[2] now becomes the goal of history. Mays (p. 101) says of them: 'by reason of their nature they are a supernatural and invincible reality within world history (see 5:7–9)'. Philistia did not survive God's judgment because God did not make it a remnant (Am. 1:8); Israel has and will because that is his will (*cf.* Rom. 11). *Strong nation* echoes verse 3. Israel will merge into the future as one of the strong nations, albeit a spiritual nation, drawn to Zion.

7b. Israel is not restored to her pre-fallen state of expressing her own will and power. Rather, she will manifest the Lord's reign over her. According to the New Testament the church has become the strong nation in view here (1 Pet. 2:9–10).

F. Jerusalem's dominion restored (4:8)

This oracle promising the restoration of Jerusalem's former imperial power serves as a hinge between 4:6–7 and 9–13. With the former it shares the symbolism of the flock and of Jerusalem as the watchtower guaranteeing the flock's survival. The movement from the regathering of Israel to Jerusalem comes naturally to a focus upon the latter. It is marked off from it by the phrase 'forever and ever' that terminates verse 7 and by its own form. It is linked by the vocative *you* (masculine in v. 8 and feminine in 4:9–13) with the correlative focus upon Jerusalem. It stands out from verses 9–13 both in form and content. The latter is characterized by 'and now' and moves between Jerusalem's present distress and its future glory whereas verse 8 refers only to Jerusalem's glory.

Westermann[3] noted that 4:8 and 5:2 reuse a very old form of 'tribe saying', such as one can still detect in Genesis 49 and Deuteronomy 33. Note these similarities with 5:2: the

---

[1] R. Martin-Archard, 'Un exégète devant Gen 32, 23–33', dans *Analyse Structurale ex Exegese biblique* (Delachaux et Niestlé, 1971), p. 6.

[2] G. Hasel, *The Remnant: The History and Theology of the Remnant Idea from Genesis to Isaiah* (Andrews University Press, 1972).

[3] C. Westermann, 'Micah 5:1–13' in G. Eichholz, *Herr tue meine Lippen auf,* 5 (E. Mueller, 1964), pp. 54–55.

prophecy starts with 'and you' followed by the name of the addressed city; then comes the promise of the sovereignty to come, followed by the evocation of the days of old – 'the former dominion' (v 8) and the remote origins of the Messiah in 5:2.

Watchtower is a fortified tower around which a group assembles itself for protection. As Israel's heretofore greatest king watched over his flock from invincible Jerusalem, so once again, when kingship is restored, the new Jerusalem will serve the same purpose. Did not the Great Shepherd of the sheep, now ascended to the heavenly Jerusalem with its myriad of angels, proclaim that the gates of hell could not prevail against him (*cf.* Mt. 16:18)? Did he not say that none could snatch his sheep out of his hand (Jn. 10:28)? Did he not promise that he would always be with his people, to the end (Mt. 28:20)? *Stronghold* is literally *Ophel*, an acropolis (*cf.* 2 Ki. 5:24 = 'hill'). Originally it was a Jebusite stronghold taken by David, more particularly the strongly defended eastern slope of the old city of David. Here it is used as a *pars pro toto* to connect the new city with the primitive city of David and to evoke the notion of a strongly defended city (*cf.* Is. 32:14). The figure slides into the new imagery for the city, *the Daughter of Zion*, used in 4:9–13. Because 'city' is feminine in Hebrew, Jerusalem is personified as a daughter (*cf.* Is. 47:1). Mays (p. 103) comments: 'By this combination of names from traditions of the past the little population grouped around Jerusalem is given a vision of what they have been so that they can hear a promise of the restoration of that past.' The reference to *kingship* prepares the way for the full development of this theme in 5:1–4 (esp. 5:2, which shares the same form).

G. God's secret strategy (4:9–13)

The oracle is developed in two stages, 4:9–10 and 11–13, with similar forms pointing to a coherent meaning.[1] Israel's King has a secret strategy behind Jerusalem's present distress, which extends from the Assyrian invasion into the Babylonian exile. Through the exile he plans Zion's liberation (vv. 9–10), and through the invasion against Jerusalem he conspires the defeat of her enemies (vv. 11–13). Each stage is marked off

[1] Renaud (1977), pp. 200–202.

by 'now', the initial word in the Hebrew text (*cf.* AV and RSV), directing attention to the present distress (vv. 9, 11). Each moves from the present affliction to the glorious future by means of a vocative addressed to the 'Daughter of Zion' (vv. 10, 13), accompanied by an imperative ('writhe . . .', 'rise. . .'), followed by a causal clause introduced by 'for' and describing that future. Their unity is reinforced by their identical lengths of seven lines each. As we shall see, 'writhe in agony' (v. 10) refers to the pains of childbirth (*cf.* AV), which figure gives hope in suffering. Zion's present suffering is not locked up in misfortune, but opens the door of hope to salvation and victory. For the remnant, as with all God's children, the punishment is not penal but remedial. For them, suffering in the 'already' is part of the salvation in the 'not yet'. By contrast, God has so arranged history that what appears to the enemy as victory in battle leads to defeat in the war.

9. The *now* has a certain width of reference, embracing both the Assyrian and Babylonian crises. Prophets saw the future not diachronically but synchronically. Paul van Imschoot puts it this way: 'The tableaux by which the prophets announce the future often lack prespective, so that it is difficult at times to distinguish if heralded events, delineated on the same plane, refer to the same epoch or must be separated by centuries.'[1]

Opinions are divided on whether or not the *king* is God or a descendant of David at the time of the crisis. The latter interpretation entails taking the rhetorical question sarcastically: while challenging them with a question that on the surface seems to aim at encouraging them in their king, Micah actually means that faith in this wooden puppet is misguided. If God is intended, then he means that Zion should stop crying because God knows what he is doing in spite of the way things seem. Since, as we have anticipated, this is an oracle of salvation, not reproach, the second interpretation is better. Renaud (1977; p. 205) defends it by the parallel, second stage (see p. 177), especially verse 12, where God is named, and by Jeremiah 8:19, a close parallel in form and thought. *Counsellor* is another epithet for God (*cf.* king/counsellor in Is. 9:6). As verse 12 makes clear, the one 'wonderful in counsel' (Is. 28:29; *cf.* Je. 32:19) has a plan of salvation even in the

---

[1] Van Imschoot, *Theology of the Old Testament*, 1, p. 166.

calamity. 'Counsellor' in Hebrew refers to one who is not only able to formulate plans, but, as P. A. H. de Boer[1] shows, to perform an action that maintains or restores life and whose effect is security. Nations do not know this about God (v. 12), but Israel should. The figure of *pain. . . in labour* refers here only to the pains of captivity (*cf.* Je. 4:31; 6:24; 13:21; *etc.*).

10. *Writhe in agony* (Heb., *ḥûl*) constitutes a pun on *pain* (Heb., *ḥîl*, v. 9). The NIV obscures it by not translating the next imperative, 'labour to bring forth' (AV). The prophet turns his rebuke of Israel for crying in pain as a woman in labour into a command so to labour that she causes a new-born child to come out into the light. The kingdom of God comes through trial, and so Israel must pass through trial – leave the security of the old city (*cf.* 2 Ki. 25:2-7; *cf.* Je. 52:7), camp in the open field (*cf.* Je 6:25; 14:18), and go to Babylon – to become the new Israel. The grammar and repetition – '*there* you will be rescued, *there* the Lord will redeem you' – focuses attention not on trial but on liberation. God chose Babylon because in Micah's pagan world it functioned as the equivalent of Rome in the Middle Ages and of Mecca in Islam. The darkest land will become the place where the daylight of the new age dawns.

J. T. Willis [2] plausibly dates the composition of the oracle to 705 BC, when Isaiah predicted that, because of his folly in connection with the visit by the embassy from Merodach-Baladan, king of Babylon, Hezekiah's house would be ruined, his wealth carried to Babylon, and his sons serve the pagan king as eunuchs (2 Ki. 20:12-19 = Is. 39:1-8).

11. The prophet now shifts from the King's secret strategy regarding Jerusalem to his game-plan for the invading nations. *Many nations* fits the scenario of the Assyrian invasion better than the Babylonian. Lindblom,[3] comparing verse 11 to Isaiah 29:7 (*cf.* also Is. 8:9-10; 17:12-14; 22:6; Ho. 10:10), refers them to the various national units that made up the imperial Assyrian army (see the Introduction, p. 143). Lutz[4] calls

[1] P. A. H. de Boer, 'The Counsellor' in *Wisdom in Israel and in the Ancient Near East*, *VT* 3 (E. J. Brill, 1965), pp. 42–73.

[2] J. T. Willis, 'Review of *Structure et Attaches litteraires de Michee IV-V* by B. Renaud', *VT* 15 (1965), pp. 402–403.

[3] Lindblom, *Micha literarisch untersucht.*

[4] H. M. Lutz, *Jahwe, Jerusalem und die Voelker* (Neukirchner Verlag Erziehungsvereins, 1968), pp. 91–95. He argues for a pre-exilic date on p. 96.

attention to the songs of Zion, which may have been composed in connection with the Assyrian crisis. The Babylonian army is not represented in this way in any parallel texts which have this motif. Quite the opposite in fact, since many nations are its victims. The prophet exposes the enemy's plan by once again allowing his subjects to speak for themselves. *Defiled* means 'to make profane', that is, they desire so to destroy the walls protecting the sanctity of Zion's sacred courts and its Temple, which contains the Lord's Most Holy Place, that they will rid the earth of God's holiness. Mays (p. 109) notes: 'When nations see themselves as the centre of history and seek a destiny that fulfills their power, they can tolerate no Zion; they are gripped with a compelling need to destroy whatever stands in judgment and restraint on their pride.'

12–13. Their hubris is all part of God's plan (*cf.* Is. 10:5–11). They are unwitting tools of their own destruction, for the Lord is using their animosity and pride to bring about their own defeat, just as he outwitted Satan in the cross of Jesus Christ (*cf.* 1 Cor. 2:7–8). They gather against Jerusalem, but really it is the Lord who gathers them; they plan to lay bare the Temple precincts, but the Lord will break them; they come to strip Jerusalem, but instead they will be stripped, and the wealth they leave behind will be offered up to the Lord. *Sheaves* on *the threshing-floor* (v. 12) pictures victims brought to a place of judgment (*cf.* Is. 21:10; Je. 51:33; Ho. 13:3), and *thresh* (v. 13) pictures the punitive act itself (Am. 1:3). They exhorted one another in their self-will to rid the earth of the Lord's presence, now the Lord commands Zion to rid the earth of them. The ox pulling the threshing-sledge represents the people of God. She is supernaturally equipped with *horns of iron*, symbolizing her invincibility, and with *hoofs of bronze*, with which she treads the pride and pretensions of the enemy exceedingly fine. The prophecy began to be fulfilled when God slaughtered the Assyrian imperial horde at the gates of Jerusalem. Jeremiah may have had it in mind when he likened Babylon to a threshing-floor (Je. 51:33). The promise, not completely fulfilled, passed into the heritage of the church, where it continues to find its spiritual fulfilment (Mt. 16:18). God is appropriately called *Lord of all the earth*, for his secret strategy includes victory over all nations.

H. The once and future king (5:1–6)

Although the text is uneven, opening up the possibility that 5:1–6 is a composite of oracles, it is best treated as a whole because of its formal and thematic unity. An inclusio including the first person pronoun, 'we/us', and a reference to the Assyrian invasion (beginning with its victory and terminating in its defeat) frames the oracle. Like the preceding oracle it moves from the present distress to future salvation, more particularly from the humiliation of Jerusalem's king (v. 1) to the Messiah's victory (vv. 2–5). There is a progression in the section: from the Messiah's salvation which has its beginning with God, who raises him up as his governor (v. 2), through the faithful community that gives him birth (v. 3), to the Shepherd-King who, by faith in God, extends his rule to the ends of the earth so that his people live securely (v. 4), and finally to his subordinates who subjugate Assyria (vv. 5b–6a).

1. The oracle commences with a form like the preceding one: 'And now' (missed by the NIV), referring to the present distress, followed by vocative of address (*O daughter of troops*, AV), with imperative (*marshal your troops*), followed by *for*. But whereas in 4:10 and 13 that form introduced the promise of salvation, here it introduces the present distress. Moreover, the theme changes from God's secret strategy to God's 'once and future king'. As Merlin predicted King Arthur should come again to rule once more,[1] so Micah saw that the ideal David would reappear as the Messiah – theological shorthand for Israel's ideal future ruler.

The *siege* in view, to judge from the rest of the book and verse 6, is that of Sennacherib.[2] Accordingly the 'now' (AV, RSV) is 701 BC, and if so, the *ruler* is Hezekiah (see the Introduction, pp. 141–143). The alternative readings for the verb and noun rendered *troops*, 'walls' (NIV mg., and the RSV and NEB text) are based on the LXX, which read the root *gdr* instead of *gdd*. The MT is preferred because the verbal form in question with *gdr* is otherwise unattested. 'Daughter' (AV; *city*, NIV) with a common noun signifies that one possesses the noun's quality;

[1] Alfred, Lord Tennyson, *Morte d'Arthur*.
[2] Mays (p. 114) says that 'in descriptions of a particular historical occasion the term ["siege" (Heb., *māṣôr*)] is used only of Nebuchadnezzar's sieges of Jerusalem', but he fails to tell his reader the more significant fact that in 2 Ch. 32:10 Sennacherib is quoted as using this very word!

in this case, 'warlike'. *Troops* evokes the small remnant left of Israel's army gathered behind Jerusalem's gates (*cf.* 1:8–16; 2:12). Isaiah also likened the Assyrian army to a *rod* (Is. 10:5, 15, 24). To *strike . . . on the cheek* signifies humiliation; the victim is so defenceless he cannot even defend his face (*cf.* Jb. 16:10; Ps. 3:7; Is. 50:6; La. 3:30). The tense should be present, 'they strike' (RSV), to judge from the introductory 'now', omitted by the NIV.

2. *But* reverses the situation from one of the present defeat to one of the Messiah's triumph. The kings born in proud Jerusalem failed; the Messiah incarnated in lowly Bethlehem triumphs. The Lord addresses personified *Bethlehem* with the announcement that he will launch the Messianic age from there. He chose Bethlehem to exhibit paradoxically Messiah's inauspicious and yet at the same time his most auspicious origins. *Ephrathah*, evocatively meaning 'fruitful', is the name of a district in Judah where *Bethlehem* was located (Ps. 132:6).[1] The address, by drawing heavily upon 1 Samuel 17:12 (of the seven words in v. 2a, b three occur here: Bethlehem, Ephrathah, Judah; *cf.* Ru. 1:2), reaches back for the Messiah's origins in the pure springs of Jesse and David and ignores his later decadent and disappointing lineage born in Jerusalem. Isaiah presented the same truth by comparing the Messiah to a branch springing from the stump of Jesse (Is. 11:1). The implication becomes explicit in the last clause, *whose origins are . . . from ancient times*. The oracle is moulded into a form of an ancient tribal saying to match its content (see 4:8). Micah in this chiaroscuro takes us back to the cradle of David's line and exhibits the Messiah as representing a new beginning out of a famous heritage. As God unexpectedly anointed David and rescued his people upon the failure of Saul, so he will give his people David's true successor after the defeat of David's descendants.

The clause qualifying *Bethlehem Ephrathah* reads literally, 'insignificant with regard to its existence among the clans of Judah'; that is, as David was the least of his brothers, so Bethlehem played only a very limited role among Judah's

---

[1] The LXX reads 'Bethlehem (= Heb., *bet-lehem*], House [= Heb., *bet*] of Ephrathath'. For this reason some critics delete Bethlehem and read instead, 'But you, O House of Ephrathah' (*cf.* JB). Since all texts and versions read 'Bethlehem', it is preferable to explain 'House' with Ephrathah in the LXX as due to dittography from *bet-lehem*.

clans. The adjective rendered *small* describes here not a quantity but a quality. Elsewhere it occurs in connection with 'weak' and 'despised' (Jdg. 6:15; Ps. 119:141) and is rendered by 'least' and 'lowly' in the NIV (*cf.* 1 Sa. 9:21, where it is contrasted with the normal word for 'small'). Matthew 2:6 reformulates the text to make its meaning plain: by virtue of its divine choice as the site for the Messiah's birth the most insignificant place will bring forth the most pre-eminent person. Bethlehem, too insignificant to be mentioned by the cartographer of the book of Joshua or in Micah's catalogue of Judah's cities of defence (Mi. 1:10–15; *cf.* 2 Ch. 11:5–12), is today incredibly the centre of pilgrimages from around the world and is universally renowned because Jesus Christ fulfilled this verse. That fulfilment confirms both the word of God and its message that the Lord delights to chose the weak and despised things of this world to shame the wise and strong, that man may boast in the Lord alone (1 Cor. 1:18–31). *Clans* designates the military-political subdivisions of a tribe consisting of about a thousand men each. Matthew reads 'clans' (Heb., *b'lpy*) as 'chiefs' (Heb., *b'lwpy*; *cf.* NIV note). Again, the difference may not be textual but interpretative. By the change he aims to form a better contrast between the 'ruler' (Gk., *hēgoumenos*) who comes out of Bethlehem with the 'chiefs' (Gk., *hēgemosin*) who come out of the other tribes. Matthew also conflates 2 Samuel 5:2 into the text.

The next clause is awkward: 'from you for me he will come forth to be ruler in Israel'. *For me*, which enjoys an emphatic position, may owe its inspiriation to 1 Samuel 16:1, underscoring the fact that the Messiah, like David, serves the Lord's plans. He is not a sultan but a vicegerent under his superior. The prophets studiously avoid entitling him 'king'. Note how Micah speaks instead of a *ruler*.

'From everlasting' (AV; *cf.* NIV mg.) was probably based on a presumption of Christ's pre-existence. The Hebrew (*'ōlām*), used in connection with either the created order or God himself, can mean 'from eternity on' (*cf.* Pss. 25:6; 90:2). It can also designate 'ancient times' within history, *i.e.* the distant past. If the reference to Bethlehem aims to evoke the memory of Jesse and David, then the latter meaning fits this context best.

Origins, in cognate Semitic languages, may celebrate a supernatural, quasi-divine origin of the king. On this evidence some scholars suggest that the word here also aims to underscore the Messiah's supernatural origins. This is possible, but see the NIV mg. 'Goings out' is from the same root as the verb rendered literally in the previous line of this verse, 'he will come forth' (*cf.* AV.) There it refers to his historical origins, which is probably true also in this parallel line. The Messiah, humanly speaking, will have the finest royal blood flowing in his veins (that is, he will be a servant of the Lord) and be an heir of God's eternal covenant with David (*cf.* 2 Sa. 7:8–16; Ps. 89:35–37).

3. From God's proclamation Micah draws the logical inference (note the use of *therefore*) that *Israel will be abandoned* (*i.e.* the *now* of distress, 4:9, 11; 5:1, including the exile, 4:10) until the Messiah comes to inaugurate the new age. (The verb is best translated impersonally, 'one will give them [Israel] up', so NIV, instead of personally, 'he will . . .', AV, RSV.) *She who is in labour* to produce the new age is Zion (*cf.* 4:10), a metonymy for the covenant community. That is to say, God will use the believing community as the agent through which the Messiah will come into the world. The community and family that gave birth to Jesus Christ were characterized by faith, prayer and the fullness of the Holy Spirit (*cf.* Lk. 1:5–2:40). The nucleus of the new age centring on the Messiah will be constituted by *the rest of his brothers.* Who are they? They are the Messiah's people who were naturally joined to him by blood and history and who, by conversion, spiritually join him and the believing remnant (*cf.* 4:7). *The rest* refers to the totality of brothers of which the remnant was a part.[1] *Return* has a nuance of conversion.[2] The term *Israelites* (more literally 'sons of Israel'), came to have a religious connotation and is so used here.[3] With the conversion of elect Israel, the Messiah will inaugurate the new age that spoils the nations. One hundred and twenty of the Messiah's brothers were gathered in the Upper Room when he sent the Holy Spirit who turned the world upside down (Lk. 3:16; Acts 2).

4. Having launched his kingdom with his brothers, the Messiah *will stand* (*i.e.* endure forever; *cf.* Pss. 33:11; 111:3;

[1] R. de Vaux, 'Le reste d'Israel d'après les prophètes', *RB* 42 (1933), p. 528, n. 1.

[2] Nielsen, *Oral Tradition*, pp. 88–89.

[3] R. de Vaux, *Histoire ancienne d'Israel*, 2: *La Periode des Juges* (Lecoffre, 1973), p. 65.

130:3; Is. 14:24) because he rules in the strength of the Lord and to the ends of the earth. Unlike David's unfaithful sons who broke covenant with the Lord by trusting in their military might (*cf.* 5:10–11), the Messiah, like David (1 Sa. 17:38–47), will keep covenant by trusting God (*cf.* Pss. 91:14; 20:2–3, 6, 8; *passim*). His government is depicted under the imagery of shepherding, which again evokes memories of David's government (2 Sa. 5:2; 7:7; *cf.* Mt. 2:6). The Lord Jesus appropriated this imagery to himself to picture his just government of and care for his subjects (Jn. 10; Heb. 13:20; 1 Pet. 5:4).[1] The Messiah's *greatness* evokes the promise made to David (2 Sa. 7:9); but in contrast to David, whose kingdom consisted only of the promised land, his greater son will fulfil the greater vision of a universal kingdom (Dt. 33:17; Pss. 2:8; 22:28; 59:13; 72:8).

5–6. Verse 4 connects the peace and security of the flock with the Messiah's universal conquest of hostile forces. In verses 5–6 the defeat of Assyria and the ensuing peace are representative of the Messiah's yet wider triumph. Moreover, the mention that *seven shepherds . . . eight leaders* will defeat Assyria signifies that the Messiah will conquer through his people. By an inclusio – *he will be their peace* (v. 5a) and *he will deliver us* (v. 6b) – Micah guards against any thought that the leaders act independently of the Messiah. By using *we/us* the prophet identifies himself with the Messiah's undefeated community of faith. Micah mentions *Assyria* because the Assyrian armies were invading the land at the time of composition. We need to recall that prophets addressed their contemporaries and referred to the future in terms drawn from their own historical circumstances (*cf.* Is. 25:10; Am. 9:12). The reference to the *land of Nimrod* (= Babylonia) confirms our suggested date of composition. It is mentioned only here and in Genesis 10:8–12 (= 1 Ch. 1:10), where it clearly coincides with Babylonia. The authors of both texts probably mentioned the land of Nimrod after Assyria to suggest that Assyria prevailed over Babylonia.[2] Instructively, the word for 'leaders' (*nasîkê*) in 5:5 (Heb., 5:4) is found in Assyrian texts describing Sargon's campaign in Syria-Palestine in 720 BC (see the Introduction, p. 141). Today the Messiah defeats his arch-enemy,

[1] J. G. S. S. Thomson, 'The Shepherd-Ruler Concept in the OT and its application in the NT', *SJT* 8 (1955).
[2] E. Lipinski, 'Nimrod et Assur', *RB* 73 (1966), pp. 77–93.

Satan, and brings the world under his dominion through under-shepherds endowed with his Spirit (*cf.* Eph. 4:7–12; 1 Pet. 5:1–4).

I. A fragrance of life, a smell of death (5:7–9)

A new oracle, linked to the preceding one in the Hebrew text by the same initial word 'and it will be' (= 'will be', NIV) in 5:5, 7, 8 and 'rescue' in 5:6 (rendered 'deliver' in the NIV) and 8, foretells more specifically that the Messiah will expand his kingdom among the nations through the remnant, introduced in 4:7. Verses 7 and 8 share a strikingly similar structure: (1) *the subject*, the future presence of the remnant among the nations;[1] (2) *the predicate*, represented by a simile in two synonymous parallels ('like dew', 'like showers', in antithesis to 'like a lion', 'like a young lion';[2] and (3) *an explanation* of the similes by relative clauses ('which . . .'). The rigorously similar structures contrast radically the remnant's twofold concurrent ministries among the nations: being a source of salvation to some, and an instrument of destruction to others. In either case, God makes them triumphant. The prophecy finds its fulfilment in the early church. Paul, including himself with the other apostles, said that God always led them, the aroma of Christ, in triumphal procession. Among those being saved they were the fragrance of life, but among those perishing they were the savour of death (2 Cor. 2:14–16). This same double ministry continues to be exercised by the church today. The oracle ends with a command (v. 9, JB) to the remnant to fulfil its mission (*contra* NIV).[3]

7. The future tense, *will be*, connects the fulfilment of this oracle with the coming of the Messiah. The weak *remnant* forged out of the Babylonian captivity will become the strong nation that overturns the tables of history (4:7). After the Messiah comes, the vanquished remnant will become the victors. They conquer not in their own strength but with the

[1] The LXX and Syr. add 'among the nations' in v. 7, forming a matching parallel with v. 8. Perhaps it should be withdrawn from both verses because of its redundancy.

[2] Hebrew has six mostly indistinguishable words for 'lion'.

[3] The ancient versions read the verb form 'will be lifted up' as indicative, but the Hebrew text has an unexpected volitive form which should be honoured.

Messiah, who rules in the strength of the Lord (v. 4). Micah refers to the remnant by the name *Jacob*, for that patriarch too was 'lame' (*cf.* 4:6) before he became 'Israel' and was strong enough to fulfil the dual promise to Abraham that those who cursed him would be cursed and those who blessed him would be blessed. In either case Abraham prevails, for all nations bless themselves through his seed (Gn. 12:3; 22:17–18). Because God was faithful to the promise and fulfilled it through the remnant, Abraham today is the father of many nations (Rom. 4:16–17). *Dew* and *showers* are always signs of divine benediction. They evoke both the mysterious heavenly origin of the remnant and its life-giving efficacy that refreshes the earth. *Wait for* would be better rendered 'wait upon' (*cf.* JB). The Hebrew word does not mean to 'delay', or to 'tarry,' but 'to look for something with eager anticipation'.[1] Dew and rain do not come through the manipulations of impotent man but through the providential actions of the gracious, omnipotent, faithful God. The word rendered *linger* can also mean 'hope for' or 'expect' and is a close synonym for 'trust', the preferred meaning because of its parallel *wait for*.[2] The key to the simile's meaning is given in the phrase *from the Lord*. Allen (p. 353) remarks: 'Man is singularly impotent over water supplies. He can store rainwater and tap underground springs, but his native helplessness before the cruel sun comes to the fore in times of prolonged drought. Ultimately man can neither help nor hinder the supply of so basic a commodity.'

8. Micah had likened Zion among the nations to a threshing bull before the Assyrian horde (4:13). Now he compares the remnant among the rest of the nations to a fierce and fearsome *lion* (the NIV's 'young lion' is doubtful) wreaking a terrible carnage among sheep. Four predicates unpack the metaphor: *as it goes* (the first verb in the Heb. text) speaks of sovereignty; *mauls* (better, 'tramples') of subjugating, destructive power; *mangles* of death; and *no-one can rescue* of God's inescapable punishment (*cf.* Dt. 32:39; Jb. 10:7; Ps. 50:22; Ho. 5:14). The Spirit of Christ in his church gives her power to extend his rule universally in spite of even Satan and his minions (Mt. 12:28; 16:18–20; Jn. 16:33; *passim*).

9. In the light of the promise of verses 7 and 8 the remnant

---

[1] *TWOT* 2, p. 791.   [2] *Ibid.*, p. 374.

is now addressed directly and commanded to fulfil its mandate. The command explains that death is dished out to their *enemies* and, by implication, life distributed to those who submit to God's rule. Micah validates the command in verse 15 of the next oracle. Behind the remnant stands the command, that is, the word of God. Those who carry out the Great Commission will prevail (*cf.* Mt. 28:17–20).

J. The Lord protects his kingdom (5:10–15)

In the final oracle of the series in chapters 4 – 5, which is against the nations (note v. 15), the Lord, consistently using the first person with the initial verb of each stich or line of verse, proclaims that he will protect his kingdom. This he will do, first, by purging it from the unholiness within and so preserve it from his wrath (vv. 10–14) and, second, by punishing foes without and so protect his people (v. 15). His punishment of Israel is remedial, and of the nations penal. All Israel, not the remnant, is addressed in verses 10–14, for they need cleansing. The Aramaic translation, the Targum, made this clear by substituting 'the peoples' in verses 10, 11, 13 and 14 for the ambiguous second person pronoun. More specifically they need cleansing from the three forms of apostasy, lumped together by the anaphora 'I will destroy'; *viz.*, replacing confidence in God with military might (vv. 10–11), magic and witchcraft (v. 12), and idolatry (vv. 13–14). The Lord himself will pop Israel's titanic bubble of pomp and pride. By this proclamation he aims to sober unbelievers and to strengthen the hands of believing Israel. This theme and aim favourably fit the situation in 701 BC (see the Introduction, pp. 141–143). The oracle presumes an enemy is attacking without and that Israel is responding with human power.[1] Through the Lord's miraculous salvation Israel learns to trust him, and the enemy experiences his anger. The prophecy is generic (see 4:1), finding immediate fulfilment in 701 BC and a greater fulfilment in the Messianic age (see p. 168).

After the anacrusis marking off the new oracle (v. 10a: ' "In that day," declares the Lord'), there are two unequal halves

[1] J. T. Willis, 'The Authenticity and Meaning of Micah 5:9–14', *ZAW* 81 (1969), p. 356.

with regard to content – verses 10b to 14, and verse 15. These are formally distinguished by employing in verses 10–14 synonymous parallelism – the pronoun 'you'/'your' at the end of each half-line and the phrase 'from among you' in verses 10, 13 and 14; and, by contrast, by employing in verse 15 formal parallelism (*i.e.* lines not semantically complementing one another) without the second person pronoun.

Verses 10–15 are linked to verses 7–9 by the catch-words 'destroy' (vv. 9, 10–13) and 'your hand' (vv. 9, 13). Regarding the latter Allen (p. 357) comments: '*Your hand(s)* in vv. 12f. strikingly repeats the phrase of v. 9 as if to warn that the hands of God's people must be emptied of all that smacks of help not derived from God if he is to give victory to their hands when they strike in battle.'

10a. *In that day* (see 4:6) links the Lord's protection of his kingdom with the whole drama of Israel's future redemption as set forth in chapters 4 – 5. The Lord's slaughtering of the Assyrian in answer to Hezekiah's prayer serves as an exemplar of its fulfilment in the messianic age.

10b–11. *Destroy* (Heb., *krt*) specifically means 'to purge', that is, to remove unholiness by punishment in order to preserve the community (*cf.* Lv. 17:10; 20:3, 5–6, *etc.*). Confidence in horse-drawn chariots and fortified cities[1] threatened Israel's covenantal relationship with God, which was rooted in trust, no less than did magic and idolatry. Perhaps pride of place is given to this false security because it had first place in Israel's heart. The scriptural notices that the land bristled with military hardware at the time Sennacherib invaded the land (*cf.* 2 Ki. 18:13, 24; 2 Ch. 32:1–5; Is. 31:1) find mute support in Hezekiah's still extant water-tunnel. The church today will not prevail through her own resources – an educated clergy, the technical know-how of expositors and educational directors, inviting buildings – but only through faith in God. She must confess once again with David: 'some trust in horses, and some in chariots, but we trust in the name of the Lord our God' (Ps. 20:7). This psalm by Israel's military genius shows that the Scriptures do not decry the use of means; they discredit confidence in them (*cf.* Dt. 17:16–17; Ps. 149:6–9; Ne. 4:9, 13–14).

[1] Hebrew parallelism represents by 'horses' in one line and 'chariots' in the next two aspects of the same referent; the same holds true of 'cities' and 'strongholds' in v. 11.

12. Isaiah in his parallel oracle (Is. 2:6-8) gives pride of place to sorcery, perhaps because he wants to emphasize its foreign source. Eastern occultism and Philistine divination were totally alien to Israel's covenant (*cf.* Ex. 22:18; Lv. 19:26). Apostate Israel, like secular man, wanted to indulge her appetites in the present apart from spiritual and ethical considerations, and at the same time guarantee her continued prosperity into the future by her own might and the help of the occult. The ethical monotheism of the prophets, however, insists that future peace and prosperity are contingent on faith and ethical behaviour in the present.

13-14. Pagan religion sought to manipulate the innate forces of life within nature through magical words and ritual. *Carved images* were part of the magic. In the high places (see 1:6) the *sacred stones* (Heb., *maṣṣebôt*) served as stylized representations of the male deity, Baal (*cf.* 2 Ki. 3:2; 10:26-27), and the wooden Asherah represented the female deity. *Cities* would be better rendered with the NEB as 'blood-spattered altars',[1] perhaps a reference to the hollow in the sacred stones to receive the blood of sacrifice. The metonymy, *the work of your hands*, emphasizes that the carved stone images are the products of human engineering and as such represent another expression of man's attempt to have life apart from the Creator. Secular man more effectively manipulates life by his use of science than his ancestors did by magic, but no more than they can he secure eternal life for himself. By continuing to substitute the creation for the Creator, he individually deprives himself of eternal life and collectively hastens his eternal death.

15. *Vengeance* has negative connotations and does not adequately represent the Hebrew word (*nāqām*) which signifies that a ruler secures his sovereignty by defensive vindication. He keeps his community whole by delivering his wronged subjects and by punishing those who do not obey him. It

---

[1] Though 'cities' is the usual meaning of the Hebrew word, attested also in the LXX and Vulg., the mention of 'cities' here is curious because they have already been mentioned in v. 10 and provide a rather bad parallel to 'Asherah poles'. J. D. Michaelis, and many commentators since, understood the word as a place of trees. In certain Ugaritic texts the word occurs in parallel with 'carved images', a coupling similar to this one. Some scholars think that the Ugaritic word is related to an Arabic cognate and on that basis suggest 'blood-daubed stone' (*cf.* NEB). Others connect it with a different Ugaritic root and come up with 'god-protector'.

signifies the sole prerogative of God to redress wrongs against his kingdom.[1] Should the subject take matters into his own hand and avenge himself, he acts in unbelief, directly challenging both the sovereign's character and power to defend his interests. Israel's Sovereign responds not dispassionately but with *anger* against those who thumb their noses at him. Some things need to be said and done with passion. From Micah to the present the Lord has preserved his kingdom against attacks from without. He will finally execute his protective power on behalf of his elect when Christ returns (2 Thes. 1:8; *cf.* Lk. 18:7–8; 21:22; Rev. 6:10). Until then the church must not tarnish her Lord's glory by avenging herself (*cf.* Dt. 32:35; Heb. 10:30; Rom. 12:19) or by trusting in her own resources.

III. HOPE IN DARKNESS (6:1 – 7:20)

A. How to stay alive (6:1–8)[2]

After an anacrusis calling the people to hear the final section of his book (v. 1a), Micah's litigation speech, delivered on the Lord's behalf, bars Israel from the protection of the Temple because she has not fulfilled her covenantal obligations. The oracle's form, though dramatic and complex, can be readily analysed in the light of other lawsuits known from extra-biblical and biblical treaties (*cf.* Dt. 32:1; Jdg. 2:1–5; 6:7–10; 10:10–16; Pss. 50; 80; 81; Is. 1:2–3; Je. 2:4–13)[3] as follows:

I. A description of the judgment scene (vv. 1b–2).
   A. The Lord summons Micah to plead his case before the mountains (v. 1b).
   B. Micah summons the mountains to hear (v. 2).

---

[1] B. Anderson, *Out of the Depths* (Westminster Press, 1983), p. 90; G. Mendenhall, *The Tenth Generation: The Origins of the Biblical Tradition* (Johns Hopkins University Press, 1973), pp. 69–104.

[2] This heading is taken from E. R. Achtemeier, 'How to Stay Alive', *Theology and Life* 6/4 (1963), pp. 275–282.

[3] The literature on this form is extensive. Suffice it here to cite a more recent work with good bibliography: G. W. Ramsay, 'Speech-Forms in Hebrew Law and Prophetic Oracles', *JBL* 96/1 (1977), pp. 45–58.

II. Plaintiff's speech (vv. 3–5).
   A. Summary accusation: Israel is without excuse for not reciprocating the Lord's love (v. 3).
   B. Accusation defended (vv. 4–5).
      1. The Lord delivered them from Egypt with excellent leadership (v. 4).
      2. The Lord brought them into the promised land through the most untoward circumstances (v. 5).
         a. He transformed Balaam's curse into a blessing (v. 5a).
         b. He led them across the Jordan (v. 5b).[1]
   C. Refutation of defence (vv. 6–8).
      1. Ritual purity cannot win the Lord's favour (vv. 6–7).
      2. The Lord wants ethical purity (v. 8).

The speech is developed by the repeated use of 'what'. The Lord initiates the prosecution by asking *what* fault they find with him (vv. 3–5). A worshipper, representing the nation, asks with *what* sacrifice the Lord will be pleased (vv. 6–7). The Lord has the last word: he has made known *what* he wants (v. 8). The argument also develops in pairs as the above outline discloses. The legal complaint aims not to sentence the people to punishment but to facilitate a restoration of the covenant.[2]

We can plausibly suppose that besieged worshippers in Jerusalem, seeking access to the Temple precincts to win the Lord's favour and protection against the aggressive Assyrians, provoked this complaint. The Supreme Priest through his surrogate 'priest', Micah, protects the sanctity of his Temple by turning the apostates away, yet he concludes by opening a door of hope if they will return to their covenant obligations. Micah functions in the priests' stead because the mercenary priests are the very ones who led the people astray into false, ritualistic theology (*cf.* 3:11).

1a. The anacrusis calls Israel to hear this third division of the book with a validation of its divine source (see 1:1). The focus of the book now shifts from unfolding the future drama of Israel's redemption (chs. 4 – 5) back to Israel's sin and present crisis. Verses 1b–2 are the proper introduction

---

[1] The NIV supplies 'journey', but see Jos. 3:1.
[2] Ramsey, 'Speech-Forms'.

to the lawsuit.

1b–2. The trial scene includes the Plaintiff (the Lord), the messenger on behalf of the Plaintiff (Micah), the witnesses (the mountains), and the defendant (Israel). The command *Stand up* (masculine singular) is addressed to Micah. The prophet reports his call in order to validate his prophetic investiture. *Plead* means to 'reclaim one's rights'.[1] Instead of *your case* we ought to read 'my case', because Micah is commissioned to represent the Lord's grievances, not his own; accordingly verse 1b should begin and end with quotation marks to indicate that the prophet is addressed by God. As a literary device, the personified mountains are then called upon by the prophet to serve as witnesses that, in barring Israel from the Temple, God is acting consistently with the original terms of the covenant mediated through Moses. Israel has an unfulfilled obligation to him.

With solemn dignity Micah carries out his mission. He summons the witnesses, introduces the Plaintiff, and finally, with dramatic suspense, names the accused, Israel. The mountains are called *everlasting* (better, 'ancient') *foundations* to emphasize that they are the oldest parts of the earth and as such can best serve as witnesses. *Lodging a charge* means 'to establish the right, what is just and unjust'.[2] Again, quotation marks should begin and end verse 2 to make it clear that Micah is speaking on behalf of God.

3. The Lord opens his case by asking two questions. First, '*What have I done to you?*', a defensive question to protect his own innocence. The second question, '*How have I burdened you?*', is designed to take the initiative away from Israel and to put her on the defensive. She thinks that she has a legitimate complaint against the Lord for inflicting intolerable burdens on her, and then rejecting the sacrifices which she offered in worship in order to win his favour. Israel thought she had a complaint against God. But in reality she has wronged the Lord, and so he has a complaint against her. His command to 'testify' (AV; *answer*, NIV) against him (that is to formulate precise accusations before the Tribunal; *cf.* Nu. 35:30; 1 Sa. 12:3; 2 Sa. 1:16; Is. 3:9), is ironic.

4. With pathos and tenderness aimed straight at Israel's

---

[1] J. Limburg, 'The Root *RIB* and the Prophetic Lawsuit Speeches', *JBL* 88 (1969), pp. 291–304.
[2] *THAT* 1, pp. 730–731.

heart, he twice calls them 'my people' (vv. 3, 5). The speech, full of grace and truth, aims to reprove and to woo Israel back to her covenant obligations, not to pronounce sentence upon her with withering words. The Lord justifies his implied accusation that Israel has wronged him in not requiting his love by rehearsing his grace towards her, beginning with the exodus from *Egypt* under divinely provided leaders and concluding with the miraculous events which marked the end of her sojourn in the wilderness and the crossing of the Jordan. He probably mentions his gift of outstanding leaders at the beginning to prompt Israel to realize that something must be wrong if he has inflicted on the nation such disastrous leaders as she now has (*cf.* ch. 3). *Redeemed*, meaning 'to free someone who is bound by legal or cultic obligation by the payment of a price' (Mays, p. 134), contrasts dramatically with Israel's attempt to win God's favour. How could she think that costly sacrifices would buy her deliverance from the Assyrians when the Lord had so freely and graciously delivered her from the Egyptians?

5. He conflates the Balak-Balaam incident, which occurred at Shittim (*cf.* Nu. 22:1), with the crossing of the Jordan to Gilgal (Jos. 2:1; 3:1; 4:19) to evoke the memory that as Israel crossed the Red Sea in the face of Pharaoh with his magicians, so also she crossed the Jordan in the face of Balak with his great prophet, Balaam. If Israel's God ruled the floods and conquered Israel's political and spiritual enemies at the beginning, why could he not now deliver Israel from Sennacherib and his religious pretensions by again employing some force of nature? The problem is obviously not the Lord, but Israel. Both events occurred at the same season (*cf.* Ex. 12:1–3 and Jos. 4:19; *cf.* Dt. 6:21–23; 26:6–9; Jos. 24:2–13) and may have been celebrated at the Temple when Micah delivered this complaint.

6–7. Instead of responding to such a wonderful Lord with loving and obedient hearts, Micah's generation transformed the covenant into a contract. In a series of parallel lines, each beginning with a question, a representative 'worshipper' seeks to establish the price that will win God's favour by raising the bid ever higher. Holocausts? One-year-old *calves* (already more costly)? Thousands of *rams*? Myriads of torrents of *oil*? Or, the highest price of all, the cruel sacrifice of a child? He can bid no higher. Outwardly he appears spiritual as he bows before the Most High with gift in hand. But his insulting questions betray a desperately wicked heart. Blinded to God's goodness and character, he reasons within his own depraved frame of reference. He need not change; God must change. He compounds his sin of refusing to repent by suggesting that God, like man, can be bought. His willingness to raise the price does not reflect his generosity but veils a complaint that God demands too much; the reverse side of his bargaining is that he hopes to buy God off as cheaply as possible. What effrontery to such a mighty and gracious God!

8. The prophet addresses the blackguard as *man*, not to identify him with humanity in general but to lump him together with all such worshippers. Up to now Micah has accused Israel's leaders; now he accuses the people. Before answering the presumptuous retort, Micah first destroys any idea that the worshipper's contemptible answer can be chalked up to ignorance. In the same epoch that the Lord saved Israel he had also given her his covenant and instructed priests to transmit its stipulations to succeeding generations. The prophets took up where the priests miscarried. Nevertheless, Micah repeats the stipulations once more in order to open the door of hope and to bring Israel back into covenant and security before it is too late. The prophets referred to the covenant's moral requirements either by the shorthand word *good*, as in verse 8a (*cf.* Is. 1:17; 5:20; Am. 5:14–15; Mi. 3:2), or, as in verse 8b, by generalizing summaries of the Lord's will, composed of two or, as here, three elements (*cf.* Is. 5:7; Ho. 4:1; 6:6; 12:6; Am. 5:24). Before such love as God has shown, Israel is not free to grab what she can out of life and be indifferent to others. Rather, first, she must *act justly*, that is, when in a socially superior position, step in and deliver the weaker and wronged party by punishing the oppressor. Israel's leaders had done just the opposite (2:1–2; 3:1–3, 5–7, 9–11). Second, *to love mercy* adds the thought that anyone who is in a weaker position due to some misfortune or other should be delivered not reluctantly, but out of a spirit of generosity, grace and loyalty. Acts of justice and succour motivated by a spirit of mercy guarantee the solidity and durability of the righteous covenant. Third, *to walk humbly* should be rendered 'to walk circumspectly'.[1] This command, which is orientated

---

[1] D. W. Thomas, in 'The Root *ṣn*' in Hebrew and the Meaning of *qdrnyt* in

towards God (in contrast to the first two, which are directed towards man), does not refer to self-effacement but to bringing one's life into conformity with God's will. The prophet does not reject ritual; he simply reasserts that the moral law has priority over the ceremonial. These particulars of the moral law are eternally relevant. If God's saving acts at the founding of Israel merit a loving surrender to God, how much more should his love displayed in Jesus Christ move people to become his disciples? Christians, like Micah's contemporaries and the Pharisees of Jesus' time, are also in danger of substituting monetary gifts and a dead moralism for the radical and continuing repentance that Christ demands.

B. Curses fulfilled (6:9–16)

Micah now shuts the door that left open the possibility of restoration (6:1–8), and publicly proclaims the sentence condemning the city to destruction. They have eaten to the full the deadly fruit of unethical practices picked from the branch of ingratitude, and so must die. The oracle can be analysed typically as follows: *Address* to the city (v. 9); *accusation* of using false measures (vv. 10–11) and false speech (v. 12); and *sentence* to disease and ruin in general (v. 13); more specifically, to afflictions of the body (v. 14) and pillaging of crops (v. 15). Verse 16 recapitulates the message: *accusation* (v. 16a), *sentence* (v. 16b; note 'therefore'). Note that in verses 10–15 the accusation and sentence both span three verses and have similar structures. The symmetry of the piece argues against those who want to rearrange the lines (*cf.* JB).

9. The text of the verse is badly damaged. The Hebrew clause rendered *to fear your name is wisdom* is too uncertain to

---

Malachi 3:14', *JJS* 1 (1949), pp. 182–188, showed that the traditional rendering, 'humbly', is a secondary meaning of this rare Hebrew word. He argued from Aramaic and Arabic cognates that the root's primary meaning was 'guard', 'strengthen', and suggested the notion that man should be 'guarded, careful, in walking with his God, in carrying out the divine will'. H. J. Stoebe, *THAT 2, pp. 567–568*, countered, on the basis of the same form as in Mi. 6:8 in Sirach 16:25 and 35:3 and related forms in 34:22 and 22:8, that the root means 'to be advised, sensible, reflective, prudent' or 'to practise discernment'. The verb form here, he held, means 'to practise clear and objective judgment before given situations'. In reality, both scholars arrive at the same conclusion.

comment upon it. Read 'Hear, O tribe and assembly of the city' in verse 9b with RSV. 'Tribe' makes a better parallel with 'city' than *rod*, though the Hebrew word in question (*maṭṭeh*) is a homonym, and since *who* must be an interrogative pronoun and not a relative (*contra* AV, NIV), it is best to emend *who appointed it* to read 'assembly of the city'. The verse should read: 'Listen! The Lord is calling to the city ... "Hear, O tribe and assembly of the city!" ' In sum, in verse 9a Micah arrests the attention of the city, and in verse 9b he expands the addressees to include the whole tribe, presumably Judah, which is thronging into the capital to worship and barter. The oracle's content, accusing them of fraudulent commercial practices and consigning them to economic loss, suggests that the market-place is in mind.

10–11. God accuses the elect nation of defrauding their fellow man with false measures (v. 10) and weights (v. 11) instead of acting justly and loving mercy (v. 8). The text of the first half of verse 10 continues to be too badly damaged to comment upon it. An *ephah* is the equivalent of twenty-two litres (about half a bushel). The scanty ephah stood under the divine curse. The Lord himself, who is 'no Olympian, remote from everyday living' (Allen, p. 378), stands behind standard weights and measures (Lv. 19:35–36; Dt. 25:13–16; Ezk. 45:10). In practice the king and his officials had to set the standard (*cf.* 2 Sa. 14:26). These corrupt officials who refused to conform their lives and administration to the Lord's righteous standards took advantage of the potential for cheating their fellow men due to their powerful positions and lack of technological expertise. Ancient balances had a margin of error of up to six per cent, and archaeologists have found few weights inscribed with the same denomination to be of exactly identical weight, so only approximate modern equivalents can be given.[1] Should the Lord turn a blind eye to the unscrupulous business practices of merchants, he would become an accomplice with them.

12. The *rich* of Jerusalem include the royal family, the military élite and the land barons (*cf.* Am. 6:1–3; Mi. 2:1–3; 3:1–3, 9–11). The parallelism, *violent* (Heb., *ḥāmās*) and *liars*, suggests that they abuse the poor and powerless by bending the law to their advantage. H. Haag comments: 'That the

---

[1] D. J. Wiseman, 'Weights and Measures', *NBD*, pp. 1245–1249.

accused should experience *ḥāmās* in court is all the more perverse, because it is in court that they should find protection from *ḥāmās*.'[1] Heschel writes: 'to us injustice is injurious to the welfare of the people; to the prophets it is a death-blow to existence; to us, an episode; to them, a catastrophe, a threat to the world'.[2]

13–15. The Judge, whom they had ignored, now hands down the sentence to fit the crime (note *therefore*). He will *destroy* them with sickness and afflictions of various sorts. Instead of *I have begun*, the received text, followed by Symmachus and Targum, reads 'I will make you sick' (*cf.* AV). *Ruin* means 'physically devastate'. The NIV rightly notes that the meaning of the Hebrew rendered *your stomach will still be empty*, is uncertain. Ehrman, who has the support of Targum, Jonathan and Rashi, defends the Syriac's interpretation that they would be afflicted with 'dysentery'.[3] The verb rendered *save* can also mean 'bring to birth' (*cf.* Jb. 10:12), and the NIV's rendering of the Hebrew *tassēg* by *you will store up* is far-fetched. More probably the word means 'to reach' (as in 2:6), that is, according to G. R. Driver, 'the mouth of the womb'.[4] In sum, one should follow the Vulgate, Targum, Aquila and the rabbis and read with NEB: 'you shall come to labour but not bring forth, and even if you bear a child I will give it to the sword'. This translation admirably suits the context. As Hillers notes, the sentence fulfils the 'futility curses' threatened in the covenant[5] (*cf.* Lv. 26:16; Dt. 28:18). The curses in the covenant also threatened the pillaging of crops (*cf.* v. 15 with Lv. 26:26; v. 15b with Dt. 28:40; v. 15c with Dt. 28:51). The prophet repeats the curses as a code in order to enable Israel to interpret the horrors and devastations that reverse the order of creation (that is, the natural disasters in v. 14) and the order of history (that is, the ravaging of the

---

[1] *TDOT* 4, p. 483.

[2] A. J. Heschel, *The Prophets: An Introduction* (Harper Colophon Books, 1962), p. 5.

[3] A. Ehrman, 'A Note on Micah VI, 14', *VT* 23 (1973), pp. 103–104.

[4] G. R. Driver, 'Linguistic and Textual Problems: Minor Prophets, II', *JTS* 39 (1938), pp. 267–268.

[5] D. R. Hillers, 'Treaty Curses and the Old Testament Prophets', *Biblica and Orientalia* 16 (1964), pp. 28ff.; *cf.* F. C. Fensham, 'Common Trends in Curses of the Near-Eastern Treaties and *Kudurru – Inscriptions* compared with maledictions of Amos and Obadiah', *ZAW* 75 (1963), pp. 155–175; K. Baltzer, *The Covenant Formulary* (Basil Blackwell, 1970), pp. 10, 14–15.

land by an enemy in v. 15) as coming from the Lord who had threatened them.

16. Once again, the Lord accuses (v. 16a) and sentences (v. 16b) the city. This is the only verse in the prophetic messages that mentions kings by name. The text assumes that the sins of infamous *Omri* and *Ahab*, who lived more than a century before Micah, have become legendary and serve as a paradigm of apostasy (*cf.* 1 Ki. 16:30–33), turpitude, cupidity and injustice (*cf.* 1 Ki. 21). Ahab's swindling and extortion of property from others is in view here. *Therefore* implies that the Lord has no alternative. The wages of sin is death, regardless of the sinner. The curses of the covenant also threatened international disgrace (Dt. 28:37).

C. The ship of state breaks apart (7:1–7)

Micah's lament song, identified as such by the anacrusis 'What misery is mine!' (v. 1a), consists of two parts: *complaint* (vv. 1–6) and *confidence* (v. 7). The complaint also has two parts: *accusation* (i.e. the nation's *crimes*, vv. 1b–4a) and *affliction* (*i.e.* national *confusion*, vv. 4b–6). The crimes of the nation's leadership can also be analysed into two parts: an *illustration* describing a vineyard stripped of its grapes and figs (v. 1b), and its *interpretation* (vv. 2–4a). The interpretation has two parts: a summary statement that there are no upright men (v. 2a), and two metaphors depicting the depraved leadership: (1) *hunters* (*i.e.* those who prey upon the people, vv. 2b–3), and (2) *hedges* (*i.e.* those who obstruct justice, v. 4a). The *pronouncement* of affliction also falls into two parts: a *general* statement that the time of confusion is at hand (v. 4b), and *specific* illustrations of it (vv. 5–6). The prophetic sentinels saw the dark storm of judgment approaching, but now that it has broken loose they see the silver lining of salvation beyond it (v. 7). The oracle begins and ends in the first person as the prophet moves from lament to confidence. He begins by identifying himself with the Lord, who had been accusing and sentencing the people in 6:10–16, and ends by identifying himself with the remnant, who will lay hold of God's forgiveness in 7:8–20.

1a. He commences his song with the telltale sign of lament, the interjection *'alĕlay lî*, *what misery is mine* (*cf.* Jb. 10:15). The repetition of the liquid consonant and the placing of the interjection in an anacrusis makes the cry more heart-rending.

1b. He now gives the reason for the lament. (The Heb. reads 'because I am like . . .'; *cf.* AV, RSV.) In an allegory the prophet, who represents the Lord, compares himself to a vinedresser who after patient and assiduous labour on his vines and trees comes to his vineyard in June, looking for the first ripe clusters of sweet *grapes* and early *figs* that grow with the vine (*cf.* 4:4; Lk. 13:6) but to his dismay finds a stripped vineyard and bare trees, for vandals have stripped it clean. Every gardener longs for the first fruit of his patient effort and woe to the person who picks it before him, especially the vandal who picks it clean! The vineyard is Israel (*cf.* Ps. 80:8–16, Is. 5:1–7) and the fruit is righteous magistrates. By contrast, the true vine, the Lord Jesus Christ, promises to produce sweet fruit from those who abide in him (Jn. 15:1–16).

2–4a. The Hebrew noun *'ayin* (= *none*, v. 1, and *not one*, v. 2) links the interpretation to the allegory and makes clear that the missing fruit is godly magistrates. *Godly* refers to those who keep covenant with God and his community; *upright* are those who maintain the moral rectitude of the covenant. The limits of *all men* must be decided by the parameters set up within a discourse; here, according to verse 3, it refers to the ruler and judges, all of whom treat their subjects as quarry. Micah, who compared himself to a disappointed vinedresser, likens these decadent officials to hunters (*cf.* Ps. 10:8–9). He unfolds his metaphor by *lie in wait* (*i.e.* their practices are sinister and covert) and *hunts . . . with a net* (*i.e.* they are effectively deadly; *cf.* 2:1–2; 3:1–3, 9–11).

Although in general the meaning of verse 3 is clear, its detailed interpretation is difficult. *The powerful dictate* would be better rendered more literally with the RSV 'the great man' (*i.e.* the king) 'dictates'. The synonymous parallelism of the lines suggests that *the ruler* and *the judge* have the same referent *vis-à-vis* the officials under the king. (*Ruler* designates the official next to the king and the article refers to a class of such magistrates.) *Evil* refers to the deadly net; *both hands* refer to 'the great man' and the officials next to him; and *conspire* means literally 'weave'. In sum, verse 3 adds to the summary statement in verse 2b the thought that the king and his officials together weave the deadly net that destroys their subjects. The king and his depraved minions flagrantly pervert the covenant not merely by accepting bribes (*cf.* Ex. 23:8; Dt.

10:17; 16:19; 27:25), but by actually wringing them out of their hapless subjects. To gratify his own appetites Solomon's successor dictated policies that tore apart the nation's covenantal solidarity. The word *desire* is the same word for 'crave' in verse 1. To satisfy his own lusts the king robbed the Lord of the fruit he deserved.

The *best of them* (*i.e.* the officials of v. 3) are like a briar *hedge* (*i.e.* they *only* obstruct justice!). If an innocent person tries to find relief from an oppressor by appealing to them, he will be hurt by their stubborn complacency, indolence and indifference.

4b. By the hinge of assonance, 'hedge' (Heb., *mᵉsûkâ*), and *confusion* (Heb., *mᵉbûkâ*), Micah dramatically and abruptly swings from lament over the city's crimes proclaimed in the third person ('he/they') to a lament over the impending judgment announced in second person ('you'). *Watchmen* designates lookouts posted on a city's walls to warn of approaching danger (*cf.* Is. 21:6); here it is a metaphor for the prophets who announced the approaching day of judgment (*cf.* Am. 5:18–20). That day is called *the day God visits you*, the day his long-suffering is spent and his judgment strikes (*cf.* Is. 10:3; Ho. 9:7). Isaiah foretells that the Lord has a day of tumult (Heb., *mᵉhûmâ*), trampling (Heb., *mᵉbûsâ*) and terror (Heb., *mᵉbûkâ*), and describes it as a day of battering down walls and of crying out to the mountains (Is. 22:5). The day, about which the nation had foolishly tried to silence the prophets, *has come*, presumably with Sennacherib's besieging of the city (see the Introduction, pp. 142–143). The invasion throws the city into panic.

5–6. Social anarchy is now specified (*cf.* Is. 3:4–5). Anticipating the horrible scene of the city under siege, Micah warns its citizens not to trust even their most intimate friends. The strongest ties of social solidarity – closest friends (v. 5a) and the most intimate relationship between lovers (v. 5b) – snap apart under the strain. The prophet effectively penetrates to the core of a man's inner friendship by mentioning successively neighbour, best friend, loving wife. The sentence matches the sin. As the corrupt officials rent the fabric of national solidarity, now the invasion will so exacerbate the division that a man must not confide even to his most intimate companion how he hopes to cope with the crisis, otherwise his confidant will abuse his trust to ensure his own survival.

As a fitting sentence against a nation that preyed upon its brothers (v. 6, *cf.* v. 2b), those most closely related by blood and marriage – father, mother, son, daughter and daughter-in-law – will disdainfully rise up as enemies against one another in order to save their own hides. This passage was later used in apocalyptic literature (*cf.* 1 Enoch 56:7; 100:2; Jub. 23:19; 4 Ezra 6:24) to describe the great eschatological day of the Lord. The Lord Jesus used this application of the verse to illustrate the division that his advent would produce in Israel (*cf.* Mt. 10:35–39; Lk. 12:53).

7. The poet now swings from lament to confidence on two hinges: the adversative *but as for me* and a word-play on the verb *watch*. Whereas in verse 4b 'watch' referred to the prophetic activity of watching for judgment, here it refers to Micah's activity in watching for salvation. Basing himself squarely on God's promises to the patriarchs (*cf.* v. 20), Micah confidently looks in prayer to his *Saviour*. 'Salvation' has both a military and a judicial sense. It refers to God's intervention in delivering the oppressed because it is right that he should do so. It would not be right if God's promises to the patriarchs regarding Israel failed or if the evil Assyrian prevailed. If any force other than God has the last word, then that force is god. The world around Micah offers him no reason to hope. Only God is left, and that is reason enough. The verbs *watch* (*in hope*), *wait* and *hear* entail not a passive waiting for the victory but an active participating in it through prayer and hope. As the ship of state broke apart, first internally from corrupt officials and then externally from the Assyrian invasion, our poet-prophet, as Mays (p. 157) says so well: 'does not give up and surrender to depression, but "waits", the most powerful form of action by the helpless (Pss. 38:15; 42:5, 11; 43:5; 130:5) who express in their waiting the knowledge that God comes to them in the form of salvation (Pss. 18:46; 22:5 . . .)'.

D. Song of victory (7:8–20)

Micah concludes his book with a liturgical hymn which commences (v. 8) with the note of confidence that concluded his lament (v. 7). The composite yet coherent liturgy which involves a constant change of speakers, consists of four almost equal strophes with three verses in each one – equivalent to the NIV verse numbering (apart from verses 16–17, which belong together). In the first strophe Lady Jerusalem in her fallen state confesses her faith in the Lord to her 'enemy' (a feminine form in the Hebrew; vv. 8–10). In keeping with that confession of faith, in the second strophe the prophet promises her that she will become the sheepfold offering salvation in a world under judgment (vv. 11–13). The third strophe consists of prayer, assurance and reflection (vv. 14–17). The prophet prays that the Lord, who led Israel out of Egypt against insurmountable odds, will once again miraculously shepherd his people (v. 14), and the Lord responds that he will (v. 15). In a meditation, Micah takes up the thesis of verses 8–10 that believing Israel will be saved and the unbelieving enemy will be conquered, while widening it to include the ensemble of nations (vv. 16–17). The rising crescendo of confidence through three strophes reaches a climax in the people's hymn of praise, celebrating the wonder that God can hurl their sins into the sea in order to fulfil his covenantal promises to the patriarchs (vv. 18–20).

The last two strophes have striking similarities with Moses' victory song at the Red Sea. Both songs celebrate in similar terms the truth that the Lord saves Israel and vanquishes her enemies. As for the vanquished peoples, they 'tremble' (Heb., *rgz*, Ex. 15:14; Mi. 7:17b, and *phd*, Ex. 15:16; Mi. 7:17) and become mute (Ex. 15:16; Mi. 7:16). As for the Lord, he is the God who does 'wonders' (Ex. 15:11; Mi. 7:15), shows 'unfailing love' (Ex. 15:13; Mi. 7:18–19), and makes Israel his 'inheritance' (Ex. 15:17; Mi. 7:14, 18). Both hymns ask the rhetorical question, 'Who is a God like you?' (Ex. 15:11; Mi. 7:18), and use the picturesque and completely original imagery of a God who throws his enemies (Egyptians and sins) into the depths of the sea (Ex. 15:1, 4–5; Mi. 7:19). But whereas Moses' song looked back upon the Lord's victory, Micah's song looks forward in faith to an even greater wonder – that God will forgive Israel and make her universally victorious.

8–10. In the first strophe humiliated Lady Jerusalem commands her blasphemous rival not to *gloat* (v. 8), explains that she suffers for her sins only for a season (v. 9), and that at the time of salvation her rival will be put to *shame* (v. 10).

In this imaginary dialogue with her enemy, Jerusalem represents herself as in the dark and as fallen on the ground before her rival (v. 8). The figure of *darkness* evokes the imagery of a dungeon-prison without light, an apt figure for a trapped city under siege. The repentant city affirms in the darkness, 'the Lord is my light' (*cf.* JB, NAB, NEB).

The faithful remnant within the city accepts the prophet's inspired interpretation of history that Jerusalem fell not by chance (*cf.* 1 Sa. 6:9) nor by the Lord's impotence (*cf.* 2 Ki. 18:22–35), but because of the Lord's wrath against her sins (v. 9). With such a world-view misery can take on spiritual meaning and lead to repentance, endurance and hope. Her hope rests on God doing what is *right*. If he punished Israel for wrongdoing, then how much more will he punish those who have wronged his elect city and blasphemed him (*cf.* v. 10). Whereas *light* in verse 8 spoke of God as the present source of salvation, in verse 9 it speaks of his future act of salvation.

The Lord's *righteousness* entails both Israel's salvation, the theme of verses 8–9, and the punishment of the taunting woman, the theme of verse 10. The blasphemer will be made to blush with shame and then will be trampled upon as the mire that is trampled in the streets, so as never to rise again. History validated Jerusalem's faith. Where is Ashur, the tutelary deity of Assyria?

11–13. In response to Jerusalem's confession of faith, the Lord delivers a message of hope. The second strophe of the victory song falls into two parts: peoples of all nations will be saved within the walls of Jerusalem (vv. 11–12) while the rest of the earth will be destroyed on account of its sins (v. 13).

Walls (Heb., *gdr*), does not mean 'ramparts' (Heb., *hwmh*), but 'wall' in general, including the enclosures of vineyards (*cf.* Ps. 80:12; 89:40; Is. 5:5) and, as here, of flocks (Nu. 32:16, 24, 36; 1 Sa. 24:3; Zp. 2:6). Jerusalem's future is not one bristling with arms as in the days before its fall (*cf.* 4:3; 5:10–11), but is likened to a sheepfold (*cf.* 4:8; 7:14) where the faithful of all nations may seek refuge from the destruction God will visit on the rest of the earth on account of its sins (v. 13). The Lord will so enlarge this 'eschatological sheepfold', his divinely imposed limits on it will be so remote, that all who want salvation can find it there.

The repetition of *the/that day* signifies that the three activities – the building of the enclosure, the expanding of its limits, and the coming of the peoples within it – belong together. By specific geographical merisms (*i.e.* opposing synecdoches indicating totality) – from Assyria in the northeast to Egypt in the southwest (the limits of Micah's world) – and by general geographical merisms – *from sea to sea and from mountain to mountain* – the universalism of the salvation is projected. The verb *come* is singular, suggesting that individual choice is involved. The prophet does not envision all peoples of all nations coming; rather he envisages individuals coming *from* (repeated twice in the Heb. text of v. 12) all peoples. *From Egypt to the Euphrates* evokes remembrance of the Lord's oath to give Israel these borders (Gn. 15:18; Ex. 23:31; Dt. 11:24) and of Israel's golden age (1 Ki. 4:21, 25). The 'eschatological day' should be understood generically (*cf.* 4:1). It was partially realized in Micah's own day when Jerusalem emerged into the light after the darkness of the Assyrian invasion (note 'now' in v. 10, to which *the day* in vv. 11–12 is connected); it found a further fulfilment in the restoration from exile, and finds its fullest historical fulfilment today as the elect from all nations come to the sanctuary of the heavenly Jerusalem (Heb. 12:22–24; *cf.* Jn. 17:2; Acts. 3:25; 2 Cor. 6:2).

Outside Israel's secure borders, within which the Lord shepherds the repentant people, the Moral Governor inflicts devastation (*cf.* Zp. 1:18; 3:8) on the earth, a metonymy for its inhabitants. We may assume from the historical context and parallel passages (*cf.* Je. 49:13, 17; 50:23; Mi. 1:3, 6) that before he burns the earth in fire (2 Pet. 3:10), which is also in view here, ravaging armies are his earthly means of scarring the earth. As Allen (p. 398) well says:

> The oracle is the counterpart to the Christian doctrine of the Last Judgment. In traditional language which Israel could understand it expresses the assurance that deficits in the moral balance sheet of the world are eventually to be paid, while the kingdom of God is to be established in triumph.

14–17. In response to the oracle promising salvation to the elect, the prophet responds in prayer. *Shepherd*, a common figure in the ancient Near East for an ideal king, depicts an inward spiritual relationship of love and trust between king and people, outward protection (v. 14a; note *staff* = sceptre), and provision (v. 14b; note *feed*). *Inheritance* metaphorically signifies their permanent position by virtue of ancient right. *Carmel* (see NIV mg.) suggests a garden-like forest (*cf.* 2

Ki. 19:23 = Is. 37:24), a place fit for the King's sheep to live. *Bashan* and *Gilead* evoke both the memory that Moses at the beginning of Israel's history gave Israel these lands by mighty wonders (note *as in days long ago*), and the desire for their famous pastures and fertile lands.

The Lord, using the first person, interrupts the petition (*cf.* Pss. 12:5; 60:6–8; 87:4) and promises to show Israel in the future such salvation-wonders as when he smote the first-born of Egypt, provided a way through the Red Sea and Jordan river, preserved them in the wilderness and overthrew numerous nations mightier than they. Israel saw that same outstretched arm when the Lord miraculously smote Sennacherib's army at Jerusalem's gates; again when Cyrus commanded that the exiles be restored and their Temple rebuilt; and, above all, when the Lord Jesus vanquished death and Satan in his death and resurrection.

Micah responds to the oracle with a meditation: the nations will be humiliated, vanquished and in turn fear the Lord. Verses 16 and 17 link closely with verse 10, but widen the humiliated enemy from one (Assyria) to all nations. In verse 10 Assyria fell in defeat, here the nations renounce their power and pride. *Lay their hands on their mouths* and 'make their ears deaf' (NEB) signifies their humiliation: they themselves will no longer either taunt Israel as the rival did in verse 10, or listen to the vain boasts of others. *Lick dust*, as seen from other parts of Scripture (Gn. 3:14; Ps. 44:25) and in many reliefs from the ancient Near East, depicts the vanquished kings grovelling before their overlord. Confronted with the Lord's power, they realize their impotence and in that spiritual state prepare to move out of their old strongholds to worship the Lord. The Lord so utterly vanquished Satan and death in the resurrection of Christ that nations today also learn to fear him.

18–20. Micah, whose name means 'Who is like Yah[weh]?' (see the Introduction, p. 137), artfully shows the significance of his name by substituting the generic noun *'el* (= God) for the proper name *Yah*, and by weaving it into the opening line of the hymn of praise that concludes his song of victory. He puts it into the mouth of the faithful remnant who will survive the Assyrian onslaught. They interpret it to mean that no God compares to the Lord in pardoning sin. If God had lacked that quality, Micah's ministry would have been pointless. Of what value would his oracles of reproach have been if God stayed angry forever? He would have had the satisfaction of venting his spleen, but the people would have become hardened in sin and despair (*cf.* Ps. 130:3–4). Because God is merciful, he offers hope to the repentant, from whom a new age can be born. Because God cannot lie, there will always be a repentant *remnant* comprising his inheritance even until the end of history (Rom. 9 – 11).

Over against the pile of words for their sin (*sin, transgression, iniquities*) the people heap up God's benevolent attributes and ways: *pardons, forgives*, does *not stay angry*, has *compassion, delights to show mercy, will be true*, the last four of which are found in the great confession at the time of Israel's first egregious sin (*cf.* Ex. 34:6). That ancient creed guarantees each generation of the faithful that God will keep his promise to the fathers and not terminate Israel's history in a cul-de-sac.

Verse 18 founded the *cause* of Israel's blessed prospect in God's attribute of forgiveness; verse 19 presents the *consequence* – their sins will be removed. As God began Israel on her journey by hurling the Egyptians into the Red Sea, so he will restore them on their pilgrimage and *hurl* all their *iniquities* into the metaphorical *depths*.

God's gracious attributes catalogued in Exodus 34:6 and rehearsed in Micah 7:18–20 can be analysed into his 'grace' and *compassion* (Heb., *rḥm*), which entail forgiveness of sin, and into his *mercy* – better 'unfailing love' (Heb., *ḥsd*) – and 'truth', which entail the keeping of his promises. The first pair is celebrated in verses 18a and 19, the second in verses 18b and 20. The two pairs are related in 18b by making his 'unfailing love' 'Heb. *ḥsd*, 'mercy') the cause of his *longsuffering* (*i.e.* 'you do not stay angry forever'). In sum, his loving fidelity to the fathers constitutes the basis of Israel's hope. As God kept his promise to Abraham in the age of Moses and Joshua by bringing Israel up out of the bondage of Egypt and into their inheritance of Canaan, so also he keeps it in Micah's time by delivering them from the hand of the Assyrian. Above all he kept his promise to Abraham by raising Christ from the dead and by giving him a spiritual seed from all the nations of the earth (*cf.* Rom. 4:17; Gal. 3:6–29). The elect continue to count on this incomparable God in every trial.